A PILOT'S
Accident Review

An in-depth look at high-profile accidents
that shaped aviation rules and procedures

JOHN LOWERY

Aviation Supplies & Academics, Inc.
Newcastle, Washington

A Pilot's Accident Review
by John Lowery

Aviation Supplies & Academics, Inc.
7005 132nd Place SE
Newcastle, Washington 98059-3153
asa@asa2fly.com | www.asa2fly.com

ASA-ACC-REV
ISBN 978-1-61954-217-4

Printed in the United States of America
2018   2017   2016   2015   9   8   7   6   5   4   3   2   1

Photo credits:
All photography is by and © John Lowery, unless otherwise indicated as follows:
Page 7, courtesy of Garmin International; p.8, Chelton Flight Systems; pp.41, 43, 134, Flight Guide; p.55, IDuke at English Wikipedia (per Wikimedia Creative Commons License CC BY-SA 2.5); p.60, Associated Press Photo/Toshihiko Sato; pp.75, 106, 154, 214, National Transportation Safety Board (NTSB); p.87, Alan Redecki (per Wikimedia Creative Commons License CC BY-SA 3.0); p.89, RocketRoute; pp.103, 109 (top), 142, National Center for Atmospheric Research (NCAR); p.109 (bottom), John R. Bakksen; p.120, National Aeronautics and Space Administration (NASA); p.121, United States Air Force (USAF); p.143, National Oceanic and Atmospheric Administration (NOAA); and p.252, Alese and Morton Pechter.

Library of Congress Cataloging-in-Publication Data:
Lowery, John, author.
  A pilot's accident review / John Lowery.
     pages cm
  ISBN 978-1-61954-217-4 (pbk.) — ISBN 1-61954-217-X (pbk.)
  1. Aircraft accidents—Case studies. 2. Airplanes—Piloting—Safety measures.
  3. Airplanes—Piloting—Human factors. I. Title.
  TL553.5.L689 2015
  363.12'414—dc23
                              2015020901

CONTENTS

FOREWORD

Once again, one of the most insightful, knowledgeable professional pilots in today's sphere of aviation has probed and poked the annals of aircraft accidents to unveil the causes of flyers killing themselves and others.

A long list of accidents spanning the spectrum of flight, from bug smashers to high-performance military and professional aviation, is examined in detail, providing solid foundations for drawing meaningful conclusions. Author John Lowery's research and experience as pilot, instructor, check airman and writer across that spectrum-of-wings are clearly evident, as he dissects an impressive array of incidents. That background is brought to bear in myriad subtle ways, such as avoiding temptations to zero-in on mechanical, training, decision making, weather, or other factor as *the* cause of a mishap. Lowery fully appreciates that most accidents are attributed to a cascade of equipment and/or human failures, and skillfully interweaves myriad elements, showing how they interact and contribute to a smoking hole.

Of particular interest to professionals, the author raises the intriguing probability that otherwise healthy pilots may suffer from an unrecognized degradation of cognitive abilities. Even experienced, proficient pilots can mentally "lose it," as they age. However, ego, complacency and a press-on proclivity that characterizes far too many aviators can lead to bad decisions and, ultimately, disaster.

Lowery addresses perennial topics associated with aircraft accidents, such as faulty training, poor judgment, fatigue, inadequate nutrition, compulsion (e.g., "get-home-itis"), and complacency. However, he also builds a compelling case for instructors and check pilots having to shoulder a portion of the blame for fatal accidents that kill innocent passengers and crew members. Time and again, training professionals in all sectors of aviation have identified deficiencies in a pilot's aptitude or cognitive capabilities, but were either reluctant to ground a career aviator, or were pressured into passing a pilot that they knew, on a gut level, was on a VFR-direct route to an accident. That, Lowery suggests, raises ethical concerns for everybody from individual at-risk pilots to training pros and Federal Aviation Administration regulators.

Aviation professionals, who've filled a pile of logbooks and think they've absorbed every tidbit written about aero-safety, will be impressed with Lowery's observations and insights. Real professionals will appreciate the author's discernment and incorporate this book's wisdom into their own flying.

— William B. Scott
Rocky Mountain Bureau Chief for *Aviation Week & Space Technology* (retired), author of *Space Wars, Counterspace* and *The Permit*.

INTRODUCTION

"He bears the seed of ruin in himself."
Matthew Arnold (1822-1888)

The intent of this book is to provide extra bits of knowledge to help the serious pilot in decision-making and thus enjoy a long flying career. Using the theory that we sometimes learn best by reviewing the mistakes of others, this book has been centered around aircraft accidents and why they occurred. In most cases the pilot or someone in his or her support team—mechanic, weather briefer, avionics technician, or in commercial flying, the pilot's management, even the manufacturer—made the accident inevitable. The pilot's personality too is frequently involved, with compulsion in decision-making a precipitating factor. To help understand the inherent problems, selected accidents have been analyzed in an effort to help prevent the predictable repetition that characterizes each year's record on file at the National Transportation Safety Board (NTSB).

The dictionary defines an accident as an "unexpected happening." Yet, when all factors are considered in most aircraft accidents, they cannot be called unexpected—simply because they were predictable. And, as you will note, many involve experienced pilots, which is by way of emphasizing that *it can* happen to you too.

Historically, about 80 percent of the annual general aviation accidents are attributed to pilot error. However, an in-depth analysis will usually show that a chain of errors, which included the pilot and one or more members of his or her extensive support team, culminated in an accident. It may have been the line-service person who refueled the piston-powered light twin with jet fuel instead of gasoline; or the flight instructor who signed off his student as fully trained before he/she was actually ready; or the FAA designated pilot examiner (DPE) who licensed a new pilot with a quick oral exam and short check flight that didn't adequately test the new pilot's knowledge or flying skill. Or perhaps it was the mechanic who repaired the engine and failed to properly torque the bolts holding the engine halves together, and the maintenance inspector who failed to catch the error. As a result, the engine fails over hostile terrain.

Sometimes it's the weather briefer who provided incomplete information, or the airport manager who failed to adequately maintain the runway surface and allowed an excessive rubber buildup from the landing traffic. As a result, it becomes slick during a rain, and when a pilot lands on the slick surface the airplane hydroplanes off the end of the runway resulting in major damage and serious injuries to passengers or crew.

Occasionally, it's a misunderstood clearance from the control tower—possibly combined with the pilot's inattention—that culminates in catastrophe. This is especially true with runway incursions, wherein a clearance was misunderstood; or while taxing for takeoff, the pilot was chatting with a friend in the right seat.

Conflicting information too is sometimes a factor. For example, there's the pilot who crashes on final approach due to wing and tail ice that accumulated during cruise flight. Although his airplane was certified for flight in known icing conditions, he didn't realize that icing certification doesn't allow continuous flight within it.

Important information is available in Advisory Circular 91-74A concerning reports of "mixed-icing, freezing drizzle or rain." The circular shows that moisture droplet size is much larger than the icing certification requirements, which typically constitute severe icing. Yet, in the Pilot's Operating Handbook/Airplane Flight Manual (POH/AFM), pilots are not clearly told that the aircraft they are flying is not equipped for flight in severe icing conditions.

This book has been designed to analyze selected accidents in the statistically most vulnerable areas. Organized according to the sequence of flight, the first chapter is an overall look at general aviation's historical accident record to see what can be learned from it. Also discussed is the increasing prevalence in GA aircraft of electronic flight instrumentation systems (EFIS), typically referred to as *glass cockpits*. While EFIS instrumentation has resulted in a decrease in the number of accidents in aircraft so equipped, NTSB records show an increase in fatalities when they are involved in accidents. This implies inadequate training or improper utilization by pilots of the remarkable EFIS capabilities.

In the hazardous environment of Alaska, the FAA's introduction of the GPS-based Capstone Program in 1999 immediately proved effective in reducing accidents—particularly those classed as controlled flight into terrain (CFIT).

About 20 percent of our annual accidents happen during departure. Chapters 2 and 3 cover preflight, takeoff, and climb accidents. Chapter 4 is a special look at the Air France Concorde crash, simply because it's a classic example of an integrated chain of errors that led to a tragic accident. This included the aircraft manufacturer, Air France management, their dispatch operation, and both the line service and cockpit crews. It was ultimately precipitated by a gross maintenance error, yet the French government ignored these failures, and to protect national pride blamed a metal strip dropped a few minutes earlier from the engine of a departing Continental Airlines DC-10.

Chapter 5 covers the enroute phase, which accounts for a major share of the fatalities. With 60 percent of the accidents occurring during descent, approach and landing, Chapter 6 is especially important. Chapter 7 concerns safety problems unique to flying by instrument flight rules.

Chapter 8 discusses maintenance error and material failure. The first event discussed involves a Cessna P210 that experienced engine failure due to improper engine maintenance by a mechanic and inadequate inspection by his supervisor. The second accident concerns a Cessna Citation CJ-1 whose pilot/owner was forced to ditch in Puget Sound because of a runaway nose-down elevator trim. Cause of the trim problem was either carelessness or inadequate training of a company electronics technician. He had used pliers to install or remove a printed circuit board in the aircraft's autopilot/trim system, and unknowingly had damaged the delicate printed circuit. This led to a runaway nose-down trim during climb, which overpowered the elevator controls. Fortunately, the pilot was able to successfully ditch the aircraft without injury or loss of life.

The third accident involved an MU-2 in which eight people were killed, one of whom was the governor of South Dakota. In this case, the NTSB accident report clearly showed the cause was failure of the FAA to require the manufacturer to abide by an earlier NTSB recommendation for a one-time fleet-wide inspection of the propeller governor hubs. The Board's recommendations were based on an in-depth analysis of a previous MU-2 accident that involved propeller hub failure. Yet 30 days after the governor was killed, the inspection was suddenly accomplished.

Chapter 9 concerns human factors involved in safe flying. This includes management and design error, the pilot's personality, emotional involvement, and ethical considerations involving the pilot's physical fitness. Chapter 10 is all about flying operations unique to the special features of seaplanes and ski-planes. If you enjoy outdoor adventure, then you must be a seaplane or ski-plane pilot. In these airplanes you have almost unlimited landing capability, but you are operating continuously in an unpredictable and potentially hazardous, off-airport environment. Thus, special knowledge is needed to use them safely.

Chapter 11 concerns flying after scuba diving, with an in-depth look at the unique physiological considerations involved. And finally, Chapter 12 considers the flight instructor, FAA designated pilot examiner, and aeromedical examiner as they relate to aircraft accidents. After all, they have the last word in aviation safety.

Someone once said, "life is a group effort." And the teamwork required to make aviation safe is the embodiment of that saying; from the manufacturer's design and production teams, the mechanics, avionics technicians, weather briefers, the line service crewmen, to the company that manufactures the fuel—even the fuel truck and its driver.

Should you become interested in researching a particular accident, the preliminary accident reports or synopses of completed accident investigations can be found at http://www.ntsb.gov/_layouts/ntsb.aviation/index. aspx. Or you can get the complete report of an accident from Public Inquiries, National Transportation Safety Board, Washington D. C. 20592-2000.

To Colonel Joe Shriber (USAFR Retired), I owe a special thanks for his detailed editing and proof reading. Your sharp eye for detail has been invaluable in rewriting this book. And I am especially indebted to retired FAA Inspector Ray C. Steinkraus, for reviewing the book's content for both technical accuracy and the author's recommendations for compliance with the FAR regulations.

To quote from the late German General Adolf Galland, "Flying is more than a sport, more than a job. Flying is pure passion and desire, which fills a lifetime." The intent of this book is to provide some additional knowledge that will help you enjoy a safe flying career for your lifetime. Meanwhile, fly safe and fly smart.

— John Lowery

CHAPTER 1

The General Aviation Safety Record

The question is often asked, "is private flying safe?" The continually improving accident record shows that it certainly is. Since an unbelievable high of 4,494 accidents in 1978, of which 793 were fatal, AOPA's 24th Nall Report covering 2012 shows GA experienced 1,029 non-commercial and commercial fixed-wing aircraft accidents with 224 being fatal—the lowest number since the end of World War II. Yet, it's regrettable to note the regularity with which pilots, or members of their support team, fail to learn from the mistakes of others, and year after year continue making almost identical errors.

Two specific areas that consistently account for a high percentage of the fatalities include *maneuvering flight* and *weather*. As for maneuvering accidents, buzzing is often involved. Many weather related mishaps are what is called *controlled flight into terrain* (CFIT): the pilot flew VFR into clouds that masked high terrain. This type of accident usually involves non-instrument rated pilots who inadvertently fly into *instrument meteorological conditions* (IMC) and hit an obstruction or high terrain. Fuel starvation or fuel exhaustion is yet another regular player that continues to cause accidents and fatalities every year.

As for maneuvering flight, how many times have you read about the pilot who buzzed his buddies or relatives and flew into the ground at high speed, simply because he didn't know that control pressures increase significantly as airspeed builds toward the redline—the maximum indicated airspeed (V_{NE})? This is a typical characteristic with cable-and-pulley flight controls, and as a by-product it helps prevent structural overstress from sudden pitch control inputs. But it also reduces controllability.

There are instances too of pilots buzzing the calm surface of a lake and flying into the water. Without seaplane training they didn't know that *mirror effect* on a glassy water surface robs you of your depth perception.

One fatal accident involved the pilot of a Cessna 185 who was attempting to drop a message to his river-rafting friends who were camped on a sand bar. To keep them in sight in the narrow river canyon he got low and slow and began banking the airplane steeply. But in his zeal to communicate, he forgot that a 60-degree angle of bank increases stall speed by 70 percent, and a 70-degree bank essentially doubles the stall speed. Thus, with a wings-level stall speed of 55 knots indicated airspeed (KIAS), a 60-degree bank would have increased the aircraft's stall speed to about 94 knots; with a 70-degree bank the aircraft would have stalled at an indicated airspeed of about 110 knots. And unfortunately that's what he did: stalled out and spun-in before his horrified friends.

Have you heard about the pilot who ran out of fuel a mile or so short of the runway? It doesn't matter what year; it happens every year. The 22nd Nall Report covering 2010 shows that after decreasing for five straight years, the number of fuel management accidents in non-commercial fixed-wing aircraft increased by 20 percent in 2009 and 2010 even as the total number of accidents has decreased.

Some accidents occur when the pilot flies an instrument approach, and as the aircraft begins breaking out of the clouds, he abandons the approach procedure and attempts to find the airport visually. A classic example occurred on a dark and foggy night when a private pilot and flight instructor in a Piper Saratoga flew a VOR/DME approach to runway 13 at Beaumont Municipal Airport (BMT), Texas. While still four miles from the airport, they began breaking out of the clouds. They quickly cancelled their IFR clearance and abandoned the approach procedure, then at a very low altitude began searching for the runway visually: *scud running*, it's called.

They found the runway, but ignored the additional protection provided by the runway's visual glide slope—a PVASI. Unfortunately, they flew into power lines near the runway and were killed. Yet adherence to the VOR procedure and use of the PVASI would have prevented this fatal accident.

Figure 1-1. ILS minimums.

Accident Defined

NTSB regulation 49 CFR §830.2 defines an accident (*mishap* is used interchangeably throughout this book) as an occurrence associated with the operation of an aircraft that takes place after the aircraft has been boarded with the intention of flight and before all occupants are deplaned. In addition, it must have resulted in substantial aircraft damage, or the death of or serious injury to someone on board. An *incident* means "an occurrence, other than an accident, that's associated with the operation of an aircraft, which affects or could affect, the safety of operations."

A *serious injury* is one requiring hospitalization for more than 48 hours within seven days of the date of injury; or one that results in fracture of any bone (except simple fractures of fingers, toes, or nose); causes severe hemorrhage; damages a nerve, muscle, or tendon; injures an internal organ; causes second and third-degree burns; or any burn that affects more than five percent of the body. If death occurs within 30 days of an injury due to an aircraft accident, it is classed as a *fatality*.

Accident Trends

NTSB data for the years 1975 to 1978 shows there were more than 4,000 accidents each year, with the previously mentioned spike in 1978 to 4,494 accidents. This is more than four times the 1,160 non-commercial, fixed-wing accidents for 2012. The alarming accident rate in the 1970s was due to a soaring economy, favorable tax laws, and limited regulation and supervision by the FAA.

With about 80 percent of each year's accidents classed as pilot error, it became painfully obvious that the FAA's lax training and proficiency standards were a major part of the problem. Accordingly, more stringent regulations were implemented, along with aggressive safety programs. For example, 14 CFR §61.56 mandated the biennial flight review for all non-commercial pilots. And for aircraft requiring two crewmembers, §61.58 mandated an annual proficiency check for the pilot-in-command. Essentially, this amounts to a re-validation of his or her type rating.

Still, the biennial flight review had inherent flaws. The pilot of a turbo-prop King Air could (and still can) take his flight review in a Cessna 152. And unbelievably, such a review keeps him current under §61.56 for two more years in the much more sophisticated light twins and turboprops. Although single-pilot accidents in these more sophisticated aircraft continue to be problematic, the insurance companies stepped into the breach by requiring *annual* recurrency training in these aircraft. This, and the availability of sophisticated simulators, has helped improve our accident history.

Attempting to fly VFR into IMC continues to be a major cause of accidents. The 2010 Nall Report states that at night IMC *"was one of the most deadly accident environments."* More than 30 percent of the accidents occurring at night involved fatalities; and if the flight was in IMC, then the chance of fatalities doubled to 60 percent.

Because of the additional hazards of night flying, a night-current pilot with an instrument rating flying IFR greatly improves the odds for a safe flight. Although some disagree, the accident record shows that you simply cannot routinely fly cross-country at night safely without an instrument rating. Because sooner or later you'll encounter inky-blackness in reduced visibility due to smoke or haze, unexpected clouds, featureless terrain, or a combination of all three at once. Then spatial disorientation seals your doom. To buffer this recommendation, countries belonging to the International Civil Aviation Organization (ICAO) require that all flights after sunset must be on an IFR flight plan.

Simulators have been a major contributor to improved pilot proficiency and the reduction in accidents—especially in the sophisticated cabin-class twins and turboprop aircraft. During the seventies and early eighties, accidental spins that occurred during engine-out training and minimum control speed (V_{MC}) demonstrations were taking a heavy toll on multi-engine students and flight instructors. Now, sophisticated simulators allow multi-engine pilots to gain and maintain proficiency in these hazardous events, particularly during the takeoff and climb phases of flight. In addition, they eliminate the risk of de-tuning or thermal shock damage to engines.

Phase of Flight

For many years, accident investigators have referred to the "critical eight minutes of flight." This comprises the first two minutes of takeoff and climb and the final six minutes of flight, encompassing descent, approach, and landing. The rule of thumb is that about 20 percent of accidents occur during departure and around 60 percent during the approach and landing phase.

Loss-of-control accidents that occur on takeoff and landing often involve crosswinds which exceed the "demonstrated" figure published in the POH and/or AFM. Unfortunately, what many pilots fail to realize is that the manufacturer's published demonstrated crosswind is established from *a dry, paved runway*, and with aircraft equipped with new tires. This crosswind velocity represents the aerodynamic limit of the flight controls to maintain a straight ground track during takeoff or landing.

To illustrate the problem, on February 10, 2004, the pilot of a turboprop Cessna 208B Caravan was departing from a runway with patches of packed snow and ice on the surface. The airplane has a demonstrated crosswind of 20 knots, and in this case the surface wind was a right-crosswind of 15 gusting to 25 knots. Predictably, during takeoff roll at between 30 to 50 knots, the pilot lost control and ran off the downwind side of the runway, then nosed over.

Although slick patches of snow and ice were also involved in this accident, the record shows that the demonstrated crosswind in the manufacturer's handbook should be considered a limitation—just as it is with transport category aircraft. Because realistically, that demonstrated crosswind figure is the manufacturer's way of telling you that beyond that number there are no guarantees. Left unsaid is that snow, ice, or a wet runway surface and worn tires causes a reduction in the demonstrated crosswind figure, simply because of the reduced tire/runway surface traction.

Fatalities

Fatal accidents are most prevalent during maneuvering flight, takeoff and climb, weather, and during descent and approach—in that order. AOPA's 23rd Nall Report also shows an ever-improving trend with only 214 non-commercial fixed-wing mishaps being fatal in 2010, compared to 233 in 2009. The report for 2002 shows that of 122 maneuvering flight accidents, 66 (54 percent) were fatal. Hitting wires, terrain, trees, or the water accounted for 25 of these; more than half occurred during personal flights where the pilot was buzzing, or attempting low-level aerobatics. As in previous years, the takeoff and climb phase was responsible for about 21 percent of the fatalities, 51 of 249 mishaps. And this is a fairly consistent annual percentage.

The 2010 Nall Report shows there were 385 landing accidents, or 35.3 percent of the total, but only 4 (1.8 percent) involved fatalities. Meanwhile weather—usually VFR into IMC—accounted for 15 percent of accidents by non-instrument rated pilots. Of these, 60 percent, or 33 of 55 accidents, were fatal. Maintenance or material failure was involved in 15.5 percent of all GA accidents, with 10.4 percent resulting in fatalities.

Electronic Flight Instrumentation Systems

Aircraft equipped with electronic flight instrumentation systems (EFIS) show a major improvement in flying safety. With EFIS, the ship's instrument panel provides electronic information rather than electromechanical indications (analog, or round dial). Basically, an EFIS equipped cockpit has a primary flight display (PFD), which includes attitude and airspeed, a multifunction display (MFD), showing navigation, and an engine indicating and crew alerting system (EICAS). Originally, only the attitude director indicator (ADI) and horizontal situation indicator (HSI) were replaced. Today, however, there are few flight instruments that aren't presented electronically. (Yet the EFIS must always be backed by the critical emergency analog instruments—airspeed, attitude indicator and altimeter.) Two notable EFIS systems for GA aircraft are the Garmin G-1000 and Chelton Flight Systems EFIS-SV (synthetic vision).

The Garmin-1000 consists of an integrated flight instrument system composed of two display units. One serves as the PFD and the other as the MFD. Additional features are found in the newer and larger G-1000 units used in the business jets. This includes a copilot's PFD combined with an alphanumeric keyboard and integrated flight director/autopilot.

The Capstone Program, implemented successfully in Alaska in 1999 to 2006, utilized the Chelton Flight Systems PFD and MFD. The PFD provided the attitude, heading, airspeed, and vertical speed information. The MFD provides a satellite based GPS visual representation of the terrain. In addition, it had the additional feature of a terrain awareness and warning system (TAWS) that alerted the pilot of an impending close encounter with the ground.

In an effort to reduce airborne collisions, the system used the new Automatic Dependent Surveillance-Broadcast (ADS-B) technology to continuously show similarly equipped aircraft on the MFD. And in the Anchorage area, a system called Traffic Information Service-Broadcast (TIS-B) depicted non-ADS-B aircraft on the MFD.

Phase I of the Capstone Program implemented in the Yukon-Kuskokwim (Y-K) Delta of southwestern Alaska, was an immediate success. The Y-K Delta area encompasses an area of about 100,000 square miles with no roads to connect more than 50 villages—the largest settlement being

Figure 1-2. The Garmin G-1000 EFIS cockpit displays a multitude of information.
(Courtesy of Garmin International)

Figure 1-3. The Chelton Flight System, introduced in Alaska in 1999, was an immediate success in reducing accidents. (Courtesy of Chelton Flight Systems)

Bethel. Consequently, aviation is the primary means of transportation. Because the Capstone Program involved professional pilots with lots of flying experience, during its first year of operation Phase I saw a 40 percent reduction in aircraft accidents. In 2002, Phase II became operational in the challenging terrain and weather of the southeast area of the state, around Juneau. From 2000 to 2004 FAA data show the Capstone Program reduced accidents by 47 percent.

Phase III which covered the entire state was activated in 2006, but in December that year the Capstone Program was incorporated into the FAA's nationwide ADS-B program. As the Capstone Program shows, the increased use of this modern-day technology has continued to significantly improve the safety of both private and commercial flying operations.

An NTSB statistical analysis for the period 2002 to 2008 of accidents involving light single-engine aircraft equipped with EFIS, found that "light single-engine aircraft, equipped with glass cockpit displays, experienced lower total accident rates, but higher fatal accident rates, than the same type equipped with conventional analog instrumentation." Accidents in the glass cockpit equipped aircraft typically involved pilots with a higher level of certification and with more total flight time than pilots flying with older analog instrumentation. Mishaps in glass cockpit aircraft were typically associated with personal/business flights, longer flights, instrument flight plans, and single-pilot operations. Accidents in airplanes equipped with conventional analog instrumentation occurred on shorter two-pilot instructional flights, and the pilots involved had less flight time than those flying with EFIS.

Age Groupings

Safety educators talk of the 18-through-23-year age group as most prone to risky flight behavior. But youth as an accident cause is not supported by the general aviation accident history. For example, statistics from a June 27, 2003 FAA study showed pilots aged 40 to 49 years had the most accidents, with the 50 to 59 year-olds in second place. Rather than being caused by high-risk behavior this probably reflects inadequate training and proficiency.

The original mandatory retirement of airline pilots at age 60 (14 CFR §121.383(c)) was a hot topic after its adoption in 1959. This rule was the result of several well-publicized incidents of in-flight incapacitation due to heart attack or stroke by airline pilots at the controls during the 1950s. The precipitating event involved the captain of a Lockheed Electra who after completing an ILS in bad weather had a fatal heart attack on short final. The copilot failed to recognize the problem in time and the aircraft crashed short of the runway, killing all aboard.

Although these tragic events appeared to justify the mandatory age-60 retirement rule, later events showed the underlying reason was economic rather than safety. Prior to deregulation, airline growth was sluggish because the now defunct Civil Aeronautics Board tightly controlled competition and profitability. Consequently in the large airlines, the senior captains were making all the money and preventing the younger first-officers from progressing. In addition, many of the old-timers were having trouble converting to jet flying.

In 1992, the FAA granted a 21-month exemption from the age 60 rule for 18 pilots employed by two foreign carriers, Icelandic Air and Corse Air. In addition, there was no age limitation for copilots flying for foreign airlines into the United States.

In 1995, the commuter airlines were placed under Part 121, and their pilots were also hit by the age-60 retirement rule. Yet NTSB records for

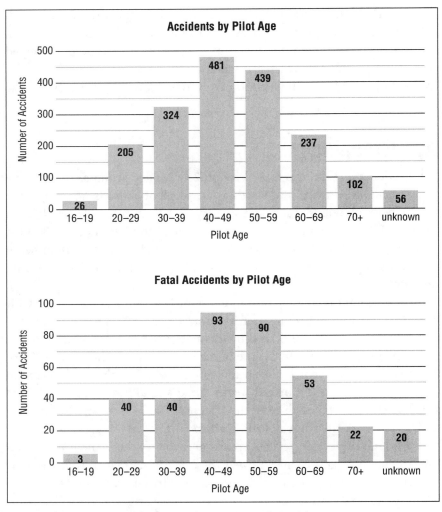

Figure 1-4. All accidents by pilot age (from a 1999 U.S. study).

these younger, erstwhile Part 135 pilots showed a higher accident rate. Consequently, the FAA delayed application of the age-60 rule to commuter crews for four years until December 20, 1999. However, during that period there were no incidents of in-flight incapacitation.

Although the Airline Pilots Association was initially against the age-60 rule, feeling the influence of a younger membership, the union reversed itself in 1980 and supported the mandatory age-60 retirement. Despite arguments to the contrary, the reasons were *strictly* economic.

On December 13, 2007, the age requirement for airline pilots was revised when congress passed the Fair Treatment for Experienced Pilots Act (Public Law 110-135). This allows both pilot and copilot on domestic flights to fly until reaching age 65. On international flights, the ICAO allows one pilot to be over age 60 provided the other is under age 60.

General Aviation Impact

The thought that a pilot could be unsafe strictly because of age, and the attendant possibility of physical impairment in flight transposed itself into general aviation. Although not mandated by the FARs, some corporations adopted the age-60 rule and forced their company pilots to retire upon reaching that magic age. But for GA pilots today, the medical basis for the forced retirement rule at a specific age is obsolete. Improved lifestyle and health habits have allowed pilots to remain vigorous and healthy to a much older age. Special emphasis placed on factors such as obesity, increased exercise, and the decreased use of alcohol and tobacco has also helped increase longevity. The medical profession too is better equipped to monitor a pilot's health.

In 1981, the Institute of Medicine stated, "Major epidemiological studies do not demonstrate a sudden increase in coronary risk at any specific age… risk-factor profiles and a more thorough testing of high-risk individuals are adequate to identify those pilots whose health status would represent a threat to safety because of possible acute incapacitation."

A look at incidents of in-flight physical impairment in GA airplanes for the years 1989 through 1994 disclosed 37 cases. Ironically they were split almost evenly by the age test: 19 cases involved pilots over the age of 60, two of whom were in their mid-eighties—one flying a Super Cub and the other a Baron 58. Meanwhile, in 18 accidents the pilots were age 59 or less, including a couple of pilots in their twenties.

In essence, the history of accidents and incidents shows that physical condition is an individual consideration. Thus, for the GA pilot there is no medical support for the FAA's age-60 retirement, or the newer age 65 rule. Nor should age worry the healthy septuagenarian. Simply put, "lifestyle" makes the difference.

In a 1975 book on aging, *Why Survive Being Old In America?*, Dr. Robert N. Butler dispelled the idea that chronological age was equivalent to physiological and psychological deterioration. In addition, he found that,

"Intellectual abilities did not decline as a consequence of the mysterious process of aging, but as the result of specific diseases."

The late Dr. T. Franklin Williams, then director of the National Institute on Aging, reported to Congress that because of "continued advances in both medical technology and research in aging, we have considerably more knowledge and understanding of health and functional ability beyond age 60 now, than we did even a few years ago...cardiac output and mental functioning may be maintained at least as late as age 80 in the same ranges as in healthy young persons...in the absence of disease, overall functioning may be well maintained at least to age 80."

Dr. Williams stated further that, "The risks of heart attack in the next four or five years in a carefully examined, healthy man [age] 60–70, is less than five percent, the same risk that exists for carefully examined, healthy men [age] 40–59." Regarding the downward trend of cardiovascular mortality, which began in the 1970s, Dr. William B. Kannel stated, "One unequivocal conclusion is that these [coronary heart] diseases are not an inevitable consequence of aging or genetic makeup, and can be prevented."

A study by the House of Representatives Public Works and Transportation Committee found, "Pilots over age 60, with more than 5,000 flight hours, have a lower accident rate than pilots of all ages with 1,000 to 5,000 flight hours." A December 1990 term paper by Embry Riddle Aeronautical University Masters Degree graduate student Kevin Riebsam, titled "*Aircraft Accident Relationship to Pilot age and Experience*," looked at the accident rate for pilots age 60 years and over, who held a Commercial or ATP certificate. Using a NTSB study (1976 to 1985) and other data, his report showed that for *professional pilots* the accident rate began to decrease in the 30-to-39 age group, accounting for 30.7 percent of mishaps. Riebsam's study found that professional pilots over 60 had the lowest number of total accidents at 5.6 percent.

Chapter 8 details the ditching of a Citation Jet following a runaway nose-down trim. Even though the 80 year-old owner/pilot lacked the elevator force to overcome the nose-down moment of a runaway pitch-trim, he maneuvered the airplane to a successful ditching off Whidbey Island, about 30 miles north of Seattle, Washington.

Nevertheless, physical incapacitation is worth some thought. Although rare, when incapacitation does occur, an accident becomes inevitable, usually with a family member or close friend aboard. This shows the great desirability of having an adequately trained copilot. For dedicated single pilot owner/operators, it should provide motivation for the AOPA's Pinch Hitter course for your spouse or frequent flying companion. Similar training is also offered by several flight schools. This course teaches the fundamentals of controlling and landing the aircraft, along with radio frequencies and the transponder code needed to get help. There have been several dramatically successful occurrences in which the pilot died, yet the pinch-hitter trained wife or passenger landed the airplane successfully, albeit with some damage.

Conclusions

The person statistically most vulnerable to having an accident is a private pilot who lacks an instrument rating, and has 1,000 hours or less flight experience. In addition, he or she will have less than 100 hours in type. Pilots with fewer than 500 hours of flight-time in type were involved in three-quarters of the general aviation accidents, 74.2 percent of which were fatal.

Preventing an accident that involves buzzing and hitting something is a matter of self-discipline. Yet, despite the continuing history of fatal accidents, it remains a problem. As for takeoff and climb accidents, because crosswinds are frequently involved, a sure way to prevent a loss-of-control accident is to use the demonstrated crosswind shown in the POH/AFM as a limitation to departure. Because above that indicated speed, you have no idea of the airplane's controllability.

When you scroll through the NTSB accident data you'll find the number of accidents involving CFIT simply unbelievable. Thus, for added capability and more quality flight time, an instrument rating is strongly recommended for all private pilots, especially before flying cross-country at night. While some will argue the point, the accident record shows that despite the official criteria for visual flight rules, without an instrument rating you simply cannot fly safely day or night with a visibility no more than one to three miles.

There are examples you'll see in this book when the weather was clearly VMC, but the pilot couldn't either maintain visual orientation or see and avoid obstructions, e.g., a white-out in snow, low visibility due to smoke, fog or rain, or simply featureless terrain on a dark, moonless night.

The John F. Kennedy Jr. accident, discussed in Chapter 7, provides a classic example. Weather conditions were legally VMC. However, after nightfall and in reduced visibility over the dark, featureless ocean, he apparently became spatially disoriented and lost control. Yet, engaging the autopilot would have leveled the wings and stopped the death-spiral, (assuming his attitude gyro was functioning properly).

In yet another classic case, despite a clear night sky, the lack of visual clues—featureless terrain—led to the death of country singer and TV star Reba McEntire's band. (Fortunately, Reba was on another aircraft.) It was a moonless late-night departure, with 50 miles visibility. To avoid San Diego's Class-B airspace, the pilot of the corporate jet attempted to fly VFR at 3,000 feet until receiving his IFR clearance. On the eastbound heading, while flying over a vast unlighted area, the two pilots were unable to see Otay Mountain (3,566 feet MSL) just east of San Diego. (This tragedy too is discussed in Chapter 7.)

The main point to remember is that the most critical phases of flight are the first two minutes of takeoff and climb, and the last six minutes of descent, approach and landing. And also remember that maneuvering flight and low-level aerobatics, or buzzing, in single-engine airplanes is consistently a predominant cause of fatal accidents.

Above all keep in mind that despite the lenient requirements of 14 CFR §61.57, you *are not* a safe or proficient pilot if you go 90 days without flying.

CHAPTER 2

The Importance of Preflight Planning

In the rush to get airborne it is often tempting to order the fuel or request a tire pressure check by line service, then hurry to the fixed-base operator (FBO) to file a clearance. But like it or not, as pilot-in-command, it is *your* responsibility to see that all pre-flight actions are accomplished correctly. After all, it's your life that's at risk, so you can't afford to take anyone's word. Look at the following example to see what I mean.

It was February 10, 1994, when a Cessna 421 on an air ambulance flight crashed shortly after takeoff from San Antonio International airport. A minute after liftoff the pilot reported a problem and said he needed to return immediately. Witnesses saw the airplane flying low with the wings wobbling and trailing black smoke. The tower cleared him to land on runway 12R, but during the pilot's futile effort to reach the airfield, the airplane crashed a half mile short of the runway, coming to rest against a four-foot diameter oak tree. The pilot and one of his two passengers was killed.

Cause of the accident was improper refueling by line service personnel. They had refueled the aircraft with 60 gallons of jet fuel rather than the 100 LL gas ordered by the pilot. Laboratory analysis showed the left tank had 43 percent gasoline and 57 percent Jet A. The right tank contained 52 percent gasoline and 48 percent Jet A.

To prevent this type of accident the FAA had issued AD 87-21-02, which mandated installation of fuel filler restrictors on the aircraft's wing tanks and the fuel truck's nozzles. This AD had been accomplished on the Cessna 421, but unfortunately the jet fuel truck had not had the modified nozzle installed. When the fuel vendor was contacted, the investigator learned that the modified nozzle had been in the warehouse for the past two years but never installed.

Yet, despite the FAA's continuing efforts to stop misfueling accidents, 20 years later it happened again on August 27, 2014 at New Mexico's Las Cruces International Airport. It was yet another Cessna 421 air-ambulance flight, registered to Elite Medical Air Transport, LLC of El Paso, Texas and operated by Amigos Aviation, Inc. of Harlingen, Texas. The aircraft crashed due to line service personnel refueling the aircraft with Jet-A instead of 100LL aviation gas. All four occupants—the pilot, two medical technicians, and the patient—were killed. According to the NTSB Preliminary Report the pilot was still seated in the cockpit when he gave the line service technician a verbal order for 40 gallons of fuel, "The line service technician drove the fuel truck to the front of the airplane putting 20 gallons in each wing [tank]. The pilot then assisted the line service technician with replacing the fuel caps, and they both walked into the office where the pilot signed the machine printed fuel ticket."

Several witnesses saw the airplane flying at a low level and emitting smoke from the right engine. Investigators found the aircraft had impacted in an upright position, but came to rest inverted whereupon it was consumed by a post-impact fire. Investigators who arrived at the accident scene the following day reported immediately smelling jet fuel. The refueling records and interviews with the line service technicians verified that the airplane had been fueled with 40 gallons of Jet-A fuel instead of 100LL aviation gasoline. Although not addressed in the NTSB's preliminary report, it seems obvious that the fuel truck operator was under-trained and neither the fuel truck nor the airplane had been modified as required years earlier by AD 87-21-02 to prevent just such an accident.

Yet in the second case, the pilot seems to have been uncommonly careless: the clearly marked Jet-A fuel truck was parked directly in front of him as he sat in the cockpit while the line service driver fulfilled his order for fuel. (This begs the question as to the pilot's age, training, and experience.) Meanwhile, it's important to remember the words of §91.3 which states, "The pilot in command of an aircraft is directly responsible for and the final authority as to, operation of that aircraft."

With single-pilot operations—in this case an air ambulance flight—the extra duties and time consuming chores required of the lone pilot-in-command is a major problem. In the rush to get something to eat, check the weather, or file a flight plan, we all sometimes fail to monitor the refueling of our airplane. Obviously, the support team's negligence led to this preventable fatal accident. But as these two Cessna 421 accidents show, the type and amount of fuel put into your tanks is critically important. And that's the responsibility of the pilot-in-command.

Because of weight and balance considerations, you'll frequently fly with a partial fuel load, but you shouldn't rely totally on the fuel gauge readings. Instead, both before and after being refueled, you should measure the fuel quantity with a calibrated dipstick and, as part of your preflight inspection, check both the color and condition of the fuel. Then make certain the fuel caps have been properly replaced.

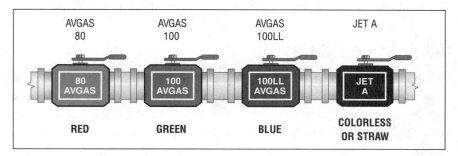

Figure 2-1. Aviation fuel color-coding system. (Source: FAA-H-8083-25A)

After re-checking the oil level make certain the dip stick and oil filler cap are secured. Line service crews are a convenience, but as accidents show, you can't be certain of their training, skill level, or attitude. In short, *never ever trust line service personnel with your life!*

It's also especially important to know the critical airspeeds at various aircraft gross weights, such as rotation or takeoff speed, best angle of climb (V_X), best rate climb (V_Y), best glide speed, flap and gear extension speeds, and final approach and landing speed. For a light-twin, it's important that you know the minimum single-engine control speed (V_{MC}) and the speed for single-engine best rate of climb (V_{YSE}). These speeds represent the only way to get optimum control and performance from the airplane.

For a single-engine airplane, a good example concerns best glide speed. If the engine fails in flight you'll be exchanging altitude for airspeed. Then, in order to get *maximum distance* from your altitude, you must hold the best glide speed for the current gross weight of your aircraft. This speed provides the most lift with the least drag, and is directly related to the aircraft's stall speed at a given gross weight. Some light aircraft have only one speed published. But more advanced models will publish a glide speed for different gross weights. Gliding either too fast or too slow will shorten your attainable glide distance. The aerodynamic drag created by extending flaps or landing gear too soon *greatly* reduces your attainable glide distance.

Another important number is maneuvering speed (V_A). For a given gross weight this speed should not be exceeded when flying in heavy turbulence. A slower airspeed compromises controllability and invites a stall and loss of control. Flying faster than V_A can result in structural damage if severe gusts are encountered. (Transport category airplanes have a speed for maximum *gust intensity*, or *turbulence penetration speed*, V_B.)

Weight and Balance

With GA airplanes it's very tempting to treat them like automobiles, and load everything you can stuff aboard. Sometimes it takes a frightening incident to get your attention before you realize the benefits of calculating the weight and balance for each flight. But then again, you may not be that lucky.

Back in the 1960s, an acquaintance of mine—an Air Force colonel and graduate of the USAF Test Pilot School—flew to the Air Force Academy at Christmas-time, with his wife and his cadet-son's girlfriend. Their trip was to take their son and his girlfriend for a weekend of skiing. The Piper Cherokee Six belonged to the Eglin AFB (Florida) aero club and had six passenger seats.

With four seats occupied by adult passengers and the aft baggage compartment loaded with bags, boots, and skis, they extended one last "awww, come on and join us" invitation to another cadet who was seeing them off. And, following this last invitation, the second cadet acquiesced. After stuffing his gear inside, they taxied out.

Following an extended takeoff roll the aircraft lifted off and was seen to pitch up, wallow from side to side, then crash and burn. All but one of the occupants were killed. They had treated this airplane like an automobile and loaded it without regard to the ship's authorized weight and balance limitations.

As passengers on a Cherokee Six, my youngest son and I too were very nearly victims of a similar situation. It was a charter flight out of Zamboanga Airport, Philippines. Our pilot was a furloughed Philippine Airline First Officer. We were a hunting party, with three 200-pound adults, two children, and a 160-pound pilot. I hadn't paid attention to the loading, but was aware that all the shotguns, rifles, and ammunition had been placed in the aft baggage area. Having never been in a Cherokee Six, I wasn't aware of the forward baggage compartment behind the engine.

When we boarded the aircraft the others insisted I ride right seat beside the pilot, since I was pilot of the C-47 (DC-3) that belonged to the U.S. Military Advisory Group (MAG) to the Philippine Armed Forces. During takeoff roll the pilot drifted toward the left edge of the runway, whereupon I finally said something and pushed a bit of right rudder. By this time we had way more airspeed than needed for takeoff; the pilot startled me by roughly snatching the airplane into the air. As we got airborne I saw the pilot's eyes grow wide with fear, and I looked down to see he had the control wheel almost full forward. We were dangerously aft of the airplane's allowable center of gravity (CG). By now we were 100 feet in the air and already out of runway. In my calmest voice I leaned over to him and coached, "don't panic, just stay at full power and make nice gentle turns to downwind and base leg."

My voice seemed to calm him, and with his composure regained he flew a wide pattern using gentle 10-degree banked turns, then made a safe power-on landing. After returning to the parking area, we reloaded the baggage and carefully worked a weight and balance form and the next takeoff was normal. Because it was an air-taxi flight and he was a furloughed airline pilot, I had trusted the lad's training, proficiency, and judgment, which almost cost us our lives.

An out-of-limits *forward* CG presents the opposite problem. In this case it can be difficult or impossible to rotate and get airborne. Or upon landing you may not be able to flare adequately for touchdown. A classic example involved a Canadian registered turbo-prop Hawker Siddeley HS-748-2A. It crashed while attempting takeoff slightly over-weight, and with an excessively forward CG. At their V_R of 115 KIAS, the captain rotated and the elevator deflected, with the nose beginning to rise to a takeoff attitude. Later, he told investigators that as the aircraft approached what he felt was a takeoff attitude, he relaxed the controls somewhat. Yet the airplane failed to get airborne. He again pulled back on the controls, but the airplane still refused to lift off.

At 131 KIAS and with 1,750 feet of runway remaining, the captain initiated the reject procedure. Despite using maximum braking and props to the full-fine pitch stop (flat pitch), the aircraft over-ran the runway at approximately 100 knots. It then rolled through some soft ground, where-upon the nose gear collapsed. The right wing then hit an ILS localizer antenna and the aircraft skidded on its belly through heavy rocks—finally coming to rest about 800 feet off the end of the runway.

Investigators found that instead of weighing the extra baggage loaded into the forward baggage compartment, the loadmaster had estimated its weight. Unfortunately, he under-estimated it by 460 pounds. This put the takeoff weight 200 pounds over the certified limit, and moved the aircraft's CG well forward of its limit. As a result, the pilot couldn't get the airplane to fly.

Underestimating the passenger, baggage, and cargo weight too often has been a common practice in both private and commercial operations. And while you may get away with it some of the time, sooner or later you'll learn the hard way that you've only been fooling yourself.

Utility and Aerobatic Category

Some light planes have weight and balance limitations designed to serve a flexible purpose. For example, an airplane may be certificated in both the normal and utility category, or normal and aerobatic category. Thus, before each flight, the owner/operator must ensure that the aircraft is loaded cor-rectly for its intended use. Normal category is used during a routine flight with passengers, wherein the aircraft can be loaded up to its gross weight and CG limit. With utility category certification, the aircraft can be used for training commercial pilots and flight instructor candidates in com-mercial maneuvers and perhaps spins.

Because of the maneuvers performed in aerobatic category, the CG is more limited and usually requires a gross weight reduction, with a more restrictive CG envelope. To stay within the approved aerobatic CG usu-ally requires limiting the fuel quantity. In a four- or six-place airplane the number of people aboard would undoubtedly be limited to two on the front seats.

Thus before an aerobatic flight, a weight and balance computation must be accomplished. And it's *very important* that the *actual* weight of each occupant is used. Should you load the aircraft for the normal category CG envelope and then proceed to try some aerobatic maneuvers, you may find it impossible to recover from certain aerobatic maneuvers—specifically spins.

The Standard Average Weights

When computing the weight and balance for a flight, beware the discredited practice of using the so-called "average weight" of 170 pounds per person. In all GA aircraft, only the actual, fully-dressed weight of each individual should be used. Following the crash of an over-loaded commuter aircraft which resulted in several deaths, the FAA modified this practice for the scheduled air carriers. Investigators found the aircraft had been badly overloaded when the standard average weight for the passengers was used in figuring the airplane's takeoff gross weight. As a result, in June 2005 the FAA published Advisory Circular 120-27E for commercial operators, which in reality should be applicable to all of us. It increased the allowable average passenger weight from 170 lbs to 190 lbs summer and 195 lbs winter. However, the advisory circular prohibits using standard average weights in the following type aircraft:

- All single-engine piston-powered aircraft.
- Multi-engine piston-powered aircraft.
- Turbine-powered single-engine aircraft.

Generally speaking, airplanes with reciprocating engines can carry full fuel or full seats, but not both at once. Many pilots, when they do compute a weight and balance, are astonished to discover they have been flying routinely over the airplane's certificated gross weight. This is especially true with extended range fuel tanks installed, or in six-seat singles, wherein weight in the two aft seats can make the CG critical. A Cessna 182 equipped with extended range fuel tanks and a full fuel load becomes a three place airplane with 200-pound adults aboard. In light, single-engine aircraft having six seats you'll often find the fifth and sixth seats are limited to 70-pound children.

To get down to basics, let's consider the simple four-place, single-engine Cessna 172. There are four seats, which seem to invite four adults aboard. Then there's a baggage compartment with a posted 120-pound limitation. Trouble is, with four adults aboard the baggage compartment is limited to 26 pounds. But how many of us Americans—ladies included—weigh 170 to 190 lbs, or less? Then there's the aircraft's basic weight, which includes the installed equipment. Essentially, with four adults aboard your Cessna 172's fuel quantity is limited to 39 gallons (234 pounds at six pounds per gallon) and very little baggage. Most GA aircraft have similar limitations.

In summary, when figuring your weight and balance, *always* use the actual weight of everyone aboard. Don't try to cheat the system by figuring each person at 170 to 190 pounds. When each passenger weighs 200 to 250 pounds, you need to be certain the resulting weight and balance is within the airplane's certificated envelope. Otherwise you jeopardize the lives of everyone aboard. Although some will consider this overly restrictive, just remember that it's not the FAA you need to worry about, but the laws of physics and aerodynamics.

High Density Altitude

High density altitudes present a special hazard where weight and balance is concerned. When loaded to your maximum gross weight, hot summer temperatures and high elevation airports can cause takeoff roll to exceed runway length. Or, during the heat of the day, in some *non-turbocharged* aircraft if you fail to limit your takeoff weight, you may find that the airplane is at its absolute ceiling and unable to climb out.

The terrain surrounding the departure runway is important too. There must be room to gain altitude, especially when your climb capability is 200 feet per minute (FPM) or less. This information should be in the Operational Data section of your Cessna Owner's Manual. But would you really consider it safe to depart with family or friends and a rate of climb computed at 200 FPM or less?

A lowland pilot flying from high elevation airfields on hot days will encounter some new and interesting problems. Even though you may have read about it, you can't appreciate the performance change until you've "been there and done that." (*Note:* If your POH performance charts provide takeoff distance figures for different field elevations, pressure altitudes and ambient temperatures, then "density altitude" has been figured out for you.)

Safety considerations and Part 91 require that you compute the expected performance of your aircraft from the charts in the POH/AFM. Yet, before you release the brakes, there are still a number of special considerations. For example, the performance charts assume your engine has been leaned for maximum power at your particular density altitude (pressure altitude and ambient temperature). As a sea level pilot you may forget to do this. Then, upon departing from a high-elevation airport, the resulting extended takeoff roll often causes a pilot to rotate and attempt liftoff too early. This can place the aircraft *behind the power curve*, wherein aerody-namic drag exceeds engine thrust, and you'll be unable to climb out of ground effect. To avoid departing almost stalled and hanging on for dear life, pay close attention to the airspeed indicator. Rotate for takeoff only *after* achieving the designated takeoff airspeed. Normally, it's the same indicated speed required at sea level. However, it just takes longer (more runway) to reach it.

Once airborne from a high density altitude airport, lacking a turbo-charged engine, you'll find that acceleration to climb speed is slower. So, after liftoff, lower the nose and accelerate to best climb speed while still in ground effect. Then be prepared for a greatly reduced climb gradient (num-ber of feet traveled horizontally compared to the number of feet climbed vertically). Because your *ground speed* exceeds your indicated airspeed, you'll be traveling over the ground faster than usual, but climbing slower. In other words, your *climb gradient* is greatly reduced, and the height of surrounding terrain becomes very important.

A high density altitude may require an early morning or late afternoon departure—before sun-up or after sunset. With reciprocating-engine sin-gles and twins, a reduced fuel load is almost always required. Sometimes, even a passenger or two and some baggage must be off-loaded before you can safely depart.

To maintain an engine-out climb capability in a twin-engine aircraft you will sometimes find it necessary to severely limit the aircraft's depar-ture weight. Professional pilots routinely limit their gross weight by short-ing the fuel load at places like Aspen (elevation 7,815 feet) or Colorado Springs (elevation 6,184 feet). Then they land at the nearest lower pressure altitude airport, such as Grand Junction (elevation 4,858 feet) or Pueblo (elevation 4,728), and refuel for the remainder of the trip.

A story told in the Lake Tahoe area tells of a new private pilot from the (sea level) Oakland-San Francisco Bay area. With his girlfriend aboard, he flew a Lake Amphibian to South Lake Tahoe Airport (elevation 6,264 feet). There he topped off the amphib's fuel tanks. Then, to demonstrate his prowess with a seaplane, he landed on Lake Tahoe—elevation of around 6,000 feet, and at the time, an ambient temperature of around 80°F (28°C). Unfortunately, upon attempting to depart he couldn't get airborne, simply because of the aircraft's gross weight and the approximately 9,000 foot *den-sity* altitude. He then docked at the seaplane base where the FBO manager de-fueled it. Later in the afternoon, it was ferried down to a lower elevation airport for the embarrassed owner.

The learning objective here is simple. To fly safely, you must know your aircraft's weight and balance and performance capability each time you fly. You may get away with an over-gross weight or out of the CG takeoff occasionally. But one day you're heavy and departing with a high-density altitude and suddenly discover the runway is too short or the aircraft won't climb out. And now fate has a "gotcha."

Weather

First let's agree that there is no such thing as an "all-weather" airplane. Nature *always* has the last word. Yet each year someone challenges a thunderstorm, or "zero visibility" in fog, and comes out the loser. For years "weather" has been a major cause of fatal accidents. Yet "bad judgment" would have been a more accurate finding.

A predominant cause of fatalities involves CFIT. This is usually the result of a pilot continuing into deteriorating weather conditions and attempting to remain visual. Consequently, whether flying VFR or IFR, accurate weather information from your departure point to your destination is essential for a safe flight.

There are many sources of weather information, but for pilots a Flight Service Station (FSS) briefing is the basic authority. Today's weather forecasts are amazingly accurate, although there is an occasional miss; where upon reaching your destination, you find the weather much worse than forecast. Therefore it is good practice to begin continuously monitoring your enroute and destination weather several days before a trip. Then, the night before and again on the day of departure, get the official FSS briefing. If cost is no problem, one of the private flight-planning companies will provide very accurate winds, weather and notices to airmen (NOTAMs), along with a computerized trip planning service. Then, while enroute, regularly re-check with Flight Watch to keep track of any forecast changes or recent pilot reports. With Flight Watch available, today's GA pilot has almost the equivalent of an airline's flight dispatcher readily available.

Some years ago, the NTSB published a report entitled "Flight Service Station Weather Briefing Inadequacies" (NTSB SIR-81-3). This report looked at 72 accidents, six of which involved pertinent weather information that was not provided to the pilot. Nevertheless, the NTSB found that FSS personnel *were* adequately trained to interpret National Weather Service information, and that the relevant data were available; however, sometimes they failed to follow prescribed procedures and the new weather information didn't reach the pilot. This shows the benefit of obtaining weather information from a variety of sources, then, while airborne, continuously monitoring the weather via Flight Watch.

The winds aloft are important too, since they affect your time en route and fuel requirements. In high mountainous terrain wind speed at mountain top height is especially critical. What many pilots fail to realize is that with winds over the crests at 20 to 30 knots or greater, severe turbulence is probable, with downdrafts possible that may exceed the climb capability of the aircraft. In addition, *standing mountain waves* tend to form, which amplify the turbulence and downdraft problem. The freezing level is important too. If you'll be flying IFR in clouds without deicing/anti-icing equipment, then you must fly below the freezing level. Obviously this can't be below the minimum enroute altitude (MEA). Trouble comes when the clouds and freezing level are at or below the MEA. With non-turbocharged engines this is a common dilemma in the western states, where many airways have MEA's of 10,000 to 14,000 feet. Thus, your only option is to delay the flight, not just because it's illegal, but because it's dangerous.

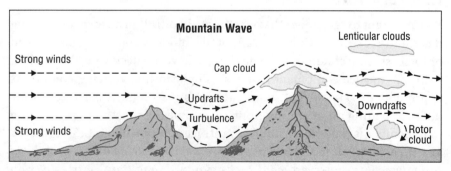

Figure 2-2. Winds at mountain peaks that exceed 20 knots will result in severe turbulence and strong downdrafts. Cap, rotor, and lenticular clouds often provide visible clues to the presence of severe turbulence.

Always have an "out" in case the weather changes. Whether flying IFR or VFR, on every cross-country flight you should identify possible en route alternates. Then, if the weather gets marginal, you can either reverse course or divert to an en route alternate.

In the western United States, another dilemma can arise. Let's say you want to depart Lancaster, California's Fox Field for Sacramento, and the weather report shows clear skies and unlimited visibility (CAVU) all the way there. But unfortunately, along your planned route on the west-side of the Sierra Nevada range, a thousand-foot blanket of fog covers the entire San Joaquin valley. Bakersfield, Fresno, Stockton, and your destination Sacramento are all at or below landing minimums. While you're en route, all stations are forecast to reach ILS minimums, but you're flying a single-engine airplane. If you decide to go, what will you do if the engine acts up or the generator/alternator quits?

In a twin you can survive an engine failure, but you'll have only one shot at landing. There are no alternates available except on the eastern side of the Sierra Nevada range; with an engine out you can't reach the 12,000 MEA to get across the mountains to an alternate with good weather. While the CAVU conditions aloft are tempting, the basic problem is you have no enroute alternates.

In-flight Ice

It's important to remember that whether VFR or IFR in an airplane lacking deice/anti-ice certification, you cannot file into an airport with *any* known or forecast icing conditions. If you don't believe it, check your POH/AFM. Without anti-ice equipment it states, "Flight in known icing conditions is prohibited." The aircraft manufacturer's instructions constitute your bible, providing all operating limitations. But the most important thing to remember is that even with deice/anti-ice equipment, *no U.S. registered aircraft is certified to fly continuously in moderate icing and is prohibited from flying into any severe icing, such as "mixed condition," or freezing rain and drizzle.* Beechcraft's *Safety Information* manual in the Baron 58 POH says it correctly: "Properly equipped airplanes are approved for flight in light to moderate icing conditions only. These aircraft *are not approved for extended flight in moderate icing conditions or flights in any severe icing conditions.*"

Finally, there's a relationship between weather and the fuel aboard. The more fuel you have the more options you have to deal with unexpected weather. But your fuel load must be balanced with your cabin load, i.e. passengers or cargo. Remember too, that with destination weather less than 2,000 feet and 3 miles, fuel to an alternate plus a 45-minute reserve must be factored into your weight and balance (per §91.167(a)).

When flying VFR during daylight hours you are legally required to carry only enough fuel to reach destination plus a 30-minute fuel reserve—or 45 minutes at night. Conversely on an IFR flight plan, the regulation requires a 45-minute reserve, day or night. But, if your cabin load will allow, just to be safe carry a one-hour fuel reserve day or night. You'll find this promotes a calmer and safer flight.

Propeller Condition

The NTSB accident record shows that a propeller's condition and how it has been maintained is often a player in our annual accident history. Ironically, the cause of almost every prop failure accident is the direct result of owner/operator ignorance and neglect. Because of inadequate emphasis during early flight training, many pilots fail to carefully check the airplane's propeller. After all, it's the owner who must ensure that any erosion or "ding" you find is within limits. But in reality, most people don't have a clue as to what they are looking for on the prop during preflight—maybe nicks or leading edge roughness from sand, or in a floatplane, water erosion. Because most pilots realize the prop's leading edge must be smooth, to save time and a few dollars some misguided souls attempt to fix a prop ding themselves, even though most require a certified mechanic to accomplish the job.

A controllable pitch prop has a flight-time limitation, or time between overhaul (TBO). In some cases, after several years of limited use, an engine and propeller may not have accumulated the expected flying hours, but there's usually a five-year (60-month) inspection requirement. Consider the following examples.

Prop Failure Accidents

Just after takeoff a Cessna 182 with five people aboard experienced complete power failure as it climbed through 800 feet. During the subsequent forced landing the aircraft flipped inverted, but fortunately no one was injured. Investigators found a fractured propeller blade caused by a fatigue crack that originated in the "tread root." In addition, internal components contained rust and rust residue. The prop's specified TBO was 1,200 hours or five years (60 calendar months). Yet it hadn't been touched in its entire 19-year service life. Advisory Directive 91-15-04, which required a modification so that a fatigue crack would leak dyed oil, also had been ignored.

Another case involved a Piper J-3 Cub cruising at 2,500 feet, when the engine began vibrating severely. The pilot told investigators, "I was afraid it was going to shake the engine off the airplane, so I shut it down." Investigators found prop de-lamination on one blade's leading edge and tip. In addition, traces of rust were found on the wood where the metal leading edge "tipping" was attached with the manufacturer's steel screws.

In a similar case, a Taylorcraft in cruise flight experienced a sudden severe vibration. This pilot too shut down the engine and made a successful forced landing. The investigation showed the brass abrasion strip and part of the blade was missing. A mechanic found dry-rot in a part of the remaining blade. Yet this kind of deterioration should have been found during its annual inspection and also pilot preflight.

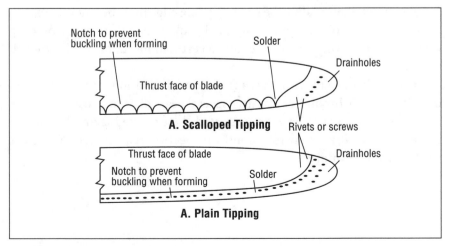

Figure 2-3. Wooden propeller blade.

Prop Strike

In most cases, following a prop strike, despite the lack of obvious damage, the propeller almost *always* requires a non-destructive inspection (NDI). Occasionally, with seemingly minor damage, the prop may be ruined. A few years back a Rockwell Commander 112TC was cruising at 9,500 when the pilot heard a loud "boom," and then the engine failed. Investigators found that the airplane had experienced two previous prop blade strikes. After each strike the engine and propeller were apparently undamaged. Yet NTSB metallurgists found, "The [prop] hub failed as a result of fatigue cracking…damage to the pre-load plate shelf indicated the hub had previously experienced a blade strike."

Another case involved a student flying a Cessna 172 on his first solo when during initial climb out the engine suddenly failed. He told investigators that he heard a loud "bang," then the engine quit. He successfully landed on a golf course, but the aircraft was substantially damaged.

Investigators found the entire prop, flange, and forward end of the engine crankshaft missing. The components were located later near the mid-point of the departure runway. An FAA investigator documented two previous prop strikes without *any* propeller or engine inspection.

In yet another case, a retired Air Force friend, his eldest son, and I were going antelope hunting. For several months we had looked forward to a week of re-living old times. Since he resided in Washington State, I joined him there for the flight in his Cessna 210 to Lewiston, Montana. John was actually a partner in the airplane, along with two other businessmen. One partner, despite several hundred hours in the airplane, seemed to be unlucky. On two occasions he had dinged the prop while taxiing too fast from their grass parking area onto the concrete ramp. In each case, when the nose-wheel hit the edge of the ramp, the prop was damaged. In a third mishap he had landed much too fast and "wheel barrowed"—again dinging the prop. However, this time the engine required inspection and replacement of the three-bladed prop.

As we approached the airplane for our trip to Montana my host said calmly, "looks like the Doc has done it again." The propeller was obviously brand new, yet the other two partners had not been informed of prop change. In fact, in only one of the three other incidents had the partners been informed, and that was because the airplane required several days of down time to accomplish an internal inspection of the engine. Nor had the insurance company or FAA been notified. The miscreant simply paid cash for the repairs and kept quiet. Now he had done it again.

We flew the trip and fortunately had beautiful weather with no turbulence over the mountains. Nor was there any hint of a problem with the airplane, engine, or prop. Yet after the trip my host kept examining the airplane from a distance. Then, without prompting, he said, "something doesn't look right. The nose looks like it droops." The airplane had looked good on both of our preflight inspections. But John wasn't satisfied. Next day, with an A&P mechanic, they opened the engine cowl and began looking for trouble. And in no time they found it. The engine firewall was buckled and the forward frame bent. That "dinged prop" incident had actually been a major accident.

The repair estimate was such that the insurance company declared it "not economically repairable." Thus, our trip to Montana had been made with a structurally damaged, un-airworthy airplane. Any moderate to severe turbulence over the mountains of Idaho and Montana could have caused airframe failure. The finely tuned Continental engine was of special concern. Internal damage could have caused engine failure during the critical takeoff and landing phase, or over the rugged mountains of Idaho and Montana.

Continental Service Bulletin M84-16 (issued December 22, 1984) advises that prop damage requiring only minor dressing of a blade does not require an engine inspection. However, if a blade or the entire propeller is removed for repair then severe internal damage to the crankshaft, prop components, counter-weights, or crank-case bearing caps may have occurred. The Service Bulletin mandated that a prop strike required complete engine disassembly and inspection. Lycoming too published Service Letter L163C, which recommends that any engine involved in a sudden stoppage event must be removed, disassembled, and inspected, prior to being returned to service. Anything less is flirting with catastrophe.

Airworthiness Directives

The importance of an Airworthiness Directive (AD) and factory Service Bulletins (SB) cannot be over-emphasized. In the Cessna 182 accident described initially, both normal maintenance and an AD had been ignored. Yet compliance with the AD would have prevented jeopardizing the lives of the occupants and loss of the aircraft. This owner's gross negligence also could have negated the insurance policy.

In yet another case, an aerobatic pilot lost his life because he failed to comply with an AD. Specifically, he was known to ignore the engine's 2,700-RPM limitation. One day during a downwind departure, he suddenly declared an emergency and began spiraling down at a 45-degree angle ultimately crashing into a residential street. The propeller, along with the severed crankshaft flange, were found near the runway still bolted together. In this case a prop blade had failed mid-span due to fatigue.

Investigators felt this resulted from the gyroscopic and aerobatic loads encountered while operating above the 2,700 RPM redline. The engine had been certificated for helicopters with a redline of 3,200 RPM. However, with aerobatic loads, it was limited to 2,700 RPM. (*Note:* Chapter 9 discusses how a manufacturer's negligence in complying with earlier NTSB recommendations, resulted in a prop hub failure that killed the governor of South Dakota, along with his pilot and five business associates.)

Fatigue Cracks

Prop blade failure due to fatigue cracks plays prominently in the accident statistics. Typically they result from a neglected nick or gouge in the leading edge of a blade. For example, a Mooney M20B was approaching the outer marker for an ILS approach. Suddenly the airplane developed a severe engine vibration. The pilot wisely shut down the engine and made a successful emergency landing. The vibration was found to have been caused by separation of a prop tip due to fatigue.

Another instance involved an Air Tractor AT-401 that was damaged in a forced landing. Investigators found that 10 inches of the prop had broken off due to a fatigue crack. In fact the blade showed fatigue cracking over 60 percent of the fractured surface. Origin of the crack was a "notch" created by a previously re-worked leading edge ding.

The accident record shows that, over the years, most all GA aircraft types have experienced a fatigue-related propeller failure. They range from the PA 24-180, Cessna 182, Cessna 421, and Beechcraft A23, to a couple in the Beechcraft 1900 Commuters.

Figure 2-4. Vibrations caused by failure of the prop-tip of this Cessna 182 forced the pilot to shut down the engine and make a forced landing.

People Strikes

No discussion of propeller mishaps would be complete without addressing human injuries from prop strikes. The first rule when walking up to a parked airplane is to always assume someone left the magnetos ON. Otherwise, during preflight, a conscientious pull of the prop blade from vertical to horizontal could cause the engine to kick over and fire momentarily.

This happened to a good friend some years ago. While preflighting an Air Force Aero Club's Navion, he pulled the prop from vertical to horizontal and the engine fired. Because he was standing up close, the prop literally chopped his legs out from under him. But thanks to a good Air Force orthopedic surgeon, he regained full use of his legs. Still, it was a close brush with sudden death and crippling injury.

Another accident potential involves loading or off-loading passengers with the engine(s) running. In a word, *DON'T!* I once watched the eight year-old daughter of my next door neighbor run through the prop of her father's newly purchased Ercoupe. He was taking his five kids to ride one at a time and didn't want to shut down the engine each time. She survived the ordeal, but with a severe head injury, and was permanently physically handicapped.

Because the general aviation fleet is aging, neglect of the prop is a potential problem. To ensure your safety, here are some of the questions you should be able to answer regarding the propeller:

1. How close is the airplane's propeller to its TBO or mandatory calendar inspection?
2. What are the factory inspection requirements and how long has it been since the fixed-pitch-prop had an NDI check?
3. With any prop strike, what action is required by the manufacturer?
4. Following a prop strike, what is the possible result of flying without the factory recommended inspection?
5. With a nick or gouge in the prop leading edge who can inspect and repair it?
6. How can you check your airplane's ignition system to be certain the magnetos are grounding in the OFF position; and what is the possible danger if one or both mags remain HOT?

Summary

The major learning objective of this chapter is that a great many of our aircraft accidents become inevitable before takeoff begins. Therefore, careful attention to all manner of detail is the responsibility of the pilot-in-command. This means supervising the refueling, accomplishing the preflight walk-around, and making certain the weight and balance is within established limits. Know the weather and keep track of it while en route. Remember too that with the wonders of the internet and other electronic aids and Flight Watch to provide weather information while en route, the GA pilot has almost the same support an airline crew enjoys with a dispatcher. And finally, don't take your propeller for granted. There is a valid reason for its inspection requirements, and many prop-related problems could and should have been caught during preflight.

Just remember, when making a hurried, cursory preflight and weather check, if you overlook something important, you'll be first to the scene of the accident.

CHAPTER 3

Takeoff and Climb Accidents

As described in Chapter 1, the takeoff phase of flight traditionally accounts for around 20 percent of the annual accidents, many of which are fatal. Some appear as the result of inadequate preflight preparation, or occasionally pilot training and/or proficiency. The following is a look at some of the more repetitive and problematic accidents and how they might have been prevented.

Airframe Ice

A major consideration during preflight in winter is deicing or anti-icing the aerodynamic surfaces, i.e., the wings and tail. Yet there is no regulation for light GA airplanes that requires this. Subpart F of Part 91, "Large and Turbine-Powered Multiengine Aircraft," forbids departure with frost, snow, or ice adhering to any propeller or windshield, or with snow or ice (or frost) adhering to the wings, or stabilizing or control surfaces (§91.527(a)(1)). Since all airfoils are affected by frost or ice contamination, realistically this rule applies to all aircraft. But in getting the surfaces cleaned, you can get either the anti-ice or deice treatment. It's important to know that there's a significant difference in the two types of treatments.

At many FBOs, *deicing* means applying a heated 50/50 mixture of water and Type I glycol. This eliminates the ice and is effective in temperatures down to about -20°C. However, Type I deicing provides very little *anti-ice* protection—called "holdover time." When it's snowing, or with a freezing drizzle, the table for "SAE Aerospace Holdover Times for Type I Fluid" shows that from 0°C to -10°C (32°F to 14°F) the holdover time is only three to six minutes. But realistically, you are unlikely to get a clearance, then taxi out and get airborne in so little time. Consequently, Type I fluid offers almost no anti-icing value.

Figure 3-1. Deicing a Cessna 208.

Airplanes with a takeoff rotation speed of 85 knots or above can get deiced and anti-iced with Type II or IV fluid. Like Type I fluid, these too can be diluted and heated to deice the aircraft. But for continued anti-ice protection during falling snow, sleet, or freezing rain, the fluid must then be re-applied cold and undiluted. When applied cold, it forms a gel-like film on the aerodynamic surfaces and provides an extended holdover time in fairly bad conditions. Then on takeoff, as the aircraft accelerates above 85 knots, the gel-film sloughs off, leaving the aerodynamic surfaces clean.

For a private pilot with no training or instruction on the problem, learning by experience can be costly. A classic example occurred on December 5, 2001, when two people came to grief in a Cessna 182 at the Prescott, Arizona airport. The temperature was -4°C with a cloudless sky and light to variable winds, but overnight the weather had been bad. One witness said the precipitation produced the "heaviest ice they had seen in a few years," and definitely "the heaviest seen this year." Another witness told investigators that, "ground icing conditions were quite severe," with the wings of parked aircraft covered with one-quarter to one-half inch of rime, with a clear-ice coating.

The accident aircraft was among the first to depart that morning. During takeoff roll it was seen to rotate slowly at the 4000-foot point. Then it lifted off into ground effect—flying about ten feet above the runway to within 1,000 feet of the departure end. Then it began to pitch up—slowly at first. But as it passed the end of the runway, it pitched up abruptly and began a right roll to about 80 degrees, ultimately crashing inverted.

Airfoil ice was the obvious cause of this crash. The pilot had made no effort to deice the aircraft. At the time, Embry Riddle Aeronautical University operated their own deice equipment at Prescott, but it was not available to the public. Thus, because he lacked the means to deice, rather than cancel the flight, compulsion lead the pilot to depart anyway.

It happened in Alaska, too, during an early-morning departure. A lineman who had serviced a Cessna Caravan described a heavy frost on the vehicles and airplanes in the area. He noted the Caravan had a thin coating of clear ice on the upper surface of the left wing; however, during preflight the pilot failed to have the wings and tail deiced. Witnesses told investigators that the pilot seemed to be in a rush to make his scheduled departure time. In addition, he ordered fuel to be added only to the left wing tank. During departure, the aircraft was seen to lift off and pass the end of the runway and begin a left turn. Then it suddenly dropped vertically into the Arctic Ocean, killing the pilot and all of his seven passengers.

Frost and/or ice on the wing increases the stall speed, but unfortunately the stall warning system *does not* compensate for the increase. Thus, with any ice on the wing or tail the aircraft can stall well before the stall warning horn sounds, or in a corporate jet, before the stick shaker activates.

Snow and Slush

Runway slush from snow or freezing drizzle can also create problems. Many pilots don't realize that U.S-licensed aircraft *are not* certified for flight in freezing drizzle. This condition is actually *severe ice*, since it involves a moisture droplet size larger than those used in the icing-certification requirement. Besides, during takeoff the runway will be coated with ice, making the published takeoff distance and accelerate-stop data totally irrelevant. More importantly, moist snow and slush cause *slush-drag deceleration*, which greatly affects your takeoff runway requirement. The following is an example of the problem.

It was a miserable evening in Minneapolis, when a Cessna 340 was preparing to depart Crystal Airport (MIC). The weather included a 600-foot ceiling, with visibility only three-quarters of a mile in light snow and fog.

Temperature was 33°F, with a dew point of 31°F and wind reported as coming from 350° at 20 knots, gusting to 30. An employee at the airport told investigators that while working outside his nearby home he had looked up when he heard a Cessna 340's engines to see who would be flying on a night like this. The tower operator said that on takeoff roll the aircraft appeared to become airborne about halfway down the runway, then it settled back down. It didn't get airborne again until crossing the end of the 3,263-foot runway. Shortly thereafter, it struck trees, crashed into two homes, and exploded. Although the two passengers were killed, the pilot survived.

The pilot told investigators that the runway was covered with one to one-and-a-half inches of snow. With an outside temperature of 33°F the snow would have been wet. While the C340's normal takeoff speed is 91 KIAS, its V_{YSE} is 100 knots. The pilot, who claimed more than 700 hours in the Cessna 340A, described how he held the aircraft down until reaching 105 knots; then rotated 200 feet from the end of the runway. He lowered the nose, he said, because the aircraft shuddered as if stalling; then, following a perceived power loss in the left engine, it hit the trees.

This pilot's takeoff technique is unbelievable for an experienced pilot. First, he had one-and-a-half inches of slush covering the runway. At a maximum gross weight of 5,900 pounds, the dry-runway ground roll (no wind) should have been 1,510 feet. The 20-knot headwind would have reduced that to 1,299 feet. To clear a 50-foot obstruction (in this case, the trees), the aircraft would have required a takeoff *distance* of just 1,724 feet—just over half the available runway. By holding the nosewheel on the runway until achieving V_{YSE} (in this case 105 knots, five knots faster than the published V_{YSE} for the Cessna 340), he maximized the *slush-drag effect*.

Using a large jet transport, NASA tests documented the effect of slush-drag on takeoff distance. They found that one-half inch of slush increased the takeoff distance by 15 percent, while one inch increased it 50 percent. One-and-one-quarter inches of slush *doubled the takeoff distance*, and with two inches *takeoff was not possible*.

The lessons from NASA's tests are very clear. First, you *must* remove all ice and snow from the aircraft during preflight. Incidentally, this includes deicing the wheel wells on retractable gear aircraft to prevent structural damage from the compacting of ice and snow when the gear retracts. It also precludes frozen up-locks or micro-switches, and locked (frozen) wheels upon touchdown. The second lesson is that slush-drag greatly extends your takeoff roll and takeoff distance. And with about one-and-a-half inches of slush, you may be unable to get airborne. While no figures or guidance are published for light airplanes, the Cessna 340 crash shows a definite relationship to NASA's demonstrated slush-drag effect on jet transports.

Runway Incursions

While taxiing in or out accompanied by friends or perhaps business clients, it is tempting to discuss the latest news or an important business deal. Yet it is of utmost importance that while in the airport environment pilots observe the *sterile cockpit rule* imposed some years ago by the FAA on airline and air-taxi crews via §§121.542 and 135.100. This means no casual conversation during taxi, takeoff, climb and landing. (As written, the rule says "below 10,000 feet." In a light plane this translates to "until reaching cruising altitude.") Unfortunately, the accident/incident record shows that too many of us indulge in affable chatter during taxi. Then we fail to comprehend our ATC instructions. The result can be a dangerous and sometimes deadly *runway incursion*, which includes entering a runway or taxiway without clearance to do so.

A common type of incursion involves crossing one runway en route to another when the tower has instructed you to hold short. (ATC requires that you read-back any hold short instruction.) According to NASA's Aviation Safety Reporting System (ASRS), "distraction" is continuously reported in ASRS reports on taxiway and runway incursions (*see* §91.25). Regardless of the perceived importance of some tasks relative to others, while taxiing, "the most important task is getting to or from the runway safely."

According to the Department of Transportation Inspector General (IG), runway incursions have increased over the years. In 1999 there were 321 incursions, but in the year 2000 that figure jumped 33 percent to 429. GA pilots were the worst offenders, accounting for 69 percent of the incidents, and in one-third of these incidents the pilot had less than 100 hours flying experience. The year 2001, however, was an exception in that the IG reports a slight decrease, showing that more pilots are paying closer attention.

In their July 2010 report, the FAA noted that the number of Category A and B incursions (those in which a collision was barely avoided) decreased after their August 2007 "Call to Action Plan for Runway Safety." The trend seemed to reverse, however, with serious incursions tripling from fiscal year 2010 to 2012. Between fiscal year 2011 and 2012 runway incursion reports increased 21 percent—and this during a period when total air traffic operations declined slightly. However, this increase may have been due to more stringent requirements for reporting runway incursions.

Highly experienced airline pilots also make these mistakes. At Seattle-Tacoma International, an airliner from Dallas had just landed; it then taxied across a runway from which another airliner was departing. The two MD-80s narrowly avoided colliding. Airport officials said the taxiing flight had been told to hold short of the runway from which the other was departing. Despite the crew's training and experience, they simply weren't paying attention. (Incidents like this motivated the FAA to require read-back of hold short instructions.)

In one incident, *Callback* reproduced the following account from the captain of a Boeing 737, noting that he encountered three problems common to taxi incidents: misunderstanding, assumption, and distraction.

> "I heard, 'Taxi to runway 19,' but I was not focused on the task at hand and missed the added phrase, 'hold short of runway 10.' The First Officer read back the hold-short instruction (I missed it again) and he then began recalculating our takeoff data. [This] caused [him] to be head-down during my approach to the hold-short point...I had switched my attention to other things. As I taxied, I began tuning the radar and formulating a weather-escape plan. I simultaneously discussed with the First Officer the bleed air and flap configurations for our heavy aircraft on a fairly short, wet runway. I was also preparing a rough mental draft of a pre-takeoff announcement about the impending turbulence on the climb-out... As I approached runway 10, I saw an aircraft in position at the other end. I assumed he was in position and hold, since I [believed I] 'had' clearance to cross. To my horror, as I crossed, I saw the other aircraft start rolling. I added power and got quickly out of the way."

ATC makes mistakes too. While flying a Sabreliner 80 out of Oklahoma City's Will Rogers World Airport, I received clearance from the tower to take off on runway 31. Before entering the runway, out of habit, I turned the aircraft slightly to view the final approach and was startled to see a King Air on short final. After obtaining a new clearance for "position and hold," I watched in horror as a Continental flight, departing on runway 35L, rotated and pulled up abruptly to avoid another airliner that had been cleared to cross its takeoff runway at mid-field. The Continental captain was audibly upset. I never learned why, but somehow the tower controller had made two grievous errors in quick succession.

Intersection Departures

Intersection departures also pose the possibility of error by either pilot or controller. A collision that occurred on March 9, 2000, at Sarasota-Bradenton International Airport, between a Cessna 152 and a Cessna 172, involved the pilots and the tower controller. The collision occurred at the intersection of runway 14 and taxiway F (*see* Figure 3-2). The weather was good, and the controller was handling a lot of traffic. The 152 had taxied from Dolphin Aviation (2) via taxiway Alpha to runway 14. The 172 had taxied from Jones Aviation (1) via taxiway F for an intersection departure. The Cessna 152 had been issued a "position and hold" clearance, while the 172 had been holding at the intersection of runway 14 and taxiway F. Seconds after the 152 was cleared into "position and hold," the 172 was cleared, "Runway 14 at Foxtrot, taxi into position and hold." After handling some other airplanes, the controller cleared the Cessna 152 for takeoff. At this time the 172, though cleared into position, had not yet entered the runway.

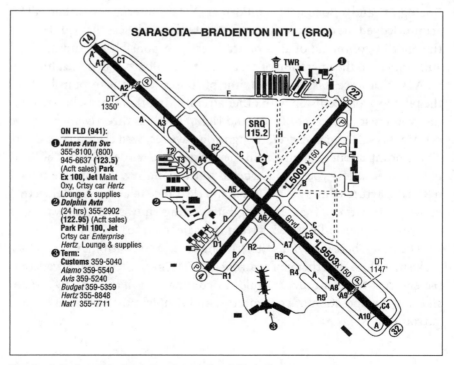

Figure 3-2. Sarasota-Bradenton International Airport. (Courtesy of *Flight Guide* ©2006)

Witnesses stated that as the 152 reached takeoff speed, the 172 entered the runway in front of it. The instructor in the 152 banked right in an attempt to avoid a collision. However, the aircraft appeared to stall, then crashed into the 172. The airplanes exploded and burned, killing both students and their instructors.

The NTSB faulted the controller for failure "to provide effective separation between the accident airplanes." A contributing factor was failure of the pilot and pilot-rated passenger of the Cessna 172 to ensure that the runway was clear of traffic before taking the runway. The Board's findings are reversed from those in similar airline mishaps. Heretofore, they have reminded pilots that it is their responsibility to ensure clearance from other airplanes and obstructions. And that remains the rule. 14 CFR §91.3 states, "The pilot in command of an aircraft is directly responsible for, and is the final authority as to, the operation of that aircraft." Thus, in reality, the pilot of the 172 departing from an intersection failed to look and listen and thus avoid the departing 152 before taxing onto the runway.

In another case where the controller erred—this during bad weather—a Boeing 747 and a Boeing 727 collided at O'Hare International. The NTSB acknowledged the controller's error but noted nevertheless that §91.3 makes the pilot-in-command of an aircraft directly responsible for and the final authority as to the operation of his aircraft. The Board stated, "…although an ATC clearance is issued for taxiing purposes…it is the responsibility of the pilot to avoid collision with other aircraft." In other words, before taxiing, you must look carefully left and right as well as directly ahead, to be certain it is safe to move, even though you have received clearance to do so. This finding applies equally in all the accidents so far described. The AIM tells us that unless you are instructed to the contrary, a clearance to taxi to the departure runway is an automatic clearance to cross all intersecting runways. However, when crossing intersecting runways or taxiways it is still your responsibility to be certain it is safe to do so.

The lesson here is obvious; "to err is human," and controllers, like pilots, make mistakes. Whether you're airborne or taxiing, you should never completely trust the controller. As pilot-in-command, *you* are *directly responsible* for the operation of your aircraft and simply must be aware of your surroundings.

The Quincy Tragedy

Awareness is even more important at nontowered airports. This tragic case of runway incursion led to the fiery death of the passengers and crew of a United Express Beechcraft 1900 and a King Air A90 at Quincy Regional Airport, Illinois. The accident occurred when United Express Flight 5925, landed on runway 13 and was hit by the King Air A90 on an instructional flight departing on runway 4 (*see* Figure 3-3). Communications at this nontowered field are conducted on the published common traffic advisory frequency (CTAF). The United Express cockpit voice recorder (CVR) documented the captain announcing her flight's position 30 miles north, with the intention to land on runway 13. The captain then broadcast in the blind, "any traffic in the area please advise." No one replied.

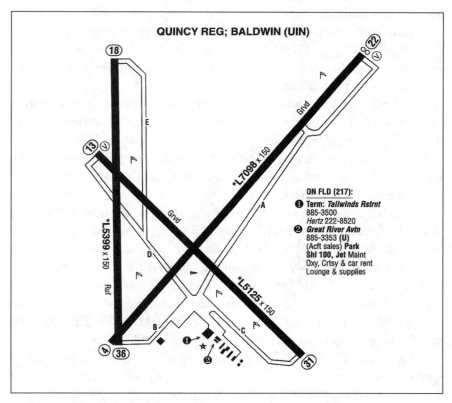

Figure 3-3. Quincy Regional Airport. (Courtesy of *Flight Guide* ©2006)

About three minutes later the pilot of the King Air A90 announced, "Quincy traffic, King Air 1-1-2-7 Delta taxiing out...takeoff on runway 4, Quincy." Then the pilot of a Piper Cherokee taxiing behind the King Air A90 announced, "Quincy traffic, Cherokee 7-6-4-6 Juliet...taxiing to runway 4, Quincy."

The United captain, who was the pilot not flying, then commented to her first officer, "they're both using runway four...you're planning on runway 13, still, right?" The first officer affirmed runway 13 and continued the approach. The captain of Flight 5925 dutifully made calls at six miles out, and again on short final for runway 13. Then she asked, "the aircraft gonna hold in position on runway four or you guys gonna take off?"

The King Air A90 was number one for takeoff on runway 4 but failed to respond. However, the Cherokee pilot, who was number two for departure, transmitted, "7-6-4-6 Juliet...holding...for departure on runway 4." The CVR recorded an interruption in this transmission by a mechanical "two hundred" announcement from the United Express ground-proximity warning system. Thus Flight 5925's crew heard "[unclear] on the uh, King Air," probably reflecting the Cherokee pilot stating that he was waiting for the King Air in front of him to depart.

The United captain replied, "okay, we'll get through your intersection in just a second sir...we appreciate that"—in the evident belief that whoever was number one for takeoff on runway four intended to hold. However, as events unfolded, and despite being on the runway ready for departure, the King Air crew was obviously not listening to any of this, nor paying attention visually to airport traffic.

It was late afternoon, and with its landing lights on, Flight 5925 made a normal touchdown on runway 13. The NTSB determined that the King Air A90 began its takeoff roll on runway four about 13 seconds before Flight 5925 touched down. They collided at the intersection of the two runways and all aboard both airplanes were killed in the ensuing fire. Rescuers reported hearing people alive inside the United Express commuter, but were unable to open the air-stair door. The two pilots in the King Air A90 survived the impact, but for some reason were unable to get out.

The crew of the King Air A90 consisted of an instructor pilot and a student pilot who was a part-time ground instructor working for Flight Safety International in St. Louis. With aspirations of attaining a job as a commuter airline pilot, she was trying to build time toward an Airline Transport Pilot certificate.

The captain was a retired TWA pilot, with a questionable track record. While still at TWA, he had been downgraded from captain to flight engineer because of "flying deficiencies." Shortly before this fatal mishap, he had made a gear-up landing with a student in a Cessna 172RG.

Two passengers who had flown into Quincy with the King Air pilot just before the accident said that he seemed "to be in a hurry," and "anxious to get home." A third passenger said that on the flight into Quincy, the two pilots seemed to have "an excellent teacher-student relationship," and that the instructor-pilot seemed to be telling her how to fly the airplane.

While the instructor-pilot's effort to help a young time-building student is commendable, the place for an extensive briefing is in the classroom. In this case, it looks as if personality traits entered the picture—the pilot was attempting to accomplish too much. He was attempting to instruct in the operation of the airplane, brief her on how to fly it, and hurry home. Clearly his attention was focused inside the cockpit. But as the AIM advises, one of the ways to avoid collisions at nontowered airports is to use both your eyes and your ears—listening to the CTAF—to keep track of traffic.

According to occupants of the Cherokee, the King Air A90 had been in position for departure for about one minute before beginning the takeoff roll. The Cherokee pilot said he did not hear a takeoff announcement from the King Air pilot, and none was recorded by the United Flight's CVR.

The Rejected Takeoff

Making a rejected takeoff (RTO) at high speed on a short runway is serious business. An in-depth Boeing study showed that in the airline fleet 76 percent of successful RTOs were initiated *before* 80 knots, 18 percent at 80 to 100 knots, and 4 percent at 100 to 120 knots. Unsuccessful RTOs—meaning there was an accident—occurred principally in the two percent initiated above 120 knots. It is noteworthy that 58 percent of the RTO accidents were initiated *after* V_1, decision speed. (In a light single or twin, rotation or takeoff speed equates to V_1.) Meanwhile, 55 percent of these high speed RTO accidents could have been avoided by continuing takeoff.

Robert Breiling Associates reported that in one year 31 percent of RTO mishaps in corporate aircraft were related to inadequate preflight planning. Many involved such factors as insufficient runway, slush-drag, locked controls, or a door opening. Seven accidents were caused by loss of steering control. The point to remember about an RTO is that the faster you are going, the more dangerous it becomes.

Takeoff roll is not the time or place to be trouble-shooting a suspected problem. While accelerating to liftoff speed, if something seems amiss, reject the takeoff early and then troubleshoot on the taxiway or ramp. A case of troubleshooting while on takeoff roll involved a King Air 300 that was wrecked at Buchanan Field (CCR) in Concord, California. The ATP-rated pilot told investigators that after beginning a rolling takeoff he noted the airspeed reading zero. Yet, instead of retarding engine power and attempting to determine the cause, he continued accelerating and watching the airspeed indicator. Finally, very late in the takeoff process, he decided to abort. He applied heavy braking and reverse thrust, but was unable to get stopped. The aircraft went off the end of the runway and skidded through a chain-link fence, then struck an automobile traveling on the perimeter road before finally coming to rest against yet another chain-link fence that bordered an interstate highway. Since the 4,600-foot runway was dry, the only possible reason for this accident was a dangerously delayed decision to reject the takeoff. Yet the pilot had identified the airspeed problem almost immediately after applying power.

A spectacular high-speed rejected takeoff accident in a luxurious Grumman Gulfstream G-IV corporate jet killed Lewis Katz, the co-owner of the Philadelphia Inquirer, along with three friends, a flight attendant, and both pilots. It was May 31, 2014, and the aircraft had landed at Laurence G. Hanscom Field (BED) in Bedford, Massachusetts, where the passengers attended a late afternoon fund raiser for the Concorde River Institute. While many details are missing from the NTSB's currently available Preliminary Report, it was a night-time departure and the weather was clear with 10 miles visibility and calm winds.

With the highly experienced copilot flying the aircraft from the left seat and the captain acting as copilot, the flight was departing on the airport's 7,011-foot long runway 11. Assuming a gross weight of around 54,000 lbs, their takeoff distance should have been 3,388 feet. The ship's CVR captured the acting copilot's callout of "80 knots," then "V_1!"—decision speed, at about 118 knots (the point to either reject or continue takeoff). Then at a V_R of approximately 122 knots the acting copilot called, "Rotate!" Takeoff speed, or V_2, was probably about 131 knots. But the flight data recorder (FDR) showed that the aircraft failed to rotate, and instead continued accelerating to 165 knots (190 mph) before the takeoff was finally rejected.

At 165 knots the thrust reversers were deployed and wheel brake pressures increased as the aircraft decelerated. Tire marks on the runway began about 1,300 feet from the end and continued for another 1,000 feet through the paved safety area (runway over-run). Seven seconds later, with the aircraft still at about 100 knots, the FDR ceased recording. It had rolled off the runway into the runway overrun area and onto the grass. It then continued on the grass until striking the approach lighting system and localizer antenna, finally coming to rest in a gully about 1,850 feet from the end of the runway where it exploded and burned.

The FDR shows the flight controls were in the locked position, yet the cockpit gust lock handle was found in the OFF position. This implies that after discovering the controls were locked at V_R, the captain and copilot frantically tried to salvage an embarrassing oversight and unlock the controls to get the aircraft airborne. But what the media failed to emphasize is that the G-IV has an interlock system that's designed to restrict throttle movement to only six percent engine RPM changes until the gust lock is disengaged. This "power lever lockout" feature was designed specifically to protect the aircraft and its occupants from just such an accident. But in this case, the protective system appears to have failed.

Thus, while the accident superficially looks like total aircrew error, the NTSB may ultimately find an equally important contributing factor was mechanical failure or maladjustment of the aircraft's power lever interlock feature that was designed to prevent this type of accident.

Once again, these accidents illustrate a very simple lesson: don't troubleshoot a problem during takeoff roll. There are too many things requiring your full attention. Know your accelerate-stop distance for each departure. Then, no later than reaching decision speed V_1—in light aircraft it's normally rotation (or takeoff speed)—reject the takeoff at the first indication that something's wrong. Otherwise, the charted accelerate-stop distance is invalid and you'll have an unknown stopping distance requirement. Perhaps the best way to remember this comes from a Boeing training film on the subject: *"Once you have reached V_1 (rotation or takeoff speed) accelerating, you have made the Accelerate-Go decision."*

Consider a typical, popular light twin with a minimum single-engine control speed (V_{MC}) of 81 knots and best-rate of climb speed with one engine inoperative (V_{YSE}) of 107 knots. The rotation speed is 86 knots, which conforms to the FAA's recommended minimum takeoff speed of V_{MC} plus five knots. Takeoff *roll* for this aircraft is shown as 2,095 feet (sea level, standard-day conditions). However, the accelerate-stop distance on a dry runway is 3,645 feet. Despite the lack of FAA mandated requirements, the accelerate-stop distance actually represents the minimum safe runway length that you should accept for departure. An aborted takeoff with anything less is likely a runway overrun incident or accident.

For GA pilots, this raises two different safety questions. First, how can you come close to the accelerate-stop performance shown on the manufacturer's chart? The answer is only by periodic practice in a simulator— ideally every six months but *not less* than yearly. Second, what about an unexpected event other than engine failure that requires a decision? It could be a blown tire, a cabin door popping open, or a generator failure. With plenty of runway ahead, the right decision is usually to reject the takeoff. However, as you approach rotation speed, the decision to stop or to continue becomes much more critical. Runway surface texture and condition—wet, dry, or snow-covered; grooved, or porous friction course (PFC)—are critical considerations too.

A tire failure anywhere near rotation or takeoff speed, for obvious reasons, will prevent you from obtaining published accelerate-stop performance. Thus, barring structural damage that makes the aircraft unsafe to fly, it is best to continue the takeoff. This allows you to reduce your weight with fuel burn-off, alert the tower, and then plan your landing. A retractable landing gear should remain extended, since retracting it could bring a smoldering tire carcass into the wheel well, or the damaged tire could hang-up on internal structure and prevent the gear from extending. You'll also want to land on the good-tire side of the runway because of the drag from the damaged tire.

Rejected Takeoff Decision

In a single-engine airplane, during takeoff roll, regardless of airspeed, with an engine failure there is no decision to make. You simply can't fly. So if you're still on the runway, brake to a stop as fast as you can. If the runway is at least as long as your *takeoff distance* (takeoff roll plus the additional distance required to reach 50 feet AGL), an engine failure at liftoff should leave you approximately the distance needed to get stopped. The POH for a Cessna 182 (at sea level and gross weight 2,800 lbs) shows a zero-wind takeoff roll of 625 feet and a takeoff distance of 1,205 feet. Thus an abort on a runway shorter than 1,200 feet will most likely result in an over-run incident or accident. Another method used in single-engine airplanes to estimate accelerate-stop distance is to add the *ground roll* for landing to the takeoff roll. At 2,800 pounds, a Cessna 182 Skylane requires a (sea level) takeoff roll of 625 feet and a landing roll of 590 feet. Adding the numbers together provides an unofficial accelerate-stop distance of 1,215 feet. Again, this becomes the minimum (safe) *dry* runway length for takeoff.

Rejected Takeoff Practice

It is best to practice high-speed rejected takeoffs in a simulator. To keep your reflexes sharp you must train not less than annually. Using your airplane is okay, but a practice RTO can be very hard on your tires and brakes. If you decide to practice aborting from takeoff speed, choose a cool day. Otherwise, with any significant brake wear and heat, you could encounter *brake fade*, wherein the brakes heat up and instead of bringing you to a decisive stop, they only slow you down—you will have exceeded their *brake energy capacity* (which is based on gross weight, field elevation, ambient temperature and wind). Also, be sure the runway is dry. Unless grooved or finished with a PFC overlay, a wet runway will be slick and greatly extend your stopping distance.

With a high speed RTO, assuming you get stopped with no problem, you must then allow the brakes to cool before returning to the hangar. Brake heat can be slow to build, normally peaking well after the event. This is especially important with aircraft that have wheel fairings. The wheel fairings trap the heat, which makes structural damage a distinct possibility. As a rule of thumb, it can take anywhere from five to 20 minutes for brake temperature to peak.

Wind Factor

A frequent cause of bent metal, bruised egos, and sometimes injured passengers involves departure with a tailwind or strong crosswind. Part of the problem is the complete lack of guidance in the typical POH or AFM. While it is basic to aviation that airplanes take off and land into the wind, a downwind departure is sometimes necessary due to such problems as traffic flow at large controlled terminals, such as JFK, La Guardia, Teterboro, or Washington's Reagan National Airport. Then there's Aspen, Colorado, which because of surrounding high terrain and a two percent downhill slope has a mandatory downhill departure on runway 33, often with a tailwind. While Aspen's two-percent slope *is* a consideration, it is the surrounding high terrain that makes the runway 33 takeoff necessary. Yet despite the lack of guidance for GA aircraft, there is a limit to how much tailwind a pilot can safely accept.

The book *Aerodynamics for Naval Aviators* shows that a headwind equal to 10 percent of takeoff or landing speed *decreases* takeoff (or landing) distance by 19 percent. Conversely, a tailwind equal to 10 percent of the takeoff or landing speed *increases* the required distance 21 percent. (Remember, takeoff distance includes ground roll plus the distance to climb 50 feet—or 35 feet for transport category aircraft. Landing *distance* assumes crossing the threshold at 50 feet, then, with idle power, a float to touchdown plus ground roll to a stop.) Because runway slope increases or decreases the runway requirement by only two to four percent per degree of slope (depending on the type of aircraft), it is always best to depart or land *into the wind*. Still, we know this is not always possible.

Transport and commuter category aircraft have a specified maximum tailwind listed in the Certificate Limitations of the AFM—most being 10 to 15 knots. In light twins, it's a different story. The Baron 58 manual does not show a limitation at all, however, the takeoff performance chart stops with a 10-knot tailwind. Thus, anything greater is an important unknown. The Cessna 421's POH says, "Increase takeoff distance four percent for each two knots of tailwind." Thus a 10-knot tailwind increases the takeoff distance—and hence runway requirement—by 20 percent. A 2,500-foot no-wind takeoff distance, with 10 knots on the tail, would require 3,000 feet.

It gets worse as the wind gets stronger. Again using the Cessna 421 as an example, a 15-knot tailwind increases the takeoff requirement 30 percent. Consequently, a 2,500-foot takeoff distance becomes 3,250 feet. Departing under these conditions from Eureka (EKA), California's 3,000-foot runway becomes impossible; and the pilot who hasn't checked the numbers with the tailwind in mind becomes a statistic. Twenty knots will increase takeoff distance 40 percent, and our benchmark 2,500-foot takeoff distance rises to 3,500 feet. If you are departing from the 3,094-foot runway 27 at Lakefront New Orleans (NEW), you are not going to make it. Failure to consider all these facts results in accidents.

Tailwind Accidents

A classic tailwind mishap involved a Cessna 172 which crashed following the end of the 27th annual airshow at Sussex Airport (FWN) in New Jersey. Onboard the 172 were three pilots headed for Republic Airport (FRG) in Farmingdale, New York. Occupying the left seat was a student pilot with 37.5 hours of dual, with his 3,244-hour flight instructor in the right seat. In back was another of the instructor's students, who had come along to see the airshow.

Surface winds, obtained later from an airport 38 miles southeast, were from 340 degrees at 10 knots, gusting to 19; several witnesses, however, told investigators the wind was predominantly from the northeast. One individual who lived on a nearby hill said that about 15 minutes before the Cessna 172 crashed, the winds began to swirl, and became unusually "strong and violent." Both during and after the airshow, the warbirds were departing eastbound on runway three, and after the show, several airplanes began taxiing to runway three. Then someone on the Unicom frequency stated, "Runway 21 will be used for departures. This is the FAA." Yet the FAA representatives had left 15 minutes earlier. UNICOM, of course, is a non-governmental aeronautical advisory station with no authority to control traffic. In fact, even with a control tower in operation, it is still the pilot's responsibility to select and request the most suitable runway for departure. Despite the stiff, gusty northeast wind, most of the airplanes dutifully taxied to runway 21 for a downwind departure. One commercial pilot, who witnessed the accident, estimated that a 20-knot tailwind was blowing. A Cherokee pilot told investigators that the wind was strong and "blowing straight down the runway." He noted that planes ahead of him were having difficulty climbing, several having "just missed the trees off the departure end." He also acknowledged taking off downwind on runway 21 and admitted coming dangerously close to the trees. When the Cessna 172 departed, it too was seen struggling to climb. The commercial pilot reported that the airplane attempted to climb at a 30-degree pitch attitude, and that it then "mushed" into the treetops and flipped forward into the ground. All three occupants were killed.

With a runway length of 3,500 feet, Sussex's runway was more than adequate for a normal departure into the wind. But the Cessna 172's POH (for aircraft manufactured in 1967) has no data for a downwind takeoff. Thus, a C172 pilot would have no idea of the runway required for a departure with a 20-knot tailwind. In addition, there was the strong gust factor. Then, with the rapidly diminishing pavement ahead—and with trees beyond—after liftoff there would have been an instinctive reaction to attempt to steepen the climb. This would explain the 30-degree pitch attitude noted by witnesses. The result was a loss of control, with a stall into the trees. The flight instructor's lack of leadership and judgment resulted in three deaths.

Engine Failure

Most commuter and all transport-category airplanes are certificated for an engine loss during takeoff. In the past, light twins were not required to have this capability. The older certification regulation—Part 23, under which many of the current fleet of light twins was certified—required only that the manufacturer document the airplane's climb or descent gradient with one engine inoperative at 5,000 feet.

Still, some light twins do have an engine–out climb capability, which will be shown on the Accelerate-Go chart in the Performance section of the POH/AFM. However, in a light twin, lacking such a chart with an engine failure on takeoff it is usually best to reject the takeoff, i.e., *accelerate-stop*. The rule of thumb is to consider your airplane a single-engine airplane with the power plant divided into two parts.

The generally recommended procedure for an engine failure at or near takeoff speed is to reject the takeoff. There are two basic reasons for this. One is the *unofficial* nature (lack of standards) of the Accelerate-Go chart. This data was compiled without any FAA-mandated standards. The second involves the drag from the landing gear, flaps, and windmilling (unfeathered) propeller. When many of the twins were certified there were no industry standards as to the specific point during the takeoff sequence when the engine was deemed to have failed. Nor was there any consideration given for the time between engine failure and the pilot's recognition and initial action.

Aircraft configuration is critical too. Most charts indicate that the landing gear must be in the process of retracting or fully up when the engine fails. Then the propeller must be feathered. However, in reality these unofficial charts are based on a flight configuration of gear-up with the propeller feathered. The most important point though, is that you must be trained and regularly re-trained in the use of the airplane's performance capability. Consider the following.

Just after takeoff, a Piper Navajo with a pilot and seven passengers aboard lost power in its right engine. The aircraft rolled and yawed, but failed to accelerate or climb. Even though the pilot feathered the propeller, he forgot to retract the landing gear and flaps. Witnesses saw the aircraft begin turning right with its nose rising slightly. Then it rolled, and in a nearly vertical nose-down attitude, crashed, killing all aboard. The NTSB said, "a successful landing on the runway could have been executed from 150 feet above the runway." But the pilot was distracted by the power loss just after liftoff and failed to execute the emergency procedure correctly. The accident report stated that he ignored outside visual references and failed to establish a configuration or pitch attitude that would maintain his airspeed at or above either V_{YSE} or V_{MC}. Thus, he could neither climb nor maintain control.

The report also showed that the pilot had 2,820 hours total time, with 214 in multi-engine aircraft. Yet the Board said he lacked adequate training to handle the engine-out emergency in this particular airplane. Indeed, the record shows that no matter how much flight time you have, thorough training in each new airplane is necessary. An Air Force study some years ago showed that with a serious emergency during the first 100 hours in a new airplane, the pilot was likely to revert to the habits established in the last airplane flown. Thus, with a new airplane, regardless your total flight time, you must re-establish your habit patterns.

An NTSB study concluded: "Accidents following engine failures in light twins generally occur due to a lack of proficiency in responding to these emergencies. Often such accidents involve some degree of panic, probably related to inadequate immediate recall of the exact emergency procedures or lack of confidence in one's ability to execute the emergency procedures. These symptoms are indicative of insufficient initial or recurrent training in engine-failure emergencies." Therefore, as said before, you are unsafe to fly a light twin without regular recurrent training the last twelve months— ideally in a simulator. Without such training, both your memory and your reflex actions in an emergency will likely be inadequate. And if you haven't flown the airplane for three months, it's not just three takeoffs and landings you need, but a couple hours' practice and a thorough review of procedures—before you take passengers with you.

Night Flying

Flying at night significantly increases a pilot's exposure to *spatial disorientation*—a condition wherein a lack of visual cues causes loss of reference to the horizon. The weather can be clear with 60 miles visibility, yet you'll find yourself unable to remain spatially oriented: unable tell which way is up, or see and observe obstructions. An example of special disorientation can sometimes occur during a dark night takeoff. As the pilot lifts off and leaves the lighted runway environment, he or she will erroneously perceive an increasing nose-up pitch attitude and apply forward pressure on the controls. This results in beginning a slight rate of descent. Or, just after liftoff, because of a cockpit distraction and possibly an inadequate nose-up trim setting, the pilot may fail to note a diminishing rate of climb that evolves into a slight descent. Then too, sometimes the terrain ahead has an uphill slope. Then, after leaving the lighted runway environment, the pilot flies into the ground or water in the departure path.

A classic example involved a Sabreliner 40, that was departing New Orleans Lakefront Airport (NEW) with the only passengers being the aircraft owner and his adult son. It was a dark, moonless night, with visibility reduced to two miles by smoke and haze. The departure was over the inky black expanse of Lake Pontchartrain and the captain was letting the as-yet-untrained copilot, who was new to jet aircraft, make the takeoff. After liftoff, the copilot, who was also a licensed mechanic, said, "Don, your altimeter's not working." With that, they both bent over and began trouble-shooting the captain's altimeter. As to what happened next, the tower operator and four fishermen in a boat all told the same story. The airplane climbed to about 400 feet, then began a slow descent into the water. On impact the aircraft exploded, with only the captain surviving.

Midair Collisions

Over the years, statistics have shown that most midair collisions occur between general aviation aircraft in VFR conditions during daylight hours and on weekends—usually with slow closure rates and at low altitude, and usually near uncontrolled airports. The NTSB had expressed concern previously about the ever-increasing air-traffic congestion around airports. The Board noted that most midair collisions "could have been prevented by the 'see and avoid' concept if the pilots had conformed to the existing flight rules, or followed sound cockpit procedures." Still, in 22 percent of the accidents they found that some limitation prevented one pilot or the other from using the see and avoid concept effectively.

An example involved a MU-2B turboprop twin which collided with a Piper Saratoga while departing from Greenwood Municipal Airport (HFY), an uncontrolled airfield outside Indianapolis Class C airspace to the east. The MU-2's 19,000-hour corporate pilot was known to prefer obtaining his IFR clearance after getting airborne so that his passengers wouldn't have to wait. On this trip, he had four passengers on a flight to Columbus, Ohio.

While the Greenwood Municipal uses a left-hand traffic pattern, the MU-2B pilot turned right almost immediately after liftoff. Once airborne, he quickly checked in with Indianapolis Approach Control. The controller then assigned him a transponder code and instructed, "Maintain at or below 5,000 feet." Shortly thereafter, at 2,100 feet and about two miles east of the airport, the MU-2 collided with the descending Saratoga.

Although very close to Greenwood airport, both airplanes were talking to Indianapolis Approach Control, instead of monitoring the CTAF, as recommended by the then-current AIM. In addition, neither pilot was complying with the AIM's recommended traffic-pattern procedures. The Saratoga pilot and his passengers were preparing to film an office building close to the airport. A Saratoga survivor told investigators they were looking down instead of scanning for other airplanes. Both pilots no doubt felt secure since they were being handled by ATC.

Figure 3-4. Mitsubishi MU-2B. (Photo by IDuke at English Wikipedia)

In reality, the MU-2 pilot's cockpit duties left him unable to comply with the see and avoid concept. First, the MU-2B is a *very difficult* airplane to fly. In addition, the cockpit is so wide that for a pilot seated in the left seat to see and avoid traffic on the right side of the airplane is unrealistic. Complicating the problem is the MU-2's high wing and extended engine nacelles that greatly restrict the pilot's vision on either the left or the right side of the cockpit. In this case, ATC was obligated to inform the Saratoga pilot of the MU-2 departing Greenwood airport, yet the controller failed to do so.

Unfortunately, this accident is typical. Even though you are on an IFR flight plan and working with ATC, you are still obligated to look around and watch for other traffic while in VMC. In addition, flying single-pilot in an airport traffic pattern and looking up frequencies or copying an IFR clearance is a sure ticket to disaster.

Remember too that some pilots may fly with the transponder off, or with an inoperative transponder, and the controller may not notice the primary target. This was the specific cause of a fatal mid-air collision between a Citation Jet and a Cessna 172 near Atlanta. The jet was on an IFR departure under radar control, while the Cessna 172 was on pipeline patrol with his transponder turned off.

Summary

This chapter has discussed some of the major factors affecting safety in the taxi and takeoff phase of flight. Safe taxiing, especially across runways, requires constant vigilance, with no extraneous talking to passengers or accomplishing other tasks while moving. Regarding rejected takeoffs, a pilot must be prepared to abort takeoff with any suspected abnormality. Don't attempt to troubleshoot while the aircraft is accelerating toward the end of the runway. Good training and practice twice a year, but not less than annually—ideally in a simulator—is the best way to maintain your reaction time.

Accidents caused by snow and ice are avoidable too. Frost, snow, and ice on aerodynamic surfaces can prove deadly. And, as I hope you can see, it's important to know the difference between getting *deiced* and *anti-iced*. Remember too that about an inch-and-a-half of wet snow on the runway can prevent you from getting airborne.

As for night flying, you need to be a current instrument rated pilot. There are special problems involving spatial disorientation at night—particularly just after takeoff on a dark and moonless night. Because without instrument flying skills, you'll be in great jeopardy. Research shows that the pilot most likely to have a serious accident holds a private certificate with 200 to 500 hours total flying time, and is not instrument rated. So think about getting an instrument rating—because realistically, it's life insurance.

Training every two years with just a casual flight review is inadequate to keep you knowledgeable, proficient, and safe. A university study done some years ago showed that after two years without refresher training, the private pilot's knowledge had degenerated to below that of a solo-student. So despite the lenient flight review requirements of §61.56, we all need thorough training and an academic review *every year* to become and remain competent airplane pilots.

CHAPTER 4
The Air France Concorde Debacle

In the preceding chapters we discussed how errors by the pilot and his support team often compound themselves to precipitate accidents. While you may wonder how the Air France Concorde mishap relates to general aviation, it is the embodiment of support-team failures—from the mechanics who inadvertently omitted a wheel spacer during heavy maintenance, to the dispatcher who allowed the aircraft to push-back with the ship's weight and balance badly out of limits, to the flight crew departing with a tailwind, which made the runway too short for a safe takeoff. There was the failure, too, of officials within the airline and within the British and French governments to address long-standing and clearly documented design deficiencies of the wheels, tires, and fuel tank structure.

Officially, the French blamed the accident on a Continental Airlines DC-10 that inadvertently dropped an engine wear strip on the runway. This supposedly punctured one of the Concorde's tires and theoretically precipitated the spectacular accident. Yet, as you will see, because of the missing spacer, the Concorde's tire probably failed *before* it hit the engine part. When examined rationally the evidence clearly shows that the proximate cause of the crash was the culmination of personnel and management failures.

Air France Flight 4590

It was July 25, 2000, when the delta-wing, supersonic Concorde, dispatched as Air France Flight 4590, thundered down runway 26R at Paris' Charles de Gaulle Airport. Its destination was New York's JFK Airport. The flight was chartered by Deilmann, a German tour-group operator. On board were 100 tourists, six flight attendants and a three-man flight crew. During takeoff roll, a tire on the left main landing gear bogie blew out, with debris rupturing the forward wing fuel cell. After a horrifying display of fire from burning fuel gushing from the ruptured fuel tank, at about 200 feet AGL the aircraft pitched up, rolled inverted, and crashed. All aboard were killed, along with four people on the ground.

Investigators often refer to "the chain of errors" that ultimately lead to an aircraft accident, noting that if the chain had been broken anywhere along the line the accident would not have occurred. The Concorde mishap is perhaps an all-time classic in this regard, since the record shows a clear pattern of management failures and calculated inaction by responsible individuals.

Given the quarter-century of the Concorde's scheduled airline service, it is clear, in retrospect, that if any one agency anywhere along the line had taken the initiative to resolve a well-documented tire-wheel design deficiency the accident chain would have been broken and this accident would not have happened. But where British Airways and Air France and their respective governments were concerned, costs to modify the design would have threatened the aircraft's already marginal profitability. In addition, admission of a design problem would damage the nations' prestige. These

Figure 4-1. Debris from a blown tire on the badly skewed left landing gear bogie ruptured the forward wing fuel cell, causing a massive fuel leak and wing fire.

(Associated Press Photo/Toshihiko Sato)

two factors appear to have stymied action. How else do you account for the airplane's dubious safety record over the years before this accident? Working back from that fateful July 25, 2000 tragedy, let's examine the various links in the chain.

Dispatch Error

The Concorde was programmed for a takeoff brake-release weight of 407,851 pounds (185 metric tons). However, during taxi they used less fuel than planned and upon lineup had 2,650 pounds of excess fuel in the rearmost tank—tank number 11. This in itself is a significant dispatch-management error. When they pushed-back from the gate, the surface winds were reported as calm and Air France dispatch must have known the departure runway in use. Thus, taxi-fuel requirements should have been reduced for the runway 26R departure.

Shortly before engine-start, 19 undocumented bags were loaded into the rear cargo hold without the flight crew's knowledge. This added an additional 1,100 pounds. At first glance, 3,750 pounds overweight for a 185-ton airplane might appear inconsequential. In fact, the French BEA said this overload would have had negligible effect on the performance of the airplane. But, at 411,601 pounds, the aircraft exceeded its 408,000-pound structural weight limitation. In addition, it exceeded its *one-engine-inoperative* (second segment) maximum climb weight, along with tire speed limitations. This overload was yet another major link in the accident chain. (Its two-engine-out climb speed was 300 knots, but the aircraft never exceeded 215 knots.)

The airplane's aft CG limit was 54 percent mean aerodynamic chord (MAC). Concorde F-BTSC's departure CG was estimated by BEA as 54.2 percent MAC. However, another source estimated the true MAC as having been closer to of 54.6 percent. Thus the airplane was dispatched dangerously aft of its CG limit.

The original test pilots found that near stall speed, with a CG aft of 54 percent MAC, the Concorde would likely pitch-up and become uncontrollable. Here again, Air France's dispatch-management was responsible. Dispatching an airplane that's out of its CG envelope is both illegal and dangerous. Yet, had nothing untoward occurred, this would not have been catastrophic.

With the Concorde's rocket-like acceleration provided by the four paired Olympus 593 turbofan engines, each producing 38,050 pounds of thrust, the excess fuel would have burned off quickly, and the captain could have gotten away with an overweight and un-balanced departure. However, in worldwide airline operations the worst case scenario is *always* considered.

On its takeoff roll, the Concorde experienced an inboard tire failure on the left-front wheel pair of the left main landing gear. Chunks of rubber from the blown tire were thrown upward and ruptured the left front wing fuel tank, causing a massive fuel leak estimated at 20 gallons (134 pounds) per second. This caused the ship's CG to move further aft. The aft CG along with a total loss of thrust from the two engines on the left wing and an airspeed behind the power curve, all combined to explain the pitch-up and roll reported by witnesses.

With the airspeed less than V_{MC} (two engines out on the same side), the airplane rolled left to an inverted position. The roll wasn't completed however, since the captain reduced power on the two operating engines in an effort to recover control.

Maintenance Error

Of utmost importance in any accident investigation is the airplane's maintenance history, especially the most recent maintenance actions. Over the years, a mechanical malfunction causing an accident has often been found linked to the most recent maintenance actions. In this case, the Concorde's maintenance records proved crucial. According to David Rose, writing for London's the *Observer*, Concorde F-BTSC went into maintenance a week before the mishap. It was scheduled for a time-change replacement of the front-left landing gear "beam"—the horizontal tube that holds the wheel axles. In the middle is a low-friction pivot connected to the vertical leg extending down from the wing. Areas of the pivot supporting the load are reinforced by two steel "shear bushings."

Normally the bushings are held in position by a gray, anodized aluminum spacer, about 12 inches long and five inches in diameter. Despite an airline's normally required quality-control maintenance checks, the aircraft left the hangar on July 21, just four days before the accident, with this spacer missing in the left front wheel pair. In fact, after the accident, the spacer was found in the workshop still attached to the old beam. The missing spacer was a maintenance-management responsibility. This was a crucial link in the chain.

When the airplane was returned to service the shear bushings initially remained in position, because the aircraft successfully flew two round-trips to New York. On the ground, the shear bushings are opposite each other. However, with the landing gear retracted, the right-hand bushing is vertically above the left. After several up and down cycles, the right shear bushing began to slip down into the gap left by the missing spacer. By the day of the crash it had moved about seven inches, with the two spacers almost touching. This allowed the front wheels to swivel approximately three degrees in either direction. Lacking a snug-fitting pivot, there was nothing to keep the front wheels aligned with the back pair.

An article on the Concorde in *Air & Space* magazine quoted a study by retired Air France Concorde captain Jean-Marie Chauve and former Concorde flight engineer Michel Suaud as determining that the airplane's initial acceleration was abnormally slow, "There was something retarding the aircraft, holding it back." They theorized it was friction from the misaligned left-front undercarriage. Without the required spacer, "the left front wheels were slightly skewed on takeoff roll." From the start of takeoff, there would have been a steady pull to the left, which would explain the slow acceleration.

Driven by the massive thrust from the engines, the right front tire of the misaligned (skidding) pair wore through the casing and failed. The report by Chauve and Suaud shows that, lacking a retarding force, the aircraft should have become airborne in 5,506 feet (1,694 meters). This was well before the 5,700-foot point where the metal strip was found. Captain Chauve states, "The tire burst at around 174 knots"—14 knots *after* V_1, decision speed. Only *after* the tire failed did it roll over the metal strip, says Captain Chauve.

It is noteworthy that to achieve the 5,506 foot takeoff distance referred to by the Chauve-Suaud study, the aircraft would have achieved V_R (rotation) and V_2 (safe one engine engine-out) takeoff speed well before the metal strip. Yet the captain was forced to rotate and liftoff much slower than programmed when well passed the metal strip. This in itself validates the slow acceleration theory.

Under normal conditions, failure of one tire on a four-wheel landing gear bogie would not be noticed by the crew. (The tire-failure warning system cut out normally at 135 knots.) However, in this case, once the tire failed, the load on the three remaining tires was unbalanced, resulting in a strong pull to the left. Although the left-hand pull had been manageable *before* the tire burst, the two front wheels were now castered hard left, resulting in the overpowering left-hand pull experienced by the captain. BEA's own photographs show unmistakable skid marks from the four left tires heading off the runway towards the rough grass median. Remarkably, the French BEA insists that the left pull was due solely to asymmetrical thrust from the two failed engines.

Published BEA data shows that the number two engine failed as the aircraft neared the grass median, only one second before liftoff. Meanwhile, the number one engine continued to produce normal thrust, until ingesting parts of a frangible runway edge light hit during the takeoff rotation.

When pressured, a BEA official conceded that the wheels were "not in a symmetric trajectory." In other words, they were out of alignment. Using David Rose's analogy, like a shopping cart with it front wheels skewed full left, the aircraft couldn't be steered by the captain and was being dragged toward the left edge of the runway. As one industry insider told Rose, "You would not see four skid marks if the wheels had been straight…and you would not see such marks at all after a normal takeoff. This plane was skidding sideways. It was out of control."

Regarding the yaw caused by asymmetric engine thrust, retired Concorde Captain John Hutchinson told Rose that a double engine failure on one side is "no big deal. The yaw is totally containable."

The Concorde's engines are mounted closer to the fuselage than, say, the more widely spaced engines on a Boeing 747. Thus, asymmetric thrust from a double-engine failure on one wing of the Concorde does not present a serious control problem. As Captain Hutchinson said, "You're not using anything like the full amount of rudder to keep the plane straight."

Still, the French BEA insists that the left pull was due to asymmetric thrust caused by the two failed engines on the left wing. Yet the data recorder showed the engines were running normally until the liftoff sequence began, as it edged towards to left side of the runway.

No Rejected Takeoff

A rejected takeoff was out of the question. The Concorde had long since passed the 160 knot V_1 decision speed. Unable to steer the aircraft, and facing a potential collision with the taxiing Air France Boeing 747 looming ahead—which coincidentally carried the French head of state, Jacques

Chirac and his wife—in desperation the captain attempted to fly it out of the problem. It was his only logical choice.

The CVR records the co-pilot screaming, "watch out!" Approaching the grass median, the desperate captain rotated at 187 knots, 11 knots below the programmed V_R of 198 knots. One second before liftoff, the number two engine failed due to ingested fragments of the tire and wheel.

BEA photos document the smashed yellow runway edge light, hit by the left landing gear during rotation. The number one engine then ingested fragments from the light fixture and, shortly thereafter, it too surged and failed, tried to recover, and then failed again.

Crew Factor

Earlier, when the Concord taxied out, the winds at Charles de Gaulle International Airport had been calm. During taxi, however, the tower advised of a newly detected eight-knot tailwind on runway 26R. Based on the airplane's brake-energy capability and balanced field length (BFL, the runway required to continue or reject the takeoff at decision speed), the airplane was now officially 11,000 pounds too heavy for runway 26R; and this figure overlooks the undocumented baggage and excess fuel. Clearly, the runway was too short for a safe departure. This determination was the responsibility of both the flight-crew and Air France's dispatcher.

If they had changed runways for an easterly departure this would have consumed the excess taxi fuel. More importantly, with an easterly departure and a headwind, the 13,550-foot runway would have been adequate. At the Concorde's programmed departure weight of 407,851 pounds the projected BFL with an eight-knot headwind was 12,140 feet, well suited to the runway length.

Still, given management's pressure for on-time departures and arrivals, it is easy to sympathize with the captain in his decision to continue with a downwind departure. The delay involved in a 180-degree runway change would have disrupted the IFR traffic flow. Thus, his decision was operationally realistic. There's not a captain among us who hasn't—on occasion—departed JFK, La Guardia, Washington National, O'Hare, London, or Paris, with a tailwind and BFL exceeding the limitations stipulated in the AFM. At the major airports, a request for a runway change inevitably involves an additional 60 to 90 minute (or greater) delay, while ATC reroutes other traffic into and out of the airport.

Yet, here again inaction by Air France dispatch looks culpable. An airline dispatcher's role is almost totally involved with the safety of each flight. The dispatcher had an obligation to warn the crew of the wind change and of their now badly over-grossed condition for runway 26R. Still, the captain had the ultimate responsibility.

Management's Responsibility

Despite all these now documented human errors, the real factor that made this catastrophe inevitable involved management at the highest levels. The Concorde's incident record showed clear evidence of a deficient design in the wheels and tires. The very first such failure on June 14, 1979 made these deficiencies apparent. Subsequently, the Concorde experienced 57 tire-wheel failures during its operational history (1976 to 2000): 30 were in Air France's operations and 27 with British Airways. Thirty-two of these blowouts damaged structure, hydraulic systems, and engines. In six instances, the wing fuel tanks were penetrated. Ironically, the July 25 accident was almost identical to the mishap on June 14, 1979—including a much smaller wing fire. This left 21 years during which the problem could have been fixed.

It wasn't until the July 25, 2000, conflagration that Britain's CAA Chairman Sir Malcolm Field said, "What is uniquely different in this case is that tire debris alone is thought to have led to this catastrophe." The Air France and British Airways fleets were then grounded.

Dangerous Trend

The Concorde entered scheduled service in 1976. Since that time, while departing from U.S. airports, Air France experienced four wheel-tire explosions. Meanwhile British Airways had five incidents, four at Heathrow and one at JFK; however, only three of these occurred during takeoff.

The June 14, 1979, Air France incident occurred during departure from Dulles International Airport. In that incident, tires number five and six blew out on the left main landing gear. The resulting debris and shrapnel punctured three fuel tanks, severed several hydraulic lines and electrical wiring, and damaged the number-two engine. A month later on July 21, yet another almost identical mishap occurred once again during departure from Dulles. There were two more U.S. incidents, one in October 1979 and the other in February 1981.

In a November 15, 1985, British Airways incident, a left-hand landing gear tire failed and both of the left engines were damaged. Another incident occurred during landing and one during taxi. Although the latter was thought to have been caused by a locked brake, the number-one fuel tank was punctured by a piece of the wheel's water deflector. Thus, the dangerous trend was readily visible to anyone who cared to look.

Government and Airline Management

Following the first two serious U.S. incidents in the summer of 1979, the FAA urgently telegraphed Airworthiness Directives to both the British and French airlines, providing procedures for improved checks of tires, wheels, and brakes. Thereupon, the French Director General of Civil Aviation issued an airworthiness directive, and Air France issued a Technical Information Update. Both of these called for a pre-takeoff inspection of wheels and tires, including both tire pressure and temperature. In addition, after takeoff, if a tire problem was suspected, crews were to leave the landing gear extended. Later, all Concordes were equipped with roll-on wheel rims, strengthened tires, and cockpit-mounted tire-failure warning lights.

The NTSB agreed with these actions by the French government. Yet, as then NTSB Chairman James B. King noted, the tire failures continued. In October 1979, during a departure from JFK, another incident occurred. Then again, in February 1981, a Concorde experienced tire failure damage departing Dulles. In both cases, the Air France crews ignored the new technical instructions and retracted the landing gear. In fact, after the October 1979 tire failure, the flight continued to Paris. In the 1981 failure, the gear was retracted and an attempt made to continue, however, the number-two engine was damaged which forced the crew to make an emergency landing at JFK.

It should be emphasized that retracting the landing gear with a blown tire is dangerous in any airplane. The tire carcass and wheel are probably very hot, even smoldering (or sometimes actively burning). At the least, the distorted shell can hang up and damage plumbing in the wheel well, and prevent later gear extension.

An NTSB investigation into the 1981 Concorde tire failure incident disclosed that the passengers had not been briefed for an emergency landing.

In addition, the CVR had been inoperative for several weeks: even more evidence of very lax management.

Still worried about the clearly hazardous design deficiency, the NTSB asked the French BEA to change the AFM. For a wheel or tire problem, the Emergency Procedures section was to include a "mandatory requirement to leave the landing gear extended; to return to the takeoff airfield; to advise cabin attendants of intended action; and to brief passengers for a precautionary landing." Unfortunately this didn't help.

Manufacturer

Lacking export orders for the Concorde, the manufacturer had terminated further design refinement. Late in the 1970s, however, engine air intakes were optimized to enhance airflow, and the elevons, vertical stabilizer, and rudder were modified, with fuel tank capacity increased slightly. These changes enhanced the economic aspects of the airplane's operation by reducing fuel consumption and improved handling. Nothing, however, was proposed to fix the continuing problems with the wheels and tires.

After the July 2000 accident, Michelin quickly developed new tire technology that essentially eliminated the risk of blowouts. With lighter radial tires, combined with other major structural improvements, the Concorde's major design deficiencies were resolved. It is noteworthy, however, that these badly needed changes were not considered economically feasible until an airplane-load of people, along with four persons on the ground, had been killed. (The settlement package offered relatives was $120 million. However, some opted to sue Continental in hopes of a larger individual settlement.) The ultimate savings from delaying safety modifications to wheels and tires is now far outweighed by the legal costs, the more extensive and expensive modifications (around $25 million), and the loss to revenue service by this marginally profitable, but spectacular, supersonic transport airplane. Alas, no monetary value can be placed on the unspeakable grief of those who lost loved ones and close friends in an accident that was so clearly preventable.

Conclusions

The single factor making this tragedy inevitable was the obtuseness of decision-makers—in both the French and British airline management and also in the associated government agencies—in not promptly modifying a clearly unsafe design when it first became apparent in June 1979. Then they continued to pass up the opportunity following every other almost identical mishap thereafter.

Still, the French BEA insists that a metal strip dropped by a Continental Airlines aircraft shortly before the Concorde's departure was the cause of the accident. Such a transparent finding is an obvious attempt to camouflage the clearly documented incompetence of high-ranking individuals in both government and airline management in order to protect the national honor. Ultimately, the missing spacer was the precipitating link in the accident chain. And that link was supplied by Air France's maintenance management.

This crash on takeoff by Air France Flight 4590 has provided an all-time classic example of how the actions or failures of individuals and government agencies that are part the flight crew's support team contributed to the accident chain that needlessly killed 113 people.

CHAPTER 5

Accidents En Route

The en route phase of flight accounts for the highest percentage of fatal accidents. As noted in Chapter 1, buzzing and CFIT are frequently involved. This chapter examines some of these repetitious and avoidable accidents.

Maneuvering Flight (Buzzing)

Near Juliette, Georgia, a Cessna 152 with a private pilot at the controls and student-pilot passenger were buzzing the calm surface of Lake Juliette. A witness reported that the airplane was flying very low "and going in and out of the coves." Then the right wing struck the lake's surface and the airplane hit the water. The NTSB classed it as an "ostentatious display [by the] pilot-in-command." Fortunately, both pilot and passenger escaped without injury.

In another case of buzzing over glassy water, the pilot was not so lucky. It was 9:00 AM on a clear, calm Sunday morning. A Part 135 cargo-laden Beechcraft Travelair was en route from Waco to San Angelo, Texas. A witness fishing on Lake O. H. Ivie, near Paint Rock, Texas, told investigators that about 9:50 AM, "the airplane appeared from the Elm Creek slough, flying straight towards me at 50 to 100 feet above the water. I watched it closely because it seemed to be buzzing the lake. I saw no indication of engine trouble…The plane skimmed the top of the water, much like a floatplane landing. I saw a spray explode around the airplane, and heard a loud 'clap' noise…[then] it immediately began to climb. I noticed the plane had a climb attitude but did not gain much altitude." With both propellers and engines damaged, the Travelair missed all the boats and fishermen, but crashed along the shoreline, killing the pilot. In his euphoria in buzzing the lake, the pilot forgot that a mirror smooth body of water robs you of your depth perception. As a result, he collided with the lake's surface.

Another tragic mishap involved a Beechcraft King Air A90 with eight parachutists aboard. It crashed into the Great Salt Lake while returning to Tooele Airport, Utah. The turboprop A90 had been stripped of all avionics except a transceiver and hand-held GPS—clearly insufficient for IFR flight. In his weather briefing, the pilot was advised of IMC at his destination: visibility was only a quarter of a mile in light snow, haze, and fog. This would have been challenging weather for even a fully equipped airliner.

Members of the skydiving team told investigators that the pilot usually handled IFR conditions by descending over the Great Salt Lake until he could see the water or ground. He would then proceed to the airport using well known landmarks. Unfortunately, this time the lake's surface was mirror-calm, and there was essentially no visibility in the light snow and fog. All aboard were killed when the pilot flew the King Air into the lake. The NTSB blamed the accident on "the pilot's over-confidence in his personal ability, in that he had reportedly done this on two previous occasions." In other words, personality factor—judgment—combined with compulsion.

Power Line Strikes

Power lines also seem to attract trouble. An incident near Pope Valley, California, involved a Cessna 172 that was seen buzzing the lake by two Sheriff's deputies. Unfortunately, the pilot failed to see the high-tension wires that spanned the lake, and they snagged the aircraft. The Cessna plunged into the lake and sank, killing the pilot. The NTSB classed it as poor judgment and inadequate lookout while buzzing.

In another case, two people were killed and one seriously injured when their Cessna 180 crashed while buzzing a friend. A passenger in the airplane had used a cell phone to call an acquaintance to say they would buzz the curio shop adjacent to an interstate highway where he was located. The aircraft made a low pass, and all exchanged waves. Unfortunately, the airplane collided with power lines that crossed the highway and impacted 480 feet from the horrified acquaintance.

Low Altitude Acrobatics

The continuous and needless deaths due to low altitude acrobatics bring to mind a poem handed down from the World War II era:

> A very hot pilot was Henry Hightower.
> He claimed to have over 400 hours.
> To prove it he dived on his girl's house one day.
> They were to be married the fourteenth of May.

A recent example involved the pilot of a Beechcraft Musketeer II who was seen doing acrobatics over his home. The maneuvers included steep turns, inverted flight, and wingovers. Then the Musketeer pilot made a steep right turn over the home of a neighbor. The NTSB report stated, "When the wings leveled, the nose dropped and the airplane's wingtip struck an 80-foot-tall pine tree." It then crashed inverted, killing the pilot.

Minimum Safe Altitudes

14 CFR §91.119, "Minimum Safe Altitudes," requires the pilot to maintain an altitude that, following engine failure, allows an emergency landing, "without undue hazard to persons or property on the surface." Over congested areas, such as a city or town, the regulation requires an altitude of at least 1,000 feet above the highest obstacle within 2,000 feet of the flight path. This rule was written many years ago, and considering the urban sprawl found in most metropolitan areas, it is now *much* too generous. From a thousand feet up most light airplanes can glide about two miles. Over a large metropolitan area, an engine failure at only 1,000 feet above ground level (AGL) will likely leave you the choice of a city street, the top of a building, or someone's house.

A classic example involved the pilot of a Sacramento, California, based Cessna 172 returning to Executive Airport (SAC) from a cross-country trip. Unfortunately, the airplane ran out of fuel and the pilot crash-landed on a city street in downtown Sacramento. At 1,000 feet he was too low to glide to his destination, or even to a vacant field.

In another instance, a pilot and passenger in a Beechcraft B-23 Sierra were participating in the Palms to Pines Air Race. Their flight had originated in Santa Monica, California, and their plan was to land at Modesto City-County Airport and refuel. After an intentional low pass and go-around "for timing purposes" as the aircraft climbed through 900 feet, the Sierra's engine quit and the pilot crash-landed on a Modesto street. Fortunately, no one was injured. The pilot told investigators she could not recall "repositioning the fuel selector during the 2.2-hour flight."

To provide yet another example, after a catastrophic engine failure a pilot commuting to work from Corona to Torrance, in the Los Angeles basin, managed to guide his Cessna 177 into a Fullerton schoolyard. The airplane was destroyed, along with the fence he used to get stopped. But he and his three passengers suffered only minor cuts and bruises.

So realistically, a flight at 1,000 feet over the urban jungle does indeed subject numerous persons and property to an undue hazard. In reality, an altitude of 3,000 to 5,000 feet AGL is more realistic. It is unthinkably selfish for a pilot to jeopardize the lives of others because of his or her own self-induced dilemma.

Controlled Flight into Terrain

Some years ago, NTSB Safety Report (SR-89/01) provided a detailed study of what is now referred to as CFIT during marginal weather. This study was deemed necessary because 72 percent of the accidents involving VFR flight into IMC were fatal. The study revealed that private pilots were most often involved, with 52 percent having less than 500 hours of flight time, and 46 percent less than 100 hours. Just over half were between the ages of 40 and 59. As for the type of aircraft, six out of seven multi-engine accidents were fatal, as were eight out of nine accidents in retractable singles. In slower flying fixed-gear singles, 13 out of 20 accidents involved fatalities.

A curious example of a CFIT accident occurred on August 9, 2010 in the crash of a turboprop powered de Havilland Otter DHC-3T. The crash in mountainous terrain near Aleknagik, Alaska, killed the highly experienced pilot along with former Alaskan Senator Ted Stevens and three fellow passengers. It's identified as "curious" because the pilot had impeccable flying credentials and the aircraft was equipped with a variety of avionics that provided more than adequate situational awareness. This included terrain avoidance with two GPS units that provided a moving map and terrain displays, along with a radar altimeter having both a visual annunciator and aural tone capability.

A surviving passenger told investigators the weather consisted of broken clouds at about 2,000 feet with some blue sky and good visibility. Another passenger said he could see only whiteout conditions outside the airplane. The highest terrain in the area was Jackknife Mountain across from their destination, which was the General Communication, Inc., (GCI) fishing lodge on Lake Nerka.

A passenger in the third seat behind the pilot said that the airplane flew below the clouds along the tree line, and maneuvered to avoid terrain. Both he and another surviving passenger said that at no time was there any unusual maneuvering. Strangely, in the final few minutes of the flight, the pilot turned the aircraft east-northeast away from its destination and *towards* mountainous terrain (Figure 5-1). Then, about 16 NM southeast of the GCI lodge, with the aircraft in a climbing left turn, it impacted the Muklung Hills.

This seemingly irrational event caused NTSB investigators to look at the pilot's background. He had only recently retired from a major airline and had just lost a close family member. In addition, four years previously he had experienced an intracerebral hemorrhage (ICH), yet the FAA still allowed him to fly with an unrestricted first-class medical certificate.

Figure 5-1. About 16 miles southeast of their destination, the pilot inexplicably turned the aircraft towards the cloud-shrouded mountainous terrain. (From NTSB Report NTSB/AAR-11/03)

A more classic example of CFIT involved a sleek twin engine Beechjet 400 that departed Rome, Georgia, VFR, with the crew intending to get their IFR clearance after becoming airborne. When they departed, Rome's automated weather system was reporting a 1,000-foot overcast with 10 miles visibility. The overcast obscured nearby hilltops that exceeded 1,600 feet MSL. Once they were airborne the ATC Center provided a transponder code and told the crew to maintain VFR, as there was inbound traffic southeast of Rome. The controller advised, "we'll have something for you later." Two minutes later the Center asked for the BE 400's altitude. The captain, who was acting as copilot, replied, "We're at thirteen hundred feet VFR, just south of Rome airport."

The CVR recorded the captain as he then began directing the pilot-flying (PF) to turn: "We're gonna have to get away from that mountain down there pretty soon. You're getting close. You're gonna have to go right." The captain then mentioned there was a mountain in one direction and an antenna in another, both hidden by the fog.

The PF was clearly uneasy, and replied, "I can't see over there." He even suggested they "punch up" through the clouds, since the tops were only 2,000 feet. But the captain persisted, and instructed, "Fly back to the right." Forty-eight seconds later, the CVR stopped recording. They had hit the 1,701-foot summit of Mount Lavender. All seven executives and the two-man crew were killed. The captain was in too big a hurry and made a fatal mistake in judgment.

Carburetor Ice

There's an old saying, "'tis an unhappy captain, made wise by many ship-wrecks." If you fly with a carbureted engine, NTSB statistics show you have a good chance of joining several unhappy captains who have experienced a carburetor-ice accident or forced landing. A three-year NTSB study showed 119 aircraft damaged or destroyed because of carburetor ice. While Cessna and Piper aircraft lead the pack, most aircraft equipped with carbureted engines—helicopters included—were involved.

The Piper J-3 Cub figured in several accidents. This caught my eye since my only dead-stick landing was in a Cub due to carburetor ice. It was early in my career and I was in Air Force pilot training at Greenville Mid-Delta Airport (GLH), Mississippi, flying the T-6 Texan. A friend had washed out of the program and I was introducing him to private flying in

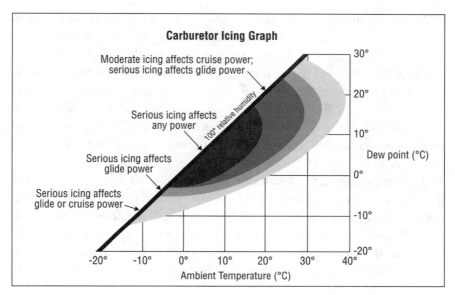

Figure 5-2. CAT chart.

the Cub. While I was demonstrating a spin, the engine quit and the prop stopped turning. Very simply, I had forgotten to pull the carb heat to hot *before* retarding the throttle. A dive during recovery to make the prop windmill was unsuccessful. Fortunately, the Mississippi delta near Greenville is replete with large pastures. And after a successful forced landing, I hand-propped the engine and away we went. Inwardly, I was euphoric at having successfully accomplished my first emergency landing. I couldn't talk about it though, since the Air Force frowned on a student making extracurricular flights. But, over the years, I have never again forgotten carburetor heat.

A very similar incident near Cedar Rapids, Iowa, involved the pilot of a Cessna 182 on his second flight of the day to off-load skydivers. He was at 3,500 feet, with an outside air temperature of 70°F and a dew point of 59°F. As the jumpers got ready, he pulled the power to idle, then out they went. Unfortunately, he had forgotten to pull the carburetor heat to ON. Although the engine continued to run at idle power for a time, there was no response from the throttle. Then he misjudged his landing pattern and hit short, badly damaging the airplane. To make matters worse, the aircraft's owner sued him—successfully—for the damage to his airplane.

When carburetor ice begins to form it restricts airflow at the throat of the venturi. Fuel in a float-type carburetor is vaporized at the narrowest portion of the venturi, immediately downstream of the throttle (butterfly) valve. At the throat of the venturi, the vaporizing fuel and decreasing air pressure (per Bernoulli's principle) create a sharp drop in temperature—as much as 60° to 70°F. Any humidity such as found with a high dew point or visible moisture, e.g., clouds or fog, quickly forms ice at the venturi and on the throttle butterfly valve. This begins literally throttling the engine's power output.

In cruising flight, the technique usually taught to combat this venturi ice involves pulling carburetor heat full hot every 30 minutes, or by watching for a drop in RPM or manifold pressure before applying carburetor heat. Yet the accident record shows that awaiting symptoms of imminent engine failure before applying carburetor heat can be counter-productive. The sudden application of hot and less dense inlet air, to an engine already

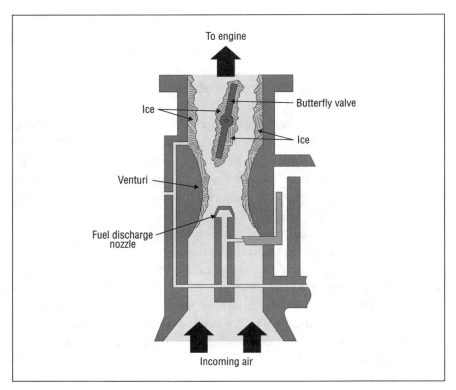

Figure 5-3. Carburetor icing.

choking due to reduced airflow, greatly enriches the mixture and can precipitate sudden stoppage.

The worry has been that too much carburetor heat causes high cylinder-head temperatures (CHT) which can lead to burnt valves or detonation. While this *can* be a problem with high-compression engines, such as the Pratt & Whitney R-985 found on the de Havilland Beaver, or the R-1340 installed on the Otter, it should not a problem with light airplane engines. In fact, without a carburetor air-temperature (CAT) gauge, when flying in conditions conducive to carburetor ice and at 75 percent HP or less, it is best to climb, cruise, descend, and land with the carburetor heat full hot. If your aircraft is equipped with a CAT gauge, then the CAT should be kept continuously at 10° to 20°C. (See your airplane's POH/AFM. 20°C is the maximum recommended for the Cessna 180/182 series.)

After applying heat you must re-lean the mixture, because it will be richer with the carburetor heat ON. The leaner mixture in turn reduces your fuel consumption. The application of carburetor heat should be done *slowly*, and will result in a slight power decrease. However, this slight power loss can be recovered by simply adding more throttle to regain the lost manifold pressure or RPM. If you are out of throttle, this technique is still recommended, since in most cases it provides an eight-percent improvement in fuel consumption with only a three-percent loss in TAS. (This ratio may vary with different airplanes.)

Induced Enrichment

The NTSB accident briefs show all too clearly that waiting and watching for symptoms of ice before applying carburetor heat can be dangerous. Several pilots told investigators that upon noticing a decrease in manifold pressure or RPM, they quickly applied full carburetor heat, whereupon the engine quit and wouldn't restart. The engine undoubtedly flooded from the suddenly enriched mixture.

A classic example involved a Cessna 150. About two hours into the night cross-country flight the engine began running rough. The flight instructor promptly applied full carburetor heat, whereupon the roughness disappeared. But, instead of leaving the carb heat ON, he pushed the heat lever to OFF. About 30 minutes later, the engine again began running rough. Yet all instruments were normal and with very little RPM fluctuation. Again, the instructor applied full carburetor heat—whereupon the engine quit and failed to restart. Because it was a nighttime emergency, they landed in trees, resulting in substantial aircraft damage. Investigators reported the temperature-dew point spread in the area was 44°F/30°F, which according to the Carburetor Icing Probability Chart is in the serious icing zone.

A few accidents occur during go-around from either a touch-and-go landing or a balked landing approach. In one case, the pilots learned the hard way why Cessna's "Pilot Safety and Warning Supplements" and their various POH/AFMs recommend that you, on go-around, apply full power first then push the carburetor heat control to COLD. Cessna advises that when relative humidity is greater than 50 percent and ambient temperature is between 20° and 90°F carburetor ice is possible. As noted earlier, the carburetor air temperature typically drops as much as 60°F *below* that of the incoming air.

A carburetor air-temperature gauge is as necessary as cylinder-head temperature or oil-pressure gauges, since each of these instruments provides critical flight safety information. The *Handbook for Pilots* published by the AOPA Air Safety Foundation states, "Accumulations [of carburetor ice] may occur at temperatures as high as 100°F, even with a very low humidity. The possibility of carburetor icing is greatest, however, with a combination of ambient temperature at 70°F or below, and a relative humidity above 80 percent." Accident briefs show only 2.4 percent of the mishaps occurring when the outside air temperature was *above* 75°F.

As the record shows, incidents of carburetor ice are most likely during cruise and descent. Thus, when atmospheric conditions are in the "serious icing" range, the cautious pilot will cruise, descend, and land with carburetor heat *full hot*. As Richard Coffey explains in *Skylane Pilot's Companion,* "Complete vaporization of the fuel-air mixture is dependent on carburetor temperatures (measured at the throttle valve) of at least 40°F." Lacking a CAT gauge, the heat should be either full hot or full cold. *Partial heat is not recommended, since this could inadvertently put the carburetor air temperature into the icing range (0° to 21°C, or 32° to 70°F).* This advice applies to all carbureted engines, not just the Cessna Skylane.

If you operate in very cold temperatures, then you'll need full carburetor heat for both taxi and takeoff. The reason is that in super cold temperatures the air is so dense and the mixture becomes so rich that fuel vaporization becomes problematic. Thus, you'll have a hard time keeping the engine running. However, use of carburetor heat will smooth it out.

For those who fly in Alaska, the relatively warm spring-through-fall months necessitate constant attention to CAT. In my home area of Sacramento, California, the situation is reversed, with the *winter* months averaging 40° to 60°F with relatively high humidity. This too requires constant attention to the CAT gauge.

With a CAT system installed, and cruising at 75 percent HP or less, the recommended procedure is simply to keep the CAT above the yellow arc, at between 10° to 20°C (the range recommended in the 182's POH). When cruising at 75 percent power at 4,000 to 5,000 feet with a CAT of 15°C and leaned in accordance with your POH, your fuel consumption will be reduced by two to three gallons per hour—simply because of the improved fuel vaporization. And this reduction applies to any cruise HP setting you chose to utilize. (*Note:* while the airplane manufacturer's POH/AFM is supposed to be the ultimate authority, a Continental representative tells me his company now recommends 125 degrees rich of peak EGT at all horsepower settings. This is 75 degrees richer than recommended by the 1985 Cessna Skylane POH.)

As you can see, there's a double benefit in using carburetor heat: you avoid the hazard of sudden engine failure from carburetor ice and you realize improved fuel consumption. One caution though: when *increasing* your power setting, be sure to enrich the mixture *before* pushing the carburetor heat knob OFF. Otherwise you'll be caught with an excessively lean mixture and the engine may falter or quit.

You'll notice there has been no mention of takeoff with carburetor heat ON. The reason is two-fold. First, the application of carburetor heat at full power results in a 9 to 15 percent loss in horsepower (this varies according to engine). This is because the heated air has a reduced volumetric efficiency. In addition, the ram air feature is shut off. Thus, with less HP you'll require more runway than the POH shows for your takeoff gross weight.

The second reason is that with carburetor heat applied, the inlet air is now unfiltered. Dust and dirt ingested into the carburetor can cause all sorts of problems. Then too, at full power you probably don't need heat. The carburetor's butterfly valve is nearly parallel with the throat of the venturi. Consequently there is almost no surface area on which carburetor ice can form. It is wise, however, to apply full heat momentarily just before takeoff, to be certain the venturi is free of ice at max power. But always take off with the carburetor heat OFF.

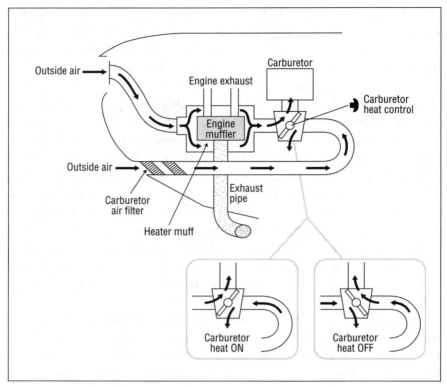

Figure 5-4. Engine compartment diagram.

Flight Instrument Failure

Vacuum pump failure in light airplanes is fairly common, and causes loss of all vacuum-operated gyro instruments—specifically the attitude indicator and heading indicator. With a failed vacuum pump, the gyros spin down gradually. While the symptoms can differ among attitude indicators (ADI and/or FD), as gyro RPM diminishes, the attitude indicator begins gradually changing pitch attitude. If you follow the indications as the aircraft enters a spiral dive, you'll have a horrendous case of vertigo—more correctly known as spatial disorientation. In other words, you won't be able to tell which way is up. And unless you have an emergency attitude indicator installed, or you're proficient with use of the turn and bank needle or turn coordinator, you are now along for the ride. This is why it's so important to regularly practice partial panel instrument flying and unusual attitude recovery.

A classic example of this problem cost the lives of Missouri Governor Mel Carnahan, his son, who was piloting the Cessna 335, and a campaign aide. It was October 16, 2000, when they departed at night on an IFR flight plan in rain and low clouds. The flight was from St. Louis to a political rally in New Madrid, Missouri. While cruising in IMC the pilot told the controller he was having problems with his primary attitude indicator and requested a higher altitude, whereupon he was cleared to 4,000 feet. Then he reported that the primary attitude indicator was not "reading properly," and that he was attempting to fly using the copilot's instrument. He then requested diversion to Jefferson City where the weather was better. But in the process of diverting, he lost control, and the aircraft subsequently crashed at high speed, killing all aboard.

In late January, 2002, a Conquest II (Cessna 441) was lost for the same reason. The aircraft was IFR from Springdale, Arkansas, to Rifle, Colorado, cruising at FL280. Then the pilot advised ATC the airplane's attitude gyro had malfunctioned which affected the autopilot, and that he was now hand-flying the aircraft. The controller wisely provided the pilot with a block altitude of FL270 to FL280. During the next 13 minutes, the airplane was noted to make a series of climbs and descents. This indicated he was flying by reference to the turn and bank indicator, located on the left side of his instrument panel. Yet, across the cockpit, the copilot's vacuum-powered ADI should have been available. Unfortunately, the pilot finally lost control and the airplane crashed.

For pilots who fly IFR in single-engine aircraft, having either a standby vacuum capability, or a standby attitude indicator is simply life insurance. In fact, don't leave home without it—unless, of course, you enjoy playing career roulette. Consider the case of a Cessna U206 out of Marion, Illinois, flown by an instrument-rated private pilot. The flight was in IMC when the pilot told ATC the vacuum pump had failed. While making a turn he reported being "completely disoriented," before losing control and crashing near Salem, Missouri.

Another case involved a non-instrument-rated private pilot flying a Piper Lance. He had departed Hornell, New York, for Lancaster, Pennsylvania, with an enroute stop at Wellsville Municipal Airport (ELZ), New York. There was no record of a weather briefing, nor was a flight plan filed with FSS. Upon taxi-out from Hornell, the pilot advised the FBO that his vacuum annunciator light was illuminated. Then, after an engine run-up, he reported the suction gauge read zero. He was advised that his attitude indicator, directional gyro, and autopilot would be inoperative. Both instruments are vacuum-powered, and the autopilot relies on their input. The pilot was told to stay away from clouds, whereupon he asked whether their mechanic had arrived for work. After receiving a negative reply, he announced he was departing for Wellsville with four passengers.

It was mid-morning, and with a 2,000-foot ceiling and six miles visibility, the weather seemed adequate for the VFR flight. At Wellsville, with the engine still running, he off-loaded two passengers and picked up three more. The weather at Wellsville was estimated as a 900-foot overcast and 1.5 to 2 miles visibility—clearly instrument conditions. The aircraft departed and climbed to around 200 feet, with witnesses noting the landing gear remained extended. A dense fog now blanketed nearby Beech Hill where the aircraft crashed, killing all aboard. Ironically, about 30 minutes later, the fog lifted.

This 400-hour pilot had owned the airplane for about a month. He had made the trip from Hormel to Lancaster on a weekly basis, and had accumulated about 20 hours in the Lance. Interestingly, he had received about 37 hours of simulated and two hours of actual instrument time towards his instrument rating. However, he had not had training on partial-panel techniques. Meanwhile, he had become over-confident in his own ability and let compulsion override good judgment. Once again, it is noteworthy that he was in that statistically dangerous category: a private pilot *without* an instrument rating, and 200 to 500 hours of flying experience.

Fuel Management Errors

Among the most avoidable mishaps are those involving fuel starvation or fuel exhaustion. Still, if you monitor the NTSB accident briefs, they continue to occur almost monthly. All of us have no doubt flirted with this danger at one time or another. We fall into the trap when we pass up the opportunity to refuel at a major metropolitan airport because of the price of fuel. Or, in a hurry and worried about traffic delays, we rationalize that we can make it with good leaning, or with the help of tailwinds. But the winds turn out to be different than forecast. Then too, in our haste we fail to recheck the weather and arrive to find our destination below minimums.

These fuel starvation accidents bring to mind some basic principles that need discussing. First, when you flew as a student pilot in Cessna 152s or Piper Warriors your instructor probably told you to "always fly with full fuel tanks." That is true *only* for those specific training airplanes. In the real world of aviation you'll frequently need to tailor your fuel load to the trip in order to accommodate all your passengers and their baggage or cargo. In single- and twin-engine aircraft equipped with reciprocating engines, when all seats are filled with adult passengers, the allowable fuel load is almost always limited by both gross weight and CG considerations. Then, because the fuel gauges in most light-airplanes are notoriously unreliable, to be certain of your fuel load you must physically measure the fuel in your tanks. With the fuel accurately measured, you can then be certain of your range and fuel reserve.

In an aircraft certified for aerobatic maneuvers in utility or aerobatic-category, full fuel may be okay with passengers for a routine trip. But when performing spins and other aerobatic maneuvers it may be necessary to limit the fuel load to keep it in the aerobatic category CG envelope. Otherwise, a spin may be unrecoverable.

What we can't anticipate in cases of fuel management problems is a fuel cap that siphons in flight, or a leaky sump drain, or loose fuel-line B-nut. Any of these conditions significantly increases the fuel consumption. Thus, it is prudent to be constantly watching for signs of abnormal fuel burn, e.g., a rapidly developing fuel imbalance, or excessively rapid decrease in the quantity, as shown on the gauges. Despite the half-hour VFR fuel reserve (45 minutes at night) required by §91.151 or the 45-minute IFR reserve (§91.167), a full one hour reserve of fuel is recommended—provided your cabin load allows it. This is just to handle unforeseen contingencies like headwinds stronger than forecast, or unanticipated bad weather.

Fuel Starvation

Failing to follow the manufacturer's procedures for fuel tank usage as outlined in the POH/AFM is often the cause of a fuel starvation mishap. An example involved the pilot of a twin-engine Cessna Skymaster (C-337H) practicing approaches and landings at his home airport. During what ended up being his last approach, both engines suddenly quit. The aircraft crashed into the outer marker beacon, then collided with a chain-link fence and skidded across a road and hit a car, before finally coming to rest against yet another chain-link fence.

Investigators examined the cockpit and found the fuel selectors for both engines set to the right tank. A check of the fuel tanks found the left tank completely dry and the right tank with 4.5 gallons of gas. The POH for the Skymaster states, "The fuel selector valve handles must be turned to LEFT for the front engine and RIGHT for the rear engine, for takeoff and landing and all normal operations...If single-tank operation is being used when fuel levels are low the fuel quantity in the tank in use should not be allowed to drop below 50 pounds (roughly 8 gallons) prior to re-establishing normal single-engine-per-tank operation; this will avoid the possibility of dual engine stoppage due to fuel starvation."

Fuel Exhaustion

Just plain running out of gas is a highly avoidable event. This once occurred when, after 11 hours in the air, a Cessna 210 equipped with long-range tanks, ran out of fuel at night. The pilot had flown from Wisconsin to Pensacola, Florida, on an IFR flight plan. After missing two ILS approaches into Pensacola, he canceled IFR and proceeded VFR to Gulf Shores, Alabama. Then, while en route to his destination, he casually told the ATC controller he was out of gas.

Amazingly, because the aircraft set down in brushy scrub, this seemingly unconcerned pilot and his three passengers survived a forced landing at night with only minor injuries. Yet a fuel stop along the way would have prevented this otherwise irrational accident.

A review of several fuel-exhaustion incidents shows that the pilots *knew* they were about to run out of fuel, but, incredibly, failed to declare an emergency or ask for help. The AIM tells us that an aircraft is in at least an *urgency* condition the moment the pilot becomes doubtful about the remaining *fuel endurance*. The AIM's glossary advises, "Minimum Fuel— Indicates that an aircraft's fuel supply has reached a state where, upon reaching the destination, it can accept little or no delay." Yet the accident record implies that many of today's pilots fail to realize they are supposed to advise ATC the moment they recognize a fuel shortage problem.

The Pilot/Controller Glossary definition of emergency fuel has been eliminated from the AIM. However, using the term establishes a valid emergency in which the pilot must get on the ground quickly as engine failure is imminent. Waiting until engine failure occurs and then suddenly announcing your situation obviates any possibility of help from ATC or other aircraft and government agencies. Consider the following example.

A turboprop King Air E90 was operating under Part 135 as a commercial air taxi with a pilot and three passengers aboard. The flight was on an IFR flight plan from Chicago's O'Hare Field to Michigan City, Indiana. The accident report states, "Following a routine departure from runway 36 at O'Hare and a routine climb, [the aircraft] established radio contact with South Bend Approach Control." The pilot was given destination weather as "indefinite ceiling two hundred [feet], sky obscured, visibility .7 NM in fog: wind calm, altimeter 30.10."

Since the airport had only a non-directional radio beacon (NDB) approach, the weather was obviously below landing minimums. Thus his departure from O'Hare, or an attempt to accomplish the approach, was illegal under §135.219. In fact, an attempt to land in the prevailing conditions would have been challenging for an ILS approach. So, assuming any sort of preflight planning, the pilot departed O'Hare knowing the field was below NDB minimums. Of course, this was a violation of §135.219 which requires that destination weather be at or above minimums at the estimated time of arrival. Then too, there was the fuel reserve requirement for the destination airport—an alternate airport, plus 45 minutes of flight thereafter.

Figure 5-5. Beechcraft King Air E90. (Photo by Alan Radecki)

The King Air pilot flew as cleared direct to Michigan City NDB, where-upon South Bend Approach established positive radar contact. He was then instructed to turn left to heading 070 degrees and told that vectors would be provided for the approach into Michigan City. He acknowledged each transmission normally and was finally told to descend and maintain 2,500 feet. Once again he responded normally. The vectors continued until suddenly radar contact was lost about six nautical miles northeast of Michigan City, when the aircraft ran out of fuel over Lake Michigan.

Despite the dark night, the pilot managed to ditch the aircraft success-fully, and all aboard survived and exited the airplane through the emergency escape hatch. About four hours after the aircraft disappeared from radar, the Michigan City Coast Guard unit received reports from observers on shore of flashing lights in the water. South Bend ATC personnel had failed to follow established emergency procedures, which included notifying proper agencies such as the Coast Guard. Consequently, all four of the airplane's occupants died of hypothermia, but only two of the bodies were recovered.

In this case, the pilot had departed O'Hare Field *knowing* the weather was below NDB minimums, and that he had an inadequate fuel supply. Once nearing his destination he failed to declare an emergency or minimum fuel and continued in a business-as-usual manner until both engines flamed out. And in the descent to the water he *still* failed to tell ATC of his predicament. Just one "Mayday" before he disappeared would have reminded the controller to initiate rescue efforts. Oh yes, and the ship's emergency locator transmitter (ELT) was found disconnected.

Optimistic Flight Planning

Another instance that sounds equally irrational involved a Cessna P210 on a late January VFR ferry flight from Iowa, where the pilot purchased the aircraft, to Paris, France. The trip included a leg from Goose Bay, Labrador, to Narsarsuaq, Greenland. The filed alternate (required under Canadian regulations) for this leg was Nuuk, Greenland. Besides the pilot, there was one non-pilot passenger aboard. The weather briefer described the pilot as "anxious to go." Weather at Narsarsuaq—a VFR only destination—was reported as 1,000 feet scattered, 3,500 feet overcast, and visibility greater than 10 kilometers (about six miles). Temporary conditions forecast for the time of arrival were an indefinite ceiling of 800 feet, with visibility 1,500

Figure 5-6. Despite having a published ADF approach procedure, Greenland's Narsarsuaq airport is a VFR-only destination. (Photo courtesy of RocketRoute)

meters (about 4,958 feet) in rain and snow. VFR minima for the airport's single runway 8-26 are 1,500-foot ceiling and visibility 8,000 meters (about 5 statute miles) (Figure 5-6).

The visual approach chart has the following caution: "Unless the ceiling is at least 4,000 feet and flight visibility at least 5 statute miles, pilots without a good knowledge of the local topographical and meteorological conditions are advised not to make any attempt to approach Narsarsuaq through the fiords." Forecast for Nuuk, the alternate, was 600 feet overcast and freezing rain, with a visibility of 5,000 meters (about 3.1 statute miles). Temporary conditions at ETA were given as 400 feet overcast, with visibility 800 meters (about half a mile) in rain and snow. Both airports were below the VFR minima, and the forecast for Nuuk mentioned freezing rain. The POH for the P210 shows that even with deicer boots, a hot prop, and heated windshield strip, the Centurion is not certificated for flight in known icing conditions. Yet, despite all the negative indicators, the pilot chose to depart anyway. Records show he had flown the route previously, which probably gave him some unwarranted confidence.

A VFR flight plan was filed for a cruising altitude at or below 5,500 feet. His estimated time en route was five hours, with an endurance of seven

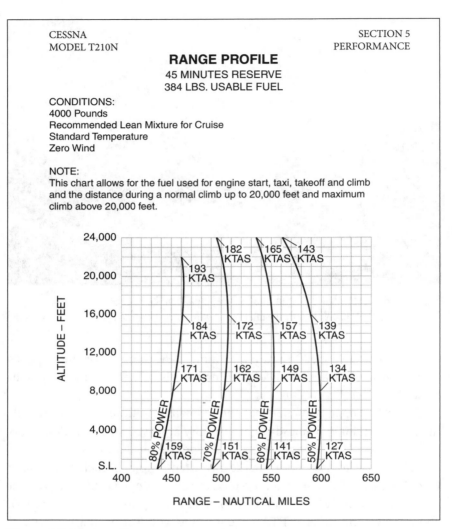

Figure 5-7. Range profile.

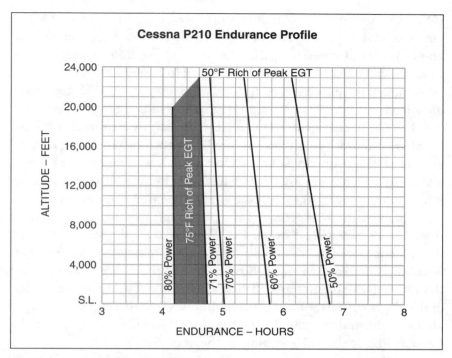

Figure 5-8. Endurance profile.

hours. As both the Range Profile and Endurance Profile charts show, this latter figure was optimistic.

Approximately two hours into the flight, the pilot was told that his destination weather had deteriorated as predicted. Surface winds were from 100 degrees at 27 knots gusting to 38 knots—a twenty-degree crosswind. The Cessna 210 has a published demonstrated crosswind capability of 21 knots. And while this is not a limitation, it's the manufacturer's way of saying that with anything greater you're on your own.

Although the airport is VFR only, it did have three NDB approaches. The minima are quite high, with a caution that "the approach should not be attempted if winds exceed 30 knots." At this point, he still could have reversed course and returned to Goose Bay.

At 1433, two hours and forty-seven minutes into the flight, the pilot advised Sondrestrom that he would divert to Reykjavik, Iceland. He estimated Reykjavik at 1717 and fuel exhaustion at 1846. At 1658, he radioed a revised ETA to Reykjavik as 1828 and reported being 150 miles west. At

1712, he was spotted on radar at 188 miles west on the 272 radial of Keflavik VOR. Winds at 5,500 feet were reported from 360 degrees at 25 to 30
knots. At 1721, after receiving a forecast of winds from 360 degrees at 10 to
15 knots above 10,000 feet, the pilot climbed to 15,000 feet.

Although the pilot had not declared an emergency, at 1723 the Icelandic Directorate of Civil Aviation initiated search and rescue operations.
A USAF C-130 rescue aircraft and Icelandic ships were directed toward
the aircraft. Surface winds near the predicted ditching point were from 33
degrees at 28, gusting to 35 knots. Ocean swells were recorded as five to
seven meters. The overcast was 900 feet with 25 miles visibility. Because
it was "dark twilight," the Air Force C-130 dispensed flares to light up the
sea. Around 1751, some 6.4 hours after departing, the 210 began a descent
from 15,000 feet, its fuel exhausted. Then, at 1826, the pilot ditched in
the Atlantic Ocean on the 268-degree radial approximately 36 miles from
Keflavik VOR. An Air Force helicopter arrived about three minutes after
the ditching with the aircraft still visible in the ocean, but there was no sign
of the two occupants. At about 1829, witnesses reported still seeing a blue
aircraft light; and by around 1834, the aircraft had disappeared. Still, the
Cessna's ELT continued operating for the next 15 minutes.

The FAA considered the flight illegal because an Export Certificate
of Airworthiness had not been obtained. The seller in Iowa reported that
the pilot was in a big hurry to depart and was unwilling to await the FAA
inspector from Des Moines who would have issued the export ferry permit.

Then the pilot attempted to depart Goose Bay without any survival gear.
But Transport Canada officials refused authorization for the trans-Atlantic
flight until the pilot had obtained the minimum required necessities. (He
had actually been planning to depart with nothing but his travel bag.)

Why the two occupants failed to exit the airplane is only speculation.
However, the U.S. Coast Guard reports that 70 percent of those who survive a ditching fail to get out due to disorientation and blind panic.

Some additional factors involved with unsuccessful egress after ditching include the streamlined doors such as found on the Cessna and Piper
single-engine series. The external water pressure will hold them closed
until cabin is flooded and the water pressure is equalized. Therefore, when
a forced landing or ditching becomes inevitable, it is wise to unlatch the
cabin door(s) before touchdown. This way they are unlikely to become
jammed if the fuselage warps or bends during the process. Although the

cabin will fill with water much faster with the door cracked open, it will make your exit quicker and easier.

With the doors closed and latched on touchdown, the occupants will be forced to hold their breath and wait until the pressure equalizes before getting out. Unfortunately, Coast Guard tests show that with a water temperature of 50 degrees or lower, even the best of us are unable to hold our breath for more than 15 seconds. And with the water temperature near freezing, the immersed human body shuts down quickly.

In this case, the Cessna P210 pilot was in such a hurry that it took Canadian Government representatives to force this pilot to acquire the required basic survival equipment. This shows he had a total disregard for the life of his passenger. And ultimately his compulsion (or obsession) to get home led him to badly overestimate the P210's range.

Had the pilot attended a water survival course, his chances of successfully escaping would have been greatly enhanced. Yet, without immersion suits, the survival of the pilot and his passenger in the cold North Atlantic for even the three minutes that elapsed before the helicopter arrived would have been problematic.

For those who fly over water regularly, a word of caution is in order. For unknown reasons the FAA does not require the general-aviation pilot to carry life preservers or survival equipment, however, the State of Alaska *does*. An NTSB investigator in Anchorage once told me that 90 percent of the fatalities involving seaplanes were due to pilots and passengers not actually *wearing* life vests. Although the life preservers were probably stored in the seat back, try finding and donning one and then finding the door or escape hatch, while upside down under 50 to 60 degree water and scared witless.

Still, §91.509, for "Large and Turbine-Powered Multiengine Airplanes," *does require* the needed equipment. Therefore, it is only smart to use that regulation as your guide and carry the equipment listed. And while no aeronautical regulation requires use of cold-water immersion suits, you'll find that all North Slope, Alaska, personnel wear them without complaint when flying over the Arctic Ocean. So take the hint.

Fire in Flight

Few things evoke panic like an aircraft fire in flight. We talk endlessly about practicing "emergency procedures," when in reality, most are "abnormal procedures" and easily handled by reading the appropriate checklist. But not with a fire in flight, because the clock is ticking for total disaster and you simply *must* accomplish the procedure 100 percent correctly while simultaneously looking for a suitable place for an emergency landing. If the POH/AFM emergency procedure puts out the fire, then you can proceed to the nearest airfield. However, if the fire continues, you must land promptly in a suitable field, or ditch in a lake or the ocean; otherwise in just a matter of seconds you could begin shedding parts—like an engine or a wing, or perhaps become totally incapacitated by the smoke.

A seven-year study of NTSB accident briefs showed a variety of unusual situations: a Cessna 172 exploded when the owner-pilot lit a cigarette; a Learjet 24 had a serious cockpit fire after one of the pilots reset a popped circuit breaker; an electrical short causes the wing leading edge of a Beechcraft 95 to explode and erupt into flames. In fact, most of the fire-in-flight accidents in the NTSB's data involved electrical-system fires, with engine

Figure 5-9. This A-36 Bonanza encountered a fire during takeoff due to an engine fuel line leak.

fires a close second. Prevalent among engine fires were those occurring during starting, usually with over-primed, flooded carburetors. These problems of course result from poor pilot starting technique. However, for this discussion, we'll deal only with engine fires in flight.

Two factors stand out in engine fires while airborne. The first is the number of malfunctioning exhaust-systems involved. The second is the frequency of maintenance error as the cause. The following are examples of engine fires in flight for various reasons.

On January 2, 2002, following extensive maintenance, a Beechcraft 58P departed Boise, Idaho on a functional test flight. The start, taxi, and run-up were normal. However, on liftoff the pilot noted a fire in the left engine. With a 10,000-foot runway, the pilot's reaction was exactly correct. He quickly rejected the takeoff and landed on the remaining runway. Neither the pilot nor his passenger was injured. The aircraft, however, was substantially damaged by an electrical short in the air-conditioner wiring which had ignited fuel vapor from a leaking fuel cell. The fire caused heat distress on the outboard upper engine mount and the structure around the engine. The bottom of the fuel tank also was found to be warped. You can visualize the result had the pilot elected to continue the takeoff. The investigation showed that faulty maintenance caused both the fuel leak and the electrical short.

In another instance, a Beechcraft Duchess on a dual training flight experienced an engine fire for an unknown cause. In this case, the flight instructor did everything wrong and ultimately precipitated a fatal accident. First, he reported a right-engine fire and requested a straight-in approach for a northbound runway at Tulsa International Airport.

Attempting to return to Tulsa with an engine fire was his first mistake, as Tulsa International was 18 miles north of their position. Yet, he was only four miles from another suitable airport. Wind at the time was south-southeast at eight knots. Witnesses saw the airplane making a fast approach to Tulsa's runway 36R. Then the pilot reported an unsafe landing gear indication and opted to go around—his second major mistake.

He was cleared to land on either runway at his discretion, whereupon he opted to land to the south. With the landing gear still extended and the right propeller still not feathered—yet another error—he added full power and began climbing which proved to be his final and ultimately fatal mistake. Witnesses said the aircraft slowed, then rolled over to the right with the nose suddenly pitching down. It crashed and burned, killing both the student and instructor. Cause of the engine fire could not be determined. But at the first sign of fire, had the pilots accomplished the correct emergency procedure and landed at the closest airport, the accident chain would have been broken.

The Board gave the probable cause of the accident as the flight instructor's failure to maintain V_{MC} during a single-engine go-around. Contributing was his failure to follow the emergency checklist and to feather the propeller. The amount of multi-engine training the instructor had received and the time period since his last multi-engine training was not addressed in the skimpy NTSB accident report. But his performance showed a distinct lack of basic multi-engine knowledge and flying skill.

In a light twin on final approach with an engine out, once you've committed to land, if the landing gear fails to check down and lock, that's just tough luck; you don't attempt a go-around. This is because light twins *are not certified* for an engine-out rejected landing (called *landing climb* in transport and commuter category airplanes). Overall, this flight instructor demonstrated fatally flawed aeronautical skill and judgment.

In another case, the pilot-owner of a Piper Aerostar departed at night with an IFR clearance from Destin, Florida. The weather was relatively good, with a 1,600-foot ceiling and seven miles visibility. About a minute after reporting out of 700 feet, the pilot advised ATC that he had lost his left engine. Witnesses saw the engine burning brightly. The pilot declared an emergency and was cleared to land at Eglin AFB on runway 12. In fact, Eglin tower advised the pilot that he was less than a mile from the runway. Then the controller advised, "You're flying right over it now." The pilot appeared preoccupied with the engine and seemed unsure of the airport's location.

Three minutes after the pilot reported the engine failure, the left wing separated and the airplane crashed one mile west of Eglin AFB. All three occupants were killed. The cause of the engine fire could not be determined. The rule of thumb has always been that if the fire can't be extinguished promptly, make an emergency landing *somewhere* immediately; because the clock is ticking on structural failure of the wings or other critical components. In addition, the fuel selector for the burning engine should be turned to OFF.

Another incident involved a corporate pilot flying a pressurized Piper Navajo. While cruising at FL240, the right engine suddenly caught fire. Immediately he began an emergency descent, while simultaneously shutting down the engine. As he passed through FL210, the fire appeared to be out. Although only 14 miles from a major metropolitan airport he opted for vectors to an airfield with a Piper dealership that was 112 miles away. He landed 50 minutes later without further problems. The engine fire problem was later traced to a faulty turbocharger.

It's difficult to fault this pilot's success and coolness with an engine fire. However, that 50-minute flight with unknown structural damage from an engine nacelle fire was—let's just say, not prudent. This pilot was playing career roulette.

Cabin Fire

Cabin fires have resulted from numerous causes, ranging from a shorted voltage regulator in a Super Cub to careless smoking in a Cessna 172. In fact, careless smoking has been involved in six percent of in-flight fires. I once witnessed a fluid-filled cigarette lighter burst into flames in a corporate jet. We were at FL390 with a cabin altitude of 8,000 feet. The pressure change had caused the lighter to leak. When the passenger attempted to light a cigarette his lighter burst into flames. A quick-thinking seatmate saved the day through deft use of a blanket to smother the flames.

The incident mentioned earlier of the Cessna 172 exploding is worth exploring. The explosion apparently occurred when someone lit a cigarette. The owner was known to habitually carry a can of highly volatile toluene-based TCP (antiknock additive) in the baggage compartment. The NTSB theorized that toluene fumes ignited "during the lighting of a cigarette." Following the explosion, three witnesses saw the aircraft trailing smoke while falling out of the sky in an "uncontrolled vertical descent."

Smoke and Fumes

The rule in aviation is that any unidentified smoke or fumes in an aircraft cabin must be considered toxic and requires immediate use of the ship's oxygen system. In cabin-class twins and turbo-props a smoldering cigarette burning that luxurious wool upholstery or carpet produces cyanide gas. An electrical fire that ignites the plastic partitions or leather-like polyvinyl headliner produces phosgene gas, along with blinding smoke laden with hydrochloric acid.

A classic example of the toxic fume hazard occurred aboard a Cessna 180. As the aircraft departed an Austin, Texas, airport it was seen trailing smoke. The commercial pilot notified the tower of his problem and said he was returning to land. A Department of Public Safety helicopter began following the Cessna, with the crew noting the Cessna's smoke trail getting progressively heavier. Suddenly the airplane nosed over and dived into the ground. Cause of the fire was identified as an excessively long ELT cable that shorted on the master switch solenoid in the aft section of the airplane. The resulting sparks ignited the highly flammable plastic baggage-compartment separator, producing an extreme amount of toxic black smoke containing phosgene gas—the gas being a byproduct of the burning plastic separator. Cause of the crash was pilot incapacitation. Investigators speculated that the pilot was probably dead before the airplane hit the ground.

A similar case involved an electrical fire aboard a MU-2. The flight was at cruise altitude when the smoke started. Unfortunately, the pilot had his oxygen mask neatly stored in a plastic bag, and due to the dense smoke, once getting it out, was unable to get it plugged into the oxygen system receptacle. The acrid smoke became so dense he had great difficulty seeing the instrument panel.

Because the smoke was originating in the aircraft's aft cabin, opening the cockpit vent made matters worse, as the vent created a suction through the cockpit. Finally, a quick-thinking passenger—who also was without oxygen—removed the emergency escape hatch. Although the electrical fire continued, the smoke diminished enough that the pilot could see to land on a short airstrip. Both the pilot and passenger got out, then stood and watched as the airplane was consumed by the electrical fire.

As mentioned earlier, the seven-year study of in-flight fires shows electrical problems are most often involved. The accident briefs suggest that the in-flight corrective action was frequently miss-handled by the pilot. But it is noteworthy that some manufacturers fail to provide a procedure for electrical fires. A few POH/AFM's simply advise to reduce the electrical load and attempt to locate the source of the problem. But in most light twins and singles, shutting down the alternator(s) or generator(s) still leaves a lot of equipment powered by the battery. (This is not true with the load-shed procedure that occurs in transport category airplanes.)

With a cockpit filled with acrid smoke, searching for circuit breakers and flipping switches in an effort to "isolate the fault" is also of doubtful value. Yet there is a quick procedure you might consider, even in IMC.

First, turn off the alternator(s) or generator(s). This will disable some electrically-powered equipment. Your vacuum powered flight instruments will continue to operate, so you can still maintain spatial orientation in IMC or at night. (Review you aircraft electrical schematic to see what is powered by the alternators/generators.) Then give the burning wires and insulation a little time to cool down. If the smoke and fumes continue unabated after about one minute, turn off the battery/electrical master switch. (In aircraft having toggle switches for the magnetos, be very careful to leave the mags ON, otherwise it will instantly get very quiet.) With alternator and battery/master switches OFF, you have induced complete electrical "failure" which hopefully will stop the electrical fire. (It didn't stop the fire in the MU-2, but that system flaw was later re-engineered.) Now you can devote your attention to flying the airplane with the vacuum-powered flight instruments and land at the closest suitable airport. (Hopefully, you planned for an enroute alternate and carry a hand held VHF radio for emergency communications with ATC.)

Thunderstorms

One of the more dangerous aviation myths is that of the "all-weather" airplane. While it's true that modern technology has done wonders in making flying more reliable and safe, it's important to remember that Mother Nature *always* has the last word. Thunderstorms, for example, contain all the major atmospheric hazards known to aviation in one violent, boiling mass. The FAA's *Aviation Weather* (AC 00-6) textbook for pilots states, *"Any cloud connected to a severe thunderstorm carries the threat of violence."* It's important for every pilot to heed that statement.

A classic case in point involved the pilot of a turbocharged Piper Saratoga SR who attempted to find his way through a band of thunderstorms. The pilot faced a line of cumulonimbi reportedly extending from northeast to southwest over central New Mexico. Two cells near the accident site were reported as "very strong and developing rapidly."

Aviation Weather notes that a squall line contains severe and steady-state thunderstorms, "and presents the single most intense weather hazard to aircraft." The accident report said the pilot was attempting to penetrate a New Mexico squall line. Unfortunately, during an inadvertent encounter with the vicious winds associated with the cumulonimbus buildups, the airplane broke apart.

The NTSB investigation team's meteorology group chairman felt the pilot probably was avoiding the cells visually until encountering the clouds surrounding the cells. The report shows that the closest cell grew from 35,000 feet to 45,000 feet in about 10 minutes. But this shouldn't have been a problem since the aircraft had a B.F. Goodrich WX-1000 Stormscope with Sky Watch (like TCAS). Following any heading change, the Stormscope continually aligns displayed electrical discharges with the airplane's course. These discharges remain displayed for approximately five minutes unless cleared manually.

After a refueling stop at Lubbock, Texas, the pilot continued to Las Vegas, Nevada, cruising VFR at 14,500 feet. Then, at 1:27 PM, he requested an IFR clearance. Shortly thereafter, he was cleared direct to Las Vegas at FL180. At 2:02 PM, the pilot requested a turn south to avoid weather. At 2:09 PM, the controller asked how much farther south he planned to go, whereupon the pilot said he would turn back northwest in five to ten miles. That was his last transmission.

Nine minutes later, the Saratoga entered instrument conditions at 17,800 feet. Only 48 seconds later, the aircraft had dropped to 15,500 feet, a descent rate of 2,875 fpm. Then it reversed course to the east. In desperation, the Saratoga pilot had violated a long-standing rule of accidental thunderstorm penetration: never turn back once you are in the thunderstorm (see AIM 7-1-29(c)(4)). At the time of the accident, a rancher near the scene reported a sharp report. Then at 2:33 PM, a Forest Service fire-watch tower reported smoke.

The FAA documented the pilot as having about 500 hours, with 100 hours in the last six months. He had obtained his instrument rating two years previously and progressed from a Piper Archer to a 1997 Saratoga. About five months before the accident he had traded for a new Saratoga. In fact, the accident airplane and engine had only 74 hours total time.

After he purchased the Saratoga, the manufacturer offered him three days of free training in the new turbocharged aircraft, which he scheduled but later canceled. The only training in the new aircraft that investigators could document was a four-hour biennial flight review four months prior to the accident. The instructor reported the pilot was "very new [to] the equipment displays, electronics operation, and airplane systems." This implies a lack of proficiency in use of the equipment. In addition, there was nothing to show that he had been trained in the use of supplemental oxygen at and above 12,500 feet (*see* §91.211(a)), or in the use of the WX-1000 Stormscope.

ATC radar data showed that the aircraft entered the weather with a ground speed of 170 knots. At maximum gross weight, V_A for the aircraft is 119 knots. The wreckage showed the left wing with an upward bend 65 inches inboard from the tip. The main spar broke at the wing root. The right wing was found parallel to the main fuselage and still attached by the control cables. The stabilator spar box showed downward bending on both ends and both leading edges showed downward bending at the outboard ends. Separated pieces of the stabilator showed compression buckling of the lower surfaces, with tension tearing on the top surfaces. In short, there was ample evidence of over-stress and structural failure—mute testimony to Mother Nature's power.

The Saratoga's WX-1000 Stormscope was top of the line. However, for it to provide the safety for which it was designed, the pilot had to be proficient in use of the system. This means both training and practice, with conservative, progressive experience. You don't just get a quick one or two-hour briefing, a then go charging into a line of thunderstorms.

Under "Thunderstorm Flying," the AIM states, "avoid by at least 20–30 miles any thunderstorm identified as severe or giving an intense radar echo" (*see* 7-1-29(a)(14)). With the Stormscope, that would translate into a cluster of plus signs showing an intense electrical charge and hence turbulence. Once you're inside the 20-mile boundary with severe storms, anything can happen. And "20 miles" means 20 miles from each cell, or 40 miles between two towering buildups. Wind-shear turbulence with up and downdrafts exceeding 6,000 fpm *may be felt 15 to 30 miles away*. In addition, once within 20 miles—even when clear of clouds—there is the possibility of encountering hail spewed out of a thunderstorm. This is especially true beneath an anvil top (Figure 5-10).

The AIM warns, "Regard as extremely hazardous any thunderstorm with tops 35,000 feet or higher whether the top is visually sighted or determined by radar" (*see* 7-1-29(a)(17)). The pilot of the Saratoga is thought to have had the storms in sight until shortly before his airplane disintegrated. In addition, the National Weather Service had issued a series of Convective SIGMETs and Center Weather Advisories for the area. The AIM further advises that "no flight through an area of strong or very strong radar echoes separated by 20–30 miles or less may be considered free of severe turbulence" (*see* 7-1-28(6)). Nor, we must add, *free of hail*.

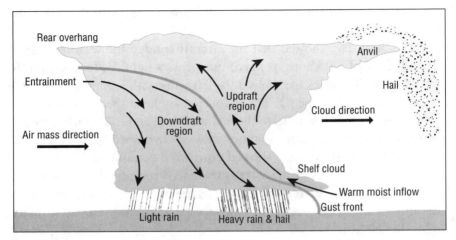

Figure 5-10. Thunderstorm diagram. Regard as extremely hazardous any thunderstorm that tops out at 35,000 or higher—within 20 miles of a cell, anything can happen.

Thunderstorm Winds

Thunderstorm winds can be divided into three categories: gust front, vertical currents (such as up and down-drafts), and tornados. First is the gust front, with winds that characteristically extend up to 20 miles from the leading edge of a storm, with velocity increasing by more than 100 knots, and changes in direction of from 40 to 180 degrees. A roll cloud, generally associated with extreme turbulence, is also a possibility. Cumulus mammatus clouds, also found in the gust front, can appear benign, but have very severe winds and turbulence. In fact, they often spawn tornados. The variations in wind direction and velocity in a gust front create wind shear, which as we know, can prove disastrous during takeoff and landing.

Vertical Currents

Another category of thunderstorm winds comprises the often violent up and downdrafts required for the storm to mature. These rising and falling currents are the result of orographic or thermal lifting, together with heat exchange inside the cloud. Flying through these transition or wind-shear areas, places major stress on both the airframe and the instrument-flying skill of the pilot.

Tornados

The final category of thunderstorm winds is the tornado, including *gust-nados*. Air is often drawn into a thunderstorm with tremendous force. In the process, it can rotate and accelerate into a funnel-shaped low-pressure vortex. If the funnel touches the ground, it is classed as a tornado. If it touches water, it is called a *waterspout*. If it remains airborne, it is classed as a *funnel cloud*. Getting involved with any form of funnel shaped low-pressure vortex can be catastrophic.

A gustnado resembles a mini-tornado, and form under a thunderstorm's shelf cloud when the strong inflow of moist air mixes with drier out-flowing air. They can appear unexpectedly like a tornado, and have a devastating effect on aircraft control.

Figure 5-11. A thunderstorm's gust-front tornado. (Photo courtesy of NCAR)

Hail

During the initial stages of a developing thunderstorm, moisture is carried aloft by rising air. Cooling as it rises, water vapor in the air condenses into droplets. These supercooled droplets can combine before freezing to become very large. Once cooling is sufficient, the moisture freezes and forms hail. This is why hailstones vary in size with the amount of moisture in the storm and the extent of its vertical development. Once their size exceeds what the updrafts can support, they fall; sometimes even ejected laterally. Thus, even in clear air, anytime you get inside of 20 miles from a thunderstorm—especially underneath the storm's *anvil*—you become vulnerable to hail damage.

Weather radar does not always paint hail. Hail thrown outside the cloud into clear air is usually invisible. The important point to remember—and this was emphasized earlier—is that *you can get hail damage in clear air when within 20 miles of the thunderstorm.*

While we all know that hail is found in thunderstorms, it is not as widely known that hail can be spewed out of the top of a cumulonimbus cloud and encountered in clear air. My first encounter was in an Air Force C-47 (DC-3) over Kansas. We were at least 10 miles from the very large cell but clearing it nicely. The hailstones that pummeled us were large, and I fully expected the windshield to shatter. We were lucky that time, but the airplane required some repair.

Another encounter involved an aging Sabreliner 40. Again, we were flying in smooth stratus clouds between two large cells. For what seemed like five minutes, we took a beating from the hail and I fully expected the engines to fail. We lucked out and were able to land safely, but repair of the damage was rather expensive. Surprisingly, the Pratt and Whitney engine compressors were found to be undamaged.

Some years ago, a Cessna 421B was knocked down by hail in New Mexico. In what should have been a fatal accident, everyone survived the uncontrolled crash landing. It was night and the aircraft was cruising at 19,000 feet in clear skies. The pilot later told investigators, "I turned on the radar and could see precipitation to the left and right of our [flight] path. However, the center area, probably 15 to 20 miles wide, was clear on the scope. This was the area [where] I planned to go through the clouds. They did not appear to be dark thunderstorms, only clouds like I had flown through many times. Before reaching the clouds, maybe 10 miles before, we encountered hail. At first it was like rain. Then within one minute of our first encounter, a large piece of ice broke through the left windshield."

The passenger in the right-seat was a private pilot, and verified to investigators that the radar, "did not indicate strong storms directly in our flight path…it showed rain on both sides, but just a small ring of rain in front." Then large hail, approximately two inches in diameter, "blew out the left windshield and dazed the pilot." He leaned right and put his head down to avoid further injury, then blacked out from hypoxia. The passenger took control and attempted to keep the wings level. He told investigators he never felt dizzy or light-headed (hypoxic). Yet, the next thing he remembered was the back-seat passenger trying to awaken him on the ground. The back-seat passenger agreed that the flight had been smooth and that "the clouds below were beautiful." He reported they encountered some "thin clouds, and the air became rougher." About that time, they encountered the hail and "it seemed the windows would burst." He related, "The pilot leaned towards the right seat about the same time his windshield failed."

With hail hitting the cabin divider and aft bulkhead, "it was very noisy," the passenger said. The pilot—still leaning right to avoid the hailstones—shouted to the right-seat passenger that he could not see the instruments. The back-seater related, "I could feel the hail hitting my left arm and decided to unbuckle and move into the aft-facing seat directly behind the copilot." The next thing the back-seat passenger remembered was the right-seat passenger shouting, "are we stalling?" He reported, "At the same time material from the floor rose up and then went back down." The airplane stalled again, then settled down for a moment.

Finally, the rush of air in the cabin became more intense. The airplane had entered a dive. The backseater related, "at that point I had given up all hope of surviving… I do not remember anything about the crash-landing. When I came around all was quiet."

None of the occupants remember the descent or crash-landing. They can only assume the airplane's inherent stability brought the nose up to a level-flight attitude. It hit, then ricocheted across the flat ranchland, skipping across the ground four times before sliding to a stop (Figure 5-12). While everyone was injured to varying degrees, they all miraculously survived the encounter with hail.

Figure 5-12. The NTSB photo shows windshield damage done by the hail encounter near a thunderstorm that downed a Cessna 421. Although everyone on board was unconscious due to hypoxia, miraculously they all survived. (Photo courtesy of NTSB)

Other Thunderstorm Hazards

All forms of icing are found in thunderstorms. Tests show that the most severe airframe icing occurs at intermediate altitudes when supercooled droplets are encountered well above the freezing level. Ice accumulation will be instantaneous. In the blink of an eye the entire airplane will be encased in all ice-forms—deadly clear ice in particular. This is why it is so critically important with turbine-engine airplanes to have engine inlet heat continuously activated, because after the accumulation occurs, activation of inlet heat will cause the ice to slough off and damage the engine compressors and fan blades. This can result in severe compressor stalls or double engine flameout. With reciprocating engines, the air inlets also can become blocked by ice and require use of alternate air or carburetor heat in order to bypass the blocked air inlets. (Alternate air is automatic in some aircraft.)

Lightning

A lightning bolt is a very long electrical spark that extends between one center of electrical charge in a cloud and another center of opposite polarity on the ground, in another cloud, or even in the same cloud. The energy produced comes from warm air rising upward into a developing cloud. As the air cools, water vapor condenses into tiny droplets. When rising air reaches a temperature of approximately -40°C, the water moisture droplets freeze and some of the ice crystals form hailstones, which then fall through the cloud. As the hailstones fall, small positively charged splinters separate, leaving the hailstones negatively charged. Vertical currents within the cell then carry these positively charged ice splinters upward, making the top of the cloud positively charged. When the potential near one of the charged areas exceeds the threshold for electrical breakdown, lightning results.

The flash of a lightning bolt can momentarily blind a pilot. Thus at night when near a buildup it's important to have the cockpit thunderstorm lights on bright. This prepares your eyes for a potential flash. Airborne lightning usually poses no physical danger since modern aircraft fuel systems are designed to prevent an explosion from a strike. However, other potential hazards include damaged electrical systems and components, instruments, radar, and the aircraft skin.

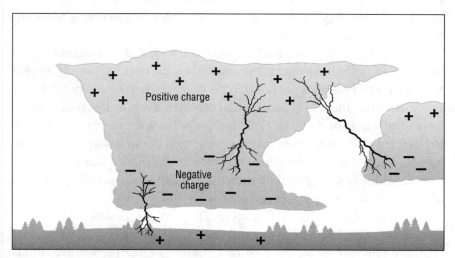

Figure 5-13. Typical thunderstorm electrical charge.

The hazard is most prevalent during prolonged flight through precipitation, when the OAT is between 5° and -5°C. Sometimes a flight through the upper level of a thunderstorm will trigger lightning that otherwise would not have occurred. However, it is most frequent at low and intermediate altitudes.

The important thing to remember is that no matter how well your airplane is equipped, you still must avoid thunderstorms by 20 to 30 miles. When approaching a squall line, this means you can go between two of them so long as they are at least 40 miles apart. Anything less is extremely dangerous. Don't let that wonderful radar or Stormscope fool you. It's for weather avoidance, *not thunderstorm penetration.*

Standing Mountain Wave

Although thunderstorms are recognized as dangerous, another weather phenomenon offers a similar potential for disaster. It's a little-known fact that the force of a mountain wave can be as strong and devastating as a downburst or a tornado. The problem arises when poorly informed pilots ignore their weather briefing regarding the winds at mountaintop height which can result in a *standing mountain wave*. It is perhaps more insidious since it can occur in clear air. At times though, it may be marked by some form of lenticular cloud. In hill country or in mountainous terrain, a mountain wave begins forming when winds blow across ridges or mountains at speeds of 15 knots or greater.

In fact, for a flight in mountainous country, AIM Paragraph 7-5-6 warns, "Don't fly light aircraft when the winds aloft, at your proposed altitude, exceed 35 miles per hour. Expect the winds to be of a much greater velocity over mountain passes than reported a few miles from them... Downdrafts of from 1,500 to 2,000 feet per minute are not uncommon on the leeward side." You'll find strong updrafts on the windward side, which may be smooth or contain severe turbulence. On the lee side you'll likely find downdrafts so strong they exceed your airplane's climb capability—often accompanied by severe turbulence.

The wave pattern may extend as much as 700 miles downwind of the mountains. Upper-air turbulence from mountain-wave effect has been recorded to above 70,000 feet. In fact, mother of pearl lenticular clouds can occur at 80,000 feet and remain stationary for long periods of time; yet

Figure 5-14. Lenticular cloud formations (top) or cap clouds (bottom) mark the presence of a standing mountain wave with severe turbulence and downdrafts.
(Bottom photo courtesy of John R. Bakkensen, ©2014; top photo, NCAR)

they can change in seconds if conditions change. A considerable amount of motion occurs around the clouds. Besides the primary wave, six or more less intense waves may be present in some geographical areas. While wind speed can increase rapidly with altitude, a strong jetstream can eliminate the wave pattern.

At lower altitudes on the windward side of the mountain range, a strong, smooth wind will flow uphill. Its velocity increases as it crests the ridgeline, and on the lee side the smooth flow often breaks up—not unlike the airflow over a stalled airfoil.

With dry air, the mountain wave may not be marked by a lenticular cloud. Yet the dry wave can be just as turbulent. Your only clue will likely be the FSS briefing, with pilot reports of moderate to severe turbulence at various altitudes, recent cold-frontal passage, or winds with a velocity exceeding 15 knots and blowing at a 30-degree angle or greater to the ridgeline.

Figure 5-15. Cloud shapes over the mountains identify the potential for dangerous winds and turbulence associated with a standing mountain wave.

Downdraft Hazards

It was late November and a Mooney 21 was navigating along V-210 through La Vita pass—roughly between Pueblo and Alamosa, Colorado. Suddenly, the pilot transmitted to Pueblo Approach Control, "Mayday! This is Mooney 977M in La Vita Pass and I'm losing altitude at one-zero thousand, squawking 7-7-0-0. I can't seem to break the downdraft." Instead of reversing course to get out of the wave, he continued straight ahead. Minimum en route altitude (MEA) on the airway through La Vita Pass was 14,000 feet. The controller responded calmly, "and your heading please?" There was no immediate reply, but moments later the pilot again transmitted a Mayday with the aircraft's call sign. It was his last transmission. The wreckage was found at 9,000 feet on a very steep slope.

During his weather briefing, the Mooney pilot had been told to expect clear skies and a strong northwesterly flow over the mountains. He was also advised that severe turbulence was a possibility. A firefighter at the scene told investigators that the surface winds in the pass were 40 to 60 mph. Shortly after the Mooney crashed, a professional pilot flying the same route in a light twin reported using full power and holding 120 knots while still descending. He lost 2,000 feet before the aircraft began maintaining altitude. He told investigators, "I have never experienced such an intensive and long-lasting downdraft situation—especially in smooth flight conditions."

It was summer in Alaska and the pilot of a Beechcraft H35 Bonanza was flying a friend on a sightseeing trip from Cordova to a private airstrip near Palmer. The weather was good and he was cruising at 6,000 feet in smooth air. But as they approached an area of snow-covered terrain the wind suddenly became stronger and turbulent. Then a strong downdraft caused the aircraft to begin descending rapidly. Although the pilot applied full power and attempted to climb, the airplane lost airspeed and continued to descend—finally crash-landing in an area of snow covered terrain. Although the airplane was a total loss, the two occupants were unhurt.

Mountain-wave patterns are not generated solely by very large mountains. They can occur in hill country with elevations as low as 300 feet. In fact, 300-foot ridges have been known to cause wave action up to 75,000 feet. Standing lenticular clouds produced by such waves can be seen readily in the rolling hills and lake country of our northern tier of states.

Flight Strength Envelope

During a severe turbulence encounter, most of us fear the threat of structural failure due to a high indicated airspeed. However, most experts will tell you that in heavy turbulence you are more likely to get in trouble by flying *too slowly* and stalling, then losing control. Yet, if you keep your speed within the aircraft's design envelope you have nothing to fear. Here's why.

The strength criteria for airplanes with reciprocating-engines are different from those for turbine-powered aircraft. Aircraft with reciprocating engines have the top of the green arc on the airspeed indicator to show V_{NO}, or maximum cruising speed. At or below V_{NO}, an aircraft certified under §23.333(c)(i) is able to handle gusts of 50 fps (3,000 fpm) up to 20,000 feet, with a linear decrease at higher altitudes. At speeds greater than V_{NO}—the yellow arc—the strength requirements diminish. For example, the Baron 58 POH states, "Do not exceed the V_{NO} except in smooth air…The redline, or 'never exceed speed,' V_{NE}, is defined by §23.1505 as being no higher than 90 percent of the airplane's maximum demonstrated dive speed (V_D). At V_D, the airplane must handle gust loads of 25 fps (1,500 fpm) to 20,000 feet, then decreasing linearly to 12.5 fps (750 fpm) at 50,000 feet."

Unlike transport-category airplanes, GA aircraft have no published turbulence-penetration speed (V_B). However, if you can stand the bumps, any speed up to the end of the green arc is your turbulence penetration speed. A more conservative procedure is to use V_A. This speed varies with gross weight, but is slower and more tolerable than V_{NO} in heavy turbulence.

Turbine-powered airplanes—jet and turbo prop aircraft—use V_{MO}, maximum operating speed, and the limiting Mach number, M_{MO}. Because jet-powered airplanes routinely cruise near their V_{MO} or M_{MO}, and because they decelerate more slowly, their limitations are based on 80 percent of V_D.

In severe turbulence most of us instinctively favor slower speeds because we are more afraid of structural failure than of inadvertent stall. Yet the record shows that because of built-in strength margins you are much more likely to encounter serious trouble due to inadvertent stall than to structural failure. Still, in the Saratoga's thunderstorm accident described earlier, the pilot was caught at a cruising speed of 170 knots, which was within the aircraft's designed structural capability. However, while reversing course in the severe thunderstorm, the pilot apparently lost control. His increasing speed and the vicious thunderstorm winds took the airplane out of its design envelope. Most likely, in blind panic while attempting to recover, he over-stressed the structure and it broke apart.

The need for careful attention to reports and forecasts of severe turbulence and thunderstorms is obvious. Professional training with the weather radar and Stormscope is an *absolute* necessity. Don't be too proud to delay a trip if extensive thunderstorms or severe turbulence is reported or forecast along your route of flight. If you are airborne and flying anywhere near a thunderstorm, then cruise at a slower speed, such as V_A. Because to avoid over-stress damage, you must be ready when the turbulence is encountered.

Emergency Landings

When the engine quits in a single, or following engine failure in a light twin, and you find that you can't maintain altitude, then you must find a place quickly in which to accomplish a forced landing. Naturally, the first priority for all of us is to find an unobstructed field where we can land without damage to the aircraft, and hence without injury. That of course is the ideal. Yet sometimes it becomes necessary to sacrifice aircraft structure so that the pilot and passengers can safely walk away. Let's look at the following examples.

A Piper Arrow departed Plymouth, Massachusetts, on a VFR flight to Block Island State Airport (BID) in Rhode Island. Twelve minutes after departure, ATC tracked the aircraft descending out of 4,300 feet and making a 180-degree turn back toward Plymouth Airport. The Arrow's engine had failed. When the Arrow's pilot asked ATC for vectors to the nearest airfield the controller gave him a heading in the opposite direction. Still descending, the pilot made yet another 180-degree turn. And due to inexperience, apprehension, and possibly lack of training, this private pilot was dissipating his life-saving altitude while frantically trying to decide what to do.

There was speculation too that the pilot was attempting to reach a cranberry bog about 300 feet from heavily traveled Interstate 495. However, the accident report shows that he made a determined approach to the interstate highway, at about a 60-degree angle. He touched down in the northbound lanes. But the aircraft slid through trees in the median strip, jumped a gully, and emerged into the southbound lanes where it collided broadside with a station wagon. The Arrow exploded on impact and the pilot and his passenger were killed. A woman and a four-year-old child died in the station wagon, while a third occupant of the vehicle was severely injured.

In another instance, a Cessna 177RG threw a rod in the number-four cylinder. The engine lost power, and white smoke billowed from the cowling. The smoke was followed by oil streaming from under the cowling onto the windscreen and passenger-side window. The pilot and front-seat passenger said later, "Our forward visibility from that moment on was almost nil." In this incident too, the pilot asked ATC for the nearest airport. The controller gave them a heading toward a nearby airfield, but unfortunately they were out of altitude. Another pilot, flying a Cessna 182 in loose formation, steered them toward a nearby interstate highway.

The acting co-pilot told investigators, "Because of the oil and smoke, we were unable to see the highway in time to make a turn aligning us with the westbound lanes." Approaching from the north, they aimed for the slightly concave dirt median. As the left wing contacted the rising ground, the aircraft slewed 90 degrees across the highway and slammed into a 50-foot

Figure 5-16. Although almost blinded by oil on the windscreen, this pilot aimed for the highway's concave dirt median, but the left wing hit rising ground and the aircraft slewed across the busy highway.

rock embankment that borders the eastbound lanes (Figure 5-16). Fortunately, traffic was unusually light and no one was injured.

The lesson in both cases is that *highways are for cars and trucks.* In each case, the pilots had other viable options. The Cardinal was over a vast, rolling plain where the pilot could have made a forced landing. The Arrow pilot also had another option: the cranberry bog, which would have been an excellent choice, albeit with aircraft damage a certainty. Yet the cranberry bushes and moist soil would have helped decelerate the aircraft, possibly allowing the occupants to survive uninjured. Best of all, landing in the bog would have prevented the needless death and severe injury of the occupants of a passing car.

The frequency of forced landings on highways seems to be increasing. The newspapers invariably make the pilot a hero for a successful street or highway landing. But these "successes" serve only to encourage others to do likewise. Highways are for cars, not airplanes.

The extreme hazard to motorists is exemplified by the collision of the Piper Arrow with the station wagon. But even if the road is deserted, it can be extremely hazardous to the pilot too. Major roads may sprout light standards, and even two-lane country highways tend to have power lines or telephone wires alongside. Fences located close to the pavement are also common. These obstructions are all hard to see. What may look to be an impending safe landing on an empty country road can turn into a deadly crash when the airplane snags invisible wires 50 feet above the asphalt.

As mentioned earlier, the real goal in any emergency off-airport landing is the protection of the cabin structure so that the occupants escape injury. A cornfield or brushy area is an excellent choice. Here, the more fragile landing gear, wings, and underside deform during contact with the vegetation to absorb the aircraft's kinetic energy. The damaged airplane can be repaired or replaced, but there is no way to live down killing innocent people while trying to save yourself.

The ideal forced-landing area is often not available, so it is the pilot's responsibility to plan his VFR flight so as to minimize flight over unsuitable terrain. And while en route, he or she must know at any given moment where to land if the engine suddenly fails. In reality, it is unthinkable for a pilot flying in VMC to ask ATC for a vector to the nearest airfield. It's something you—the pilot-in-command—are supposed to have in mind continuously during the trip.

During flight planning, we all get careless and fail to bend our route to stay over good terrain. And sometimes the rush to get going causes us to neglect identifying enroute airfields or areas suitable for a forced landing. While it doesn't happen often, with an engine failure you will experience the ultimate test of your training, flying skill, and judgment. Asking ATC to suddenly step in and save you, or landing on a heavily traveled street or highway, is simply not the way it is done. Part of being a competent pilot-in-command is being prepared to handle your own emergencies. But above all remember: *highways are for cars, not airplanes.*

Conclusions

This chapter has covered the types of accidents that occur most frequently during the enroute phase of flight. As you can see, there are many factors to consider when acting as pilot-in-command. Remember too that a biennial flight review *does not* keep you knowledgeable and up to date. Only *annual recurrency training* with a ground school review of important subjects and a flying proficiency check in the various types of aircraft you fly will keep you truly knowledgeable and proficient. While it is time-consuming and expensive, you should consider it life insurance.

CHAPTER 6

Descent, Approach, and Landing

As mentioned in Chapter 1, about 60 percent of the general aviation accidents each year occur during descent, approach, and landing. While not usually fatal, they occur so consistently that in accident investigation circles they've become known as the "magic six minutes of approach and landing." While causes vary, a principal ingredient is compulsion—otherwise identified as rash judgment. Consider the following examples.

The Approach

It was a foggy, dark night at Laconia Municipal Airport (LCI) in Sanbornton, New Hampshire, when a Piper Arrow crashed into Hopkinson Hill, killing the pilot and his three passengers. As is so often the case, the private pilot was not instrument rated. Still, he had a total flight time of 1,675 hours, of which 498 hours were at night. Over the years he had logged 27 hours of simulated instrument time—including three hours in actual instrument conditions. These are respectable totals, so this pilot could not be called inexperienced. His most recent simulated instrument training had taken place seven months earlier and consisted of a mere 24 minutes during a biennial flight review. The previous year he had received 1.4 hours of simulated instrument dual, which included ADF holding and two localizer approaches to Laconia's runway 8.

The pilot owned a business in Glens Falls, New York, and commuted daily from his home near Laconia Airport in Gilford, New Hampshire. On the night of his fatal accident, weather at his departure point, Glens Falls, was VFR. However, the FSS advised of "instrument meteorological conditions [that] prevailed throughout the Lakes Region of New Hampshire." He was told to expect 300-foot ceilings and one-mile visibility in fog, including an area of embedded thunderstorms that topped 33,000 feet. The FSS briefer finished by advising that VFR flight *was not* recommended.

Nevertheless, the pilot departed VFR at 7:56 PM, without a flight plan and with three passengers aboard. Approaching Laconia, the captain of a commuter flight about to make an approach asked for the Arrow's position. The pilot replied with his approximate location and stated that he had ground contact, and adding, "I'll be landing in five minutes." The flight impacted one-half mile west of Belknap NDB, the final approach fix for the runway eight localizer and 65 feet below the top of Hopkinson Hill.

Several things point to this pilot's apparent habit of flying in IMC without an instrument rating, and with no IFR flight plan. First, he had 498 hours of night time, which in the New Hampshire area was bound to have included frequent encounters with instrument conditions. The fact he lived near Laconia and commuted daily implies an inherent compulsion to get to work or to get home (we've all experienced it). His checkout during the previous year on holding patterns and the runway eight localizer approach, without the goal of an instrument rating, no doubt bolstered his confidence to press on into marginal conditions. In fact, he probably asked for such training specifically to help him sneak into Laconia in marginal weather.

His lack of an instrument rating probably explains why he even *considered* flying into an area of embedded thunderstorms. A pilot with IFR training would have been taught a healthy fear of thunderstorms. But scud running at night, with a 300-foot ceiling and only one mile visibility is downright scary. These conditions were more suited to a precision ILS approach, than to the localizer approach available at Laconia. And it's utterly unthinkable to have tried it VFR at night. In effect, the pilot showed an irrational self confidence. In the end his overconfidence, poor judgment, disregard for FAA regulations, inadequate instrument training, and compulsion led to his death and those of three friends.

Tire Hydroplaning

Tire hydroplaning occurs when a film of water separates the tire from the runway surface and prevents braking traction. Often, the surface is so slick that upon touchdown the wheels fail to spin-up and activate the anti-skid system. In some aircraft this means that on touchdown the ground spoilers fail to deploy to kill the wing's residual lift and the locked-wheel

Figure 6-1. A wet muddy film in light rain on the well-used and ungrooved runway surface allowed a crosswind to blow this aircraft off the side of the runway.

protection from anti-skid brakes fails to arm. This sets the stage for a tire hydroplaning accident.

While tire tread design and tread depth both play a part, runway surface texture and depth of the water film are the key factors. Although there are two formulas for calculating dynamic hydroplaning speeds, they are of little use to the pilot. For a GA airport, if the surface is wet you should expect it to be slick.

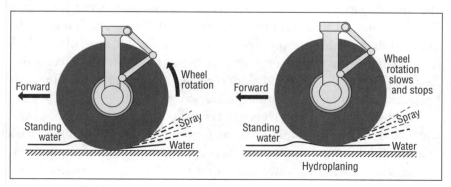

Figure 6-2. Tire hydroplaning.

Figure 6-3. NASA hydroplaning tests document the separation of the tire from the runway by a water film. (NASA photo)

On a smooth runway surface—regardless of tire tread depth—even an early-morning dew can cause slickness, resulting in so-called *thin-film skids.* This phenomenon can occur at any speed, and the skidding generates heat due to friction which vaporizes the moisture beneath the tire. This steam-heat then scalds the rubber, such that it melts and reverts to the uncured state—hence the term *reverted rubber skids.* Instead of the black tire skid marks you would normally expect, this phenomenon leaves white, so-called "steam cleaned" skid marks on the runway. Once thin-film skids begin, the condition can continue to below taxi speed.

Tire hydroplaning accidents are typically blamed on the pilot. And while landing long, or sometimes a bit fast, is often involved, in reality it's a substandard runway surface texture combined with the surface contamination, such as standing water, snow, or ice that's the real causative factor.

Figure 6-4. Thin film skids can occur at any speed and leave *white* rather than black skid marks, due to the steam generated beneath the scalding tire tread. (USAF photo)

NASA tests show that either the lateral grooves or an asphalt porous friction course (PFC) surface which are properly maintained, will provide a one-to-one, wet-to-dry stopping ratio. In other words, a runway surface so treated will provide the same stopping capability, whether wet or dry. Runways used by the airlines are required to have either lateral grooves or a PFC overlay. Conversely, GA runways have no minimum standard of slickness. Lacking FAA standards, GA runways may or may not have aggregate in the asphalt or concrete; and even if present, the aggregate may have been polished by years of long use. Thus, when wet, the runway surface becomes as slick as wet ice. Consider these examples.

The 2,600-foot runway at a small Texas airport was wet following rainfall, with standing water reported on the surface. A Cessna 172 touched down approximately 1,100 feet long. If the runway had been dry, the remaining 1,500 feet would have been more than adequate for a normal rollout. But when the pilot applied brakes, there was no deceleration—because his tires were hydroplaning. The Cessna then skidded off the right side of the 22-foot-wide runway, past the departure end and onto an uneven grassy overrun. Finally, the left wing hooked a tree, and the airplane came to rest in a drainage ditch.

In a similar instance—a wet, 2,100-foot runway with standing water—a Beechcraft Queen Air touched down normally. But when the pilot applied brakes, there was no braking action. Consequently, the airplane slid off the end, slued left, and hit the airport's boundary fence.

In another classic case of hydroplaning, a Learjet 35A completed an ILS approach at Greenville, South Carolina's Downtown Airport (GMU) and landed on runway 1. The 5,393-foot runway was wet, and in trying for a smooth landing the pilot let the plane float, finally touching down at midfield, with 2,700 feet of runway remaining. On a dry surface, this would have been enough to get stopped. However, upon applying brakes, "there was absolutely no braking action due to [tire] hydroplaning," the captain later recalled. The aircraft continued beyond the end of the runway onto a sod stopway, down a steep (70-degree) 30-foot embankment, across a service road, and into a drainage ditch.

The investigator's report commented on the lack of skid marks on the runway and the presence of skid marks in the sod overrun. This of course shows that the airplane's fully modulated anti-skid braking system was working properly, protecting the tires from skids on the wet concrete surface, which had been polished by many years of wear. It was so slick that wheel spin-up failed to occur, and the system's "locked wheel protection" feature, which prevents hydroplaning in the form of viscous and reverted rubber skids, prevented any braking action. Once the aircraft left the runway, the grassy overrun provided the traction needed to cause "wheel spin-up." This activated the anti-skid brakes and allowed the tires to mark the sod overrun. Still, once again, the pilot was blamed, yet, when the chain of errors is examined, the substandard runway surface texture made the accident inevitable.

The combined efforts of a team from NASA, FAA, and USAF conducted tests in the late 1960s and early 1970s, that showed the average runway had a wet-to-dry stopping ratio of 2:1. In other words, a wet surface would double the ground roll. Some runways were so polished and smooth that when wet they showed a six-to-one stopping ratio—the equivalent to wet ice.

The GMU runway appears to have fit this latter category. Yet either lateral groves or a PFC overlay would have prevented the problem. Based on statements in their report, the NTSB and FAA investigators apparently were unfamiliar with the tire hydroplaning phenomenon; and the runway's surface texture was not addressed in their accident report. However, it is noteworthy that the GMU runway 1 is now grooved. As noted earlier, because of the insistence of the Airline Pilots' Association (ALPA), all runways used by airlines must be grooved or have a PFC overlay.

Required Runway Length

When determining the landing-runway requirement, many GA pilots simply look at the Landing Distance chart in the POH/AFM and come up with a number. "The runway must be at least that long," they say. Yet that figure in the POH is actually just the starting point. With any airplane there are three factors that should be considered in determining the actual runway length needed for a safe landing. First is the headwind or tailwind factor. The second concerns obstructions in the approach path based on a three-degree glide slope (20-to-1 glide path ratio) to the runway threshold. The third factor is runway surface texture and condition, i.e., smooth asphalt or concrete, PFC overlay, grooved, dry or wet, standing water, snow or ice covered. Any one of these factors can make your landing runway requirement much longer than anticipated. (Runway slope normally is a minor consideration; although Nevada's Boulder City Municipal, with a 2.7% uphill slope on runway 33 is a notable exception.)

In evaluating a potential destination airport, commercial pilots are required to use the "60 percent rule" (*see* §135.385(b)). This says that the *landing distance* cannot exceed 60 percent of the available runway. Landing distance is predicated on a stabilized glide path ratio of 20-to-1 (three-degree glide slope) approach. The aircraft then crosses the runway threshold at a height of 50 feet, and at an airspeed of 1.3 V_{S0} (stall in landing configuration), followed by an idle-power float from the threshold to the 800-to-1,000-foot touchdown zone. The runway requirement is then calculated from this base figure. If the runway is wet, then 15 percent must be added. (*Note:* the wet factor additive is 15% of the calculated dry runway requirement; not 75% of the available runway.)

Thus, in a light twin or corporate jet, a 3,000-foot *landing distance* would require a 5,000-foot (dry) runway (dry, 3,000 ÷ .60 = 5,000 feet).

If it's wet, the required runway length becomes 5,750 feet (5,000 × 1.15 = 5,750 feet). (This also essentially fits with the previously mentioned rule of thumb of a 2-to-1 runway wet-to-dry stopping ratio; wherein on an ungrooved runway the landing roll is said to double when runway surface is wet.) Keep in mind that the 60 percent rule also applies to small (non-transport) airplanes flying for hire under Part 135 air-taxi rules. Still, whether you're flying for hire or for pleasure, in a Beechcraft A-36, a twin-engine B-58 Baron or Citation X, the 60 percent rule offers protection from a runway overshoot accident. (*Note:* the column on the chart for ground roll considers only the distance from the touchdown point, wherever that may be, to where the aircraft is fully stopped.)

Wind Effect

Airplanes are designed to take off and land into the surface wind. The aerodynamic rule is that a headwind that equals 10 percent of the landing speed reduces landing distance 19 percent. Conversely, a tailwind of the same velocity *increases* landing distance by 21 percent. Uphill or downhill slope is negligible, since it increases or decreases landing distance by only two to four percent per degree of slope. This is why it is normally better to ignore runway slope and land into the wind. (Aspen, Colorado, is a notable exception, because of both a two percent uphill slope on runway 15 and high surrounding mountainous terrain beyond.)

The Cessna 421C POH states, "Decrease landing distance by 3% for each 4 knots of headwind…with tailwinds up to 10 knots, increase total distance by 8% for each 3 knots of wind." Thus at a gross weight of 6,600 pound and a landing speed of 96 knots, the (no-wind, 86°F) landing distance is 2,200 feet. With a 10-knot headwind that number is *reduced* 7.5 percent or 165 feet (2,200 × .075 = 165 feet). A 10-knot tailwind extends the 2,200-foot landing distance just over 24 percent, or 528 feet; for a total landing distance of 2,728 feet. Now add the 60 percent dry runway factor and the landing runway requirement becomes 4,547 feet (2728 ÷ .60 = 4546.66 feet). If the surface is wet, runway length must be 5,226 feet (4,547 × 1.15 = 5,229 feet). Anything less is a game of "bet your struts."

Of special interest is that the manufacturer's POH Landing Distance chart list the conditions under which the data was derived. Whether it's a Cessna 185, Beechcraft Baron, or Learjet, the chart stipulates "power off (over the landing threshold), maximum braking, paved, level, dry runway, zero wind." Left unsaid is that these data points were obtained by skilled engineering test pilots under ideal conditions. And as you have seen, anything other than these conditions increases the landing distance, e.g., wet surface, ice or snow, gravel, grass, etc. Consider the following accidents.

It was a cold winter morning when the Cessna Citation was cleared for an ILS runway 23 approach to Bluefield, West Virginia. Runway 23 was listed as 4,743 feet long. Weather was reported as 700-foot overcast, with visibility of one mile in light snow and fog. Surface winds were on the tail from 070 degrees at 13 knots. The runway was reported covered with a three-quarter inch of wet snow and slush, with braking action poor to nil. Because the Citation has a 10-knot tail wind limitation, on the first approach the pilot attempted to circle-to-land on runway 5. But on downwind he encountered clouds and missed the approach.

On his second attempt, despite the 13-knot quartering tailwind, and the report of nil braking, he landed on runway 23. Witnesses said that touchdown was at around 1,000 feet beyond the threshold. During the landing roll, the pilot discovered there was no braking traction, and that it was obvious he couldn't get stopped. Nevertheless, he delayed the go-around decision until only about 1,200 feet of runway remained. At that point he applied full power, but unfortunately the retarding effect of the wet snow and slush (slush-drag deceleration) greatly diminished the aircraft's acceleration. Although he managed to rotate, the aircraft failed to get airborne until 100 feet past the end of the runway. It flew for about 100 feet, then struck the localizer antenna and trees—finally crashing 785 feet beyond the end of the pavement. The pilot and copilot were killed on impact, with the three passengers killed in the subsequent explosion and fire.

The captain of this ill-fated flight was very highly experienced, with over 10,000 hours of flight time, of which 3,642 were in the Citation. The copilot had logged 4,748 hours, with 1,216 hours in type. Yet despite their combined experience, this professional crew clearly attempted the impossible in an attempt to please the passengers. The compulsion factor again.

According to the AFM charts, with a 10-knot tailwind, their dry-runway landing distance was 2,625 feet, and on a wet runway, 3,937 feet. For an icy runway, the chart showed a 5,250-foot landing distance. Thus, discounting the excessive tailwind component, with just a 10-knot tailwind, the icy-runway landing distance exceeded the runway length by over 500 feet. Then, in a delayed attempt to go-around, slush-drag from nearly an inch of wet snow greatly extended his takeoff requirement.

Runway Surface Slush

In the late 1960s and early 1970s, NASA slush tests with a jet transport showed that when landing on a snow or slush-covered runway, three hazards await you:

1. Hydroplaning of the tires, which can prevent wheel spin-up and jeopardize both braking and directional control (discussed later in more detail).
2. Sudden slush-drag deceleration, wherein the deep snow or slush causes a rapid deceleration and can collapse the nose-gear strut.
3. Damage to landing-flaps and gear doors from the high-velocity impact of snow, ice, and slush. In addition, despite the use of chine-equipped nosewheel tires to deflect the spray, ingestion of slush can cause damage to a jet engine's fan and compressor blades.

Although the Citation's AFM allows three-quarters of an inch of slush for both takeoff and landing, Advisory Circular 91-6A, *Water, Slush, and Snow on the Runway*, which was based on NASA tests with turbojet aircraft, recommends a limitation of *one-half inch* of slush. It's a pointless debate though, since the cause of the Citation accident is perfectly clear. No prudent pilot lands with an excessive tailwind on a slushy, short runway with reported nil braking action.

As demonstrated in the NASA tests, the most important consideration is the runway surface texture and any surface contamination, such as standing water, slush, ice, or snow. The tire's tread pattern and tread-depth also play a prominent but secondary role. On a wet, smooth runway surface, worn tire tread makes it easier to encounter a traction loss. Even heavy dew can cause this. However, a runway surface with lateral grooves or PFC overlay helps provide the expected traction, regardless of a tire's tread depth.

Another important factor on every landing approach, especially in marginal conditions, is the pilot's mental preparedness to go around if conditions aren't just right. If you are high over the threshold, too fast, too long, or upon applying brakes you discover there's no braking traction, then a prompt go-around becomes necessary. Don't take a chance and attempt to salvage a flawed landing, because, as the Citation accident shows, your life and those of your passengers depends on your decision.

Approach Path Obstructions

The presence of obstructions in the approach zone is another factor that can reduce the effective runway length. In calculating an airplane's landing distance we assume a three-degree glide slope (20 feet horizontally per foot down) to 50 feet above the runway threshold. When obstructions in the approach area interfere with this glide path—trees, buildings, a fence, a windmill—the touchdown zone must be moved down the runway in order to maintain the three-degree stabilized approach. In other words, to assure the desired stabilized glide path ratio, the runway threshold must be displaced further down the runway. Unless it's a private airstrip, the airport's management considers any approach zone obstructions, then physically marks the displaced threshold (DT) on the runway surface.

A visual glide path, such as visual approach slope indicator (VASI) or precision approach path indicator (PAPI), normally provides a three-degree approach path, as does an ILS glide slope. In Class D airspace, even though you may be VFR, all airplanes

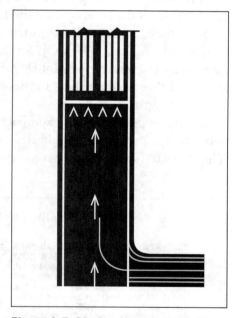

Figure 6-5. Displaced runway threshold.

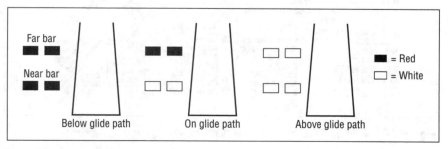

Figure 6-6. Two-bar VASI.

are required to follow the VASI to every landing. If there's an ILS, pilots of large and turbine powered aircraft *must fly* the glide slope (*see* §91.129(e)(3)). At a few locations, in order to provide obstacle clearance, the visual glide path can be as high as 4.5 degrees. California's Bakersfield Municipal Airport (L45) offers an example; wherein the runway 34 PAPI provides a four-degree approach slope because of power lines just south of the runway. However, without short takeoff and landing (STOL) capability, a glide slope greater than 3.5 degrees begins to affect your effective runway length. This is because the aerodynamic drag from flaps, spoilers or speed brakes cannot provide enough drag to maintain a stabilized airspeed. Thus you will tend to float in the landing flare and land long.

Sometimes approach zone obstructions are more subtle. For example, at Cameron Airpark (O61), California, the stopway at the approach end of runway 13 rises five percent (Figure 6-7). This necessitates a 193-foot displaced threshold on the 4,051-foot runway, leaving the pilot with an effective length of 3,858 feet.

On the opposite end, the approach to runway 31 has obstacles in the form of high terrain and tall obstructions, necessitating a 1,509-foot DT. Thus the 4,051-foot runway has an effective length (dry) of only 2,542 feet.

Figure 6-7. Flight Guide Cameron Airpark diagram. (Courtesy of *Flight Guide* ©2004)

To emphasize the problem further, suppose you were landing a Beech-craft Debonair at a private, 2,600-foot airstrip, with an elevation of 700 feet, a mild 70-degree temperature and calm winds. At a gross weight of 2,800 pounds, the performance chart shows a landing distance of 1,825 feet. This alone, accounts for 70 percent of the available runway. But it's a remote airstrip in hunting country; the rancher who owns it will tell you by telephone there are 110-foot trees only 1,000 feet from the threshold. Now, because of the obstacle (trees), your first consideration is to determine the effective runway length.

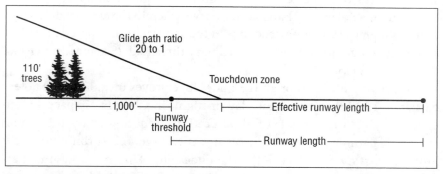

Figure 6-8. Diagram of effective runway length.

First you must determine the glide-path distance from the trees to the 50-foot threshold point. The formula is: glide path distance = obstruction height × 20 feet/1 foot. Filling in the numbers gives us: GPD = 110 × 20/1 = 2,200 feet.

To find effective runway length (ERL) we use the formula: ERL = runway length + distance from obstruction to threshold − GPD. Again, filling in the numbers, we get: 2,600 + 1,000. − 2,200 = 1,400 feet ERL. Thus, the runway is too short for the Debonair's 1,825-foot landing distance.

The point is that you must pay attention to the ancillary factors that affect your landing distance—the wind, runway surface conditions, obstructions, and displaced thresholds—all of which affect your effective runway length.

Night Operations

When approaching the runway at night over dark, featureless terrain, lacking either visual approach path guidance (VASI, PAPI, etc.) or an ILS glide slope to follow, you are exposed to a hazard known as *black-hole effect*. This visual illusion is a major cause of nighttime landing accidents. It becomes hazardous where an airport's surrounding area lacks human habitation, such as lighted buildings or homes, to provide visual cues. With the illuminated runway sitting in a sea of blackness, the pilot will attempt to maintain a constant three degree approach angle. But without visual cues, he or she will instinctively perceive that the aircraft is high on the approach path. The result is a downward banana-like curve, wherein the aircraft drops low and hits high terrain or obstructions in the approach zone, or it can lead to a landing dangerously short of the runway threshold. (See more on visual illusions in Chapter 7.)

This is where a VASI or an ILS glide slope proves invaluable. As noted earlier, §91.129 mandates that, day or night, in Class-D airspace—even though flying VFR—pilots of all aircraft are required to fly the visual approach path—VASI or PAPI. Meanwhile, large and turbine-powered aircraft *must fly* on or above the ILS glideslope. This is sound guidance for any landing approach in any type airplane. But, as you'll see, too many pilots, both professional and private, completely ignore these invaluable landing aids (*see* AIM 2-1-2).

A highly publicized airline mishap involved the black-hole effect during a late-night approach on the island of Guam. The captain of the Korean Airlines Boeing 747 abandoned the non-precision approach and attempted to fly visually over the hilly, black, featureless terrain. While the ILS glideslope was reported as inoperative, he failed to utilize either the VOR minimums—which were established specifically for terrain avoidance—or the vertical guidance to the landing zone available from his flight management system. During his visual approach, he dropped below the descent angle that would have led to a normal landing, then hit a hill off the approach end of the runway, killing all aboard.

Sabreliner 65 Accident

An almost identical accident resulted in the loss of a fanjet Sabreliner 65 during a dark, moonless, night approach into Kaunakakai Airport on the island of Molokai, Hawaii. The weather was reported by both the weather service and several witnesses at the airfield as clear with good visibility. There is ample evidence that the crew had failed to review either their navigation chart or the Kaunakakai approach plate. First, the copilot filed for 3,000 feet—presumably direct, since no route was specified in the flight plan. But mountainous terrain made flying the airways advisable, and the MEA to the airfield was 6,000 feet. They arrived after the airport's control tower had closed and failed to ascertain the correct frequency for the CTAF needed to activate the runway lights. Consequently, after unsuccessfully attempting to key-up the airport lighting, they couldn't locate the airport visually in the featureless black terrain. (The rotating beacon was either inoperative that night or wired to be activated with the runway lights.) Then the copilot thought he saw clouds below, so they opted to fly the VOR circling approach to runway five.

As they began the VOR approach, the cockpit voice recorder documented the captain having the copilot read the approach chart and provide him with the headings and altitudes. (The captain's habit of relying on the copilot to read the step-by-step approach procedure negated the safety inherent in a two-crew airplane. Only the copilot knew where they were going, and unfortunately he made a couple of fatal mistakes.) Following completion of the procedure turn, as they approached the VOR the copilot discovered his CTAF error and keyed up the runway lights. Finally, in a sea of blackness, they had the now-illuminated runway in sight.

Because of sharply rising volcanic mountainous terrain west of the airport, the airfield diagram had a notation, "Mountain located 2.8 NM from the threshold runway 5, approximately 1,280 feet high on extended centerline." But alas, neither pilot had studied the diagram during preflight, and now they were too busy to notice.

As for the VOR minimums, the copilot told the captain to maintain 2,200 feet to the VOR and then descend to 1,000 feet. This erroneous statement—the result of a hurried look at the approach chart—set the stage for the accident. The copilot had looked quickly at the circle-to-land, DME-minimums box and failed to notice the step-down procedure after pass-

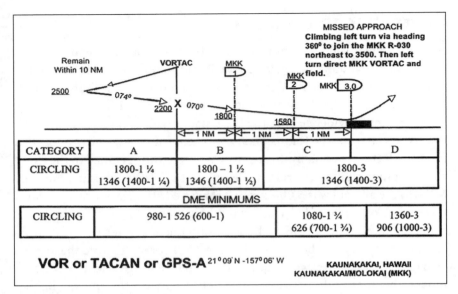

Figure 6-9. MKK VOR Approach.

ing the VOR. This procedure would have provided the necessary terrain clearance.

What the approach chart showed was an 1,800-foot MDA for the first mile past the VOR, then 1,580 feet to the 2-DME point, followed by 1,080 feet at the 3-DME point. While the captain had landed at Molokai once previously during daylight, he apparently thought the 1,000 feet MDA provided by his copilot would keep them above the high terrain.

The airport diagram noted too that during the day the PAPI was, "not available beyond 2.0 NM from the threshold due to rapidly rising terrain." And the PAPI system was noted as unavailable at night because its three-degree glide path intersected the high terrain.

With the runway in sight, at about 1.3 miles past the VOR the copilot cancelled their IFR clearance with ATC. Concurrently, the captain began a slight descending right turn off the VOR radial to visually align with the runway. Thereafter, the cockpit voice recorder documented their path towards destruction.

When the airplane was at 1.2 NM past the VOR and crossing the 111° radial, the transponder Mode C reported an altitude of 1,300 feet. About that time, the captain said, "oops." Presumably, at this point, he noted the runway lights had disappeared. (Later flight tests showed that the runway was hidden behind the ridgeline at that altitude.) The co-pilot said, "That's the clouds." When the runway lights were obscured by the mountain ridge, the young copilot had mistaken this for the clouds he had erroneously reported before the approach began. The captain then queried, "Let's have that again. That's the clouds huh? Oh!"

Having descended below the ridgeline of the high terrain west of the field, they had lost sight of the airport and were now again engulfed in a sea of blackness. The white cockpit lights are typically somewhat brightened for reading charts, and this may have been a factor too. Yet, being VFR and having lost sight of the runway—presumably due to clouds—it was the copilot's duty to immediately call "missed approach." Had the captain made an immediate full power climb for a missed-approach, the accident chain would have been broken, because at this point they still had the space to power-up and miss the ridge.

Suddenly, the now extended landing lights illuminated the light brown dead grass of the steeply up-sloping terrain. Three seconds later the captain says, "ooh, wadoyou…" A second after that, the CVR ended. All six people aboard were killed on impact.

Circling Minimums

In concept, the circling approach is designed simply to bring you into visual conditions, such that you can then fly a visual traffic pattern. Yet the circling approach is perhaps the most statistically hazardous maneuver in instrument flying. It requires that the landing runway be kept continuously in sight, while simultaneously watching the altimeter and airspeed. If visual contact with the runway is lost, this should trigger an instantaneous missed approach, with an immediate climb toward the missed approach point (MAP). Then, unless ATC has issued other instructions, you must initiate the published missed approach procedure. And it's absolutely essential that you've memorized the procedure so that it can be started without hesitation. You certainly can't look down at the approach plate and begin reading it.

One of the prime rules in a circling approach to minimums is that on the final approach you *never* descend below the published circling altitude until intercepting the visual glideslope indicator—VASI or PAPI. If the runway lacks a visual glideslope system, then hold circling minimums until you reach a point where a normal three-degree descent can be made to touchdown. As the following mishaps show, to do otherwise denies you the clearance from terrain and obstructions.

An accident involved the pilot of a Piper Comanche who had completed a VOR approach to Sidney Municipal Airport (N23), New York. Weather at the airport was VMC, with scattered clouds at 1,500 feet AGL and a 5,500-foot overcast. Visibility was seven miles, with winds from the southeast at five knots. The Comanche was circling to land on runway 7. The published MDA was 2,280 feet. With an airport elevation of 1,027 feet, this was 280 feet higher than the traffic pattern altitude of 2,000 feet. Circling minimums represent the *lowest altitude* to which you can safely descend. These higher minimums are the first clue to obstructions in the protected area. (The Flight Guide airport diagram in Figure 6-10 shows the airport surrounded by 800 foot hills.)

After breaking out of the clouds, if the weather is good enough for a normal VFR traffic pattern, the pilot is expected to fly it. And while the weather that night at Sidney Municipal airport was suitable for a VFR pattern, the lack of visual cues required that the pilot use the higher circling minimums. However, in this case he failed to monitor his altimeter and relied solely on his visual perception to see and avoid high terrain and obstructions—in this instance, dark green trees.

The airplane crashed and burned about one mile north of the airport, on the downwind leg for runway 7. Impact with trees occurred at 1,550

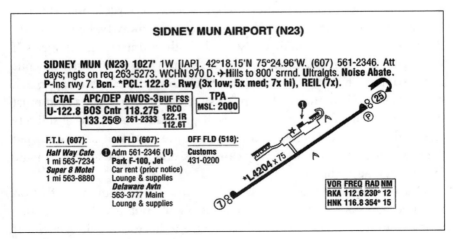

Figure 6-10. Sidney Municipal Airport (N23), New York. (Courtesy of *Flight Guide* ©2004)

feet, or 730 feet below the MDA and 450 feet below traffic pattern altitude. The dark night, featureless terrain, and airport lighting had affected the pilot's depth perception, and black-hole effect caused him to perceive the airplane's altitude as being much higher than it actually was.

Another accident involved a Learjet 23 on an air-taxi flight with four passengers aboard. The flight was at night under IFR, en route from Detroit to Pellston (PLN), Michigan. Destination weather was scattered clouds at 400 feet, measured ceiling 800 feet overcast, visibility seven miles, thunderstorms and light rain showers. The VOR approach was to runway 23, with a circle to land on runway 5. The crew reported the runway in sight and commented that they would fly a left-hand traffic pattern to runway 5. Airport elevation at Pellston is 720 feet MSL, with circling minimums of 1,320 feet—or 600 feet AGL. While descending from base leg to final approach, the aircraft struck trees at 886 feet MSL—more than 400 feet below MDA, killing everyone aboard.

Witnesses reported that the Learjet flew in and out of low scud before the crash. But the fatal error was the pilot beginning descent on base leg before intercepting the VASI glide slope, which was available for runway 5. The NTSB accident report stated: "The hazards of night approaches over areas lacking visual cues are well known." Perhaps the main hazard is the optical illusion of being higher than you actually are.

Balked Landing

The balked landing procedure—better known as a *go-around*—catches a few pilots each year. Actually, it's an utterly simple process. When approaching to land and configured for landing, aerodynamic drag is high and engine power is greatly reduced. A go-around simply requires that you add full engine power, establish a climb, then begin reducing the aerodynamic drag in reverse order in which it was added. Usually, the POH/AFM procedure requires that you first either partially or fully retract the flaps (depending on the aircraft), and second, *once climbing*, retract the landing gear. Unfortunately, NTSB investigators have found a number of pilots who were never trained in the procedure and who consequently came to grief.

A classic example involved a new private pilot on his fourth flight with passengers in a Cessna 172. His first landing attempt was much too long, so he wisely went around. Witnesses reported that, during the go-around the airplane was performing strangely. His second landing attempt was also long. Again he attempted a go-around, applying full power but failing to retract the fully extended flaps. This time, the airplane pitched-up, stalled, and crashed.

The two long landing attempts were bad enough, implying both inadequate training and proficiency. Yet it turned out the problem had deeper roots. NTSB investigators found only two entries in the pilot's logbook regarding go-around training. Both were pre-solo. Nor had the pilot been required to perform balked landings on his private-pilot flight check. When interviewed by investigators, even his flight instructor could not adequately explain the full-flap go-around procedure for the Cessna 172.

Professional pilots trip up too. Nestled in Colorado's Rocky Mountain range, Aspen's Pitkin County Airport (Sardy Field) is an interesting study. At an elevation of 7,820 feet, it lies in a narrow mountain valley. The A/FD notes laconically, "*Terrain will not allow for normal tfc patterns. High rates of descent may be required due to terrain.*" Because of the two percent uphill slope on runway 15 and sharply rising terrain southeast of the airport, regardless of wind direction, landings are normally accomplished uphill on runway 15, with departures made downhill on runway 33. A balked landing on runway 15 requires careful attention, since there's little room for error.

Aspen's runway 15 traffic pattern for light aircraft is 9,000 feet MSL, or about 1,200 feet above airport elevation. The only safe go-around procedure is a maximum-performance climb straight ahead to 8,500 feet, followed by a left climbing turn to 9,000 feet. Even at this altitude, terrain clearance is assured for only one-and-a-half miles from the field.

Weather minimums at Aspen are different too. For example, the A/FD states that flight is not recommended "unless ceilings are at least 2,000 feet above highest terrain and visibility is 15 miles or more."

A classic mishap at the challenging airport involved a commuter airline's Twin Otter. With seven passengers aboard, the IFR flight had departed Denver for Aspen with a time en route of about an hour and a cruise altitude of 17,000 feet. At 17 miles from Aspen, with scattered snow showers and some freezing rain in the vicinity, the crew canceled IFR and received clearance for a straight-in visual approach to runway 15. At about five miles out, the pilot circled to lose altitude. During this maneuver he encountered freezing rain and the windshield became coated with ice. As the aircraft approached the runway, the tower controller noted it appeared too high. Simultaneously, the pilot advised he would circle to land.

The dangerous terrain surrounding this airport is well advertised, and the captain was intimately familiar with the area. Yet he descended to about 200 feet above the runway threshold, then initiated a level left turn with a bank angle of 45 degrees. Unable to see through the windshield, and with his attention directed toward the end of runway 15, the pilot "flew into the high ground which lay in his flight-path."

The aircraft was destroyed and all aboard killed. The crash site was three-quarters of a mile from the runway at an elevation of 8,020 feet, 226 feet above the airport. NTSB's report stated, "If the standard go-around procedure had been executed, they could have gained sufficient altitude to clear all terrain." The captain had 5,865 hours, with 525 hours in this make and model of aircraft.

Landing Accidents

The rule of thumb for many years has been that a bad approach—one that has become de-stabilized for whatever the reason—leads to a bad landing. Whether you fly a Cessna 150 or a Boeing 747, you are equal at risk from three leading causes of landing accidents:

1. Attempting to salvage a bad approach.
2. An excessive rate of descent that requires lots of power to arrest.
3. A bounced landing and failure to execute a prompt go-around.

Consider the following example. Despite having a VASI available for glide-path guidance, the captain of a Boeing 727 made a steep descent and touched down about 300 feet past the runway threshold. He was on a visual approach to runway 9 at Harry S. Truman Airport, Charlotte Amalie, St. Thomas, Virgin Islands. With touchdown zone markers located 800 feet from the threshold, the 4,650-foot runway is a challenge for a Boeing 727. Yet this captain ignored the VASI, and his steep descent caused an excessive sink rate. The aircraft landed hard and then bounced nearly 50 feet into the air. Yet the captain failed to apply power. In fact, he first deployed the spoilers, but quickly retracted them.

A second bounce occurred about 1,500 feet down the runway. This one fractured the right main landing gear. After a *third* bounce—this one to about 30 feet—the aircraft touched down 2,700 feet down the runway, whereupon the right landing gear collapsed. The damaged aircraft departed the runway and crashed through a chain-link fence, then hit a truck on a perimeter highway, finally coming to rest against the side of a hill. Fire broke out, and unfortunately two of the 48 passengers perished.

The training manual for the B-727 states: "Hard or bounced landings are generally made from high approaches at higher than normal descent rates with excessive and/or late rotation. *Poor landings usually follow poor approaches.*" And, as stated earlier, in reality this is true for all airplanes.

Two lessons are immediately obvious. The first is to follow the VASI glide path. With a descent angle greater than three degrees, the landing approach is "de-stabilized," and airspeed control becomes problematic. Higher than desired airspeed leads to excessive float, with a landing touchdown well down the runway. But as this 727 accident shows, the greatest hazard is the abrupt landing flare (round-out) that's required from a steep approach, which makes a hard landing possible. Yet the VASI was designed specifically to help prevent such errors.

The second lesson is that on a marginal runway you must be mentally prepared for an immediate go-around. If anything destabilizes your approach—e.g., too steep a descent, too high over the runway threshold; either too much or too little airspeed, or a prolonged float in the flare—then *go around,* and get it right the next time. Remember too that once you float past the touchdown-zone markers, you must have plenty of runway ahead, or promptly go-around.

Crosswind Factor

Crosswinds also play a regular role in the annual aircraft accident statistics. Many aircraft have a maximum demonstrated crosswind component. Yet, as discussed in Chapter 3, some pilots seem to ignore the figure—perhaps because in light aircraft it's not a stated limitation. But realistically, if you take off or land in a crosswind that exceeds the POH/AFM demonstrated crosswind figure, you are flirting with a loss of control.

A case in point involved a Cessna 172 at Grants Pass, Oregon. The pilot had only recently qualified for a private pilot certificate, and with two passengers on board was attempting to land on runway 12. The wind direction was variable from 140 to 200 degrees—a crosswind of up to 80 degrees—gusting from 13 to 19 knots. This information was available to him from the Sexton Summit ASOS, the frequency for which can be found in both the A/FD and on the Klamath Falls Sectional Chart. In addition, the airport had a UNICOM. Still, despite these sources of information, the pilot was apparently unaware of the surface winds. And upon landing, he lost control and struck trees alongside the runway. Fortunately, no one was seriously injured.

The owner's manual for the Cessna 172 states: "With average pilot technique, direct crosswinds of 15 MPH can be handled safely." Remember, though, that surface winds are reported in knots. So we're looking at a recommended maximum crosswind component of 12 knots. It could be argued in this case that a 60-degree crosswind equates to an effective headwind of 12 knots. However, the wind was gusting and variable from 20 to 80 degrees from the right. The combination of gusts and variable direction made it much too dangerous to attempt landing a light airplane.

Wake Turbulence

Despite extensive publicity of the phenomenon, accidents resulting from wake turbulence continue—often the result of heavy traffic flow at major airports. At Philadelphia International, a Piper Navajo on final less than a minute behind a Boeing 727 suddenly rocked from side to side, pitched up, rolled inverted to the left, and then crashed, killing its three occupants. At John Wayne Airport in Orange County, California, a Westwind corporate jet crashed on short final after encountering the wake of a Boeing 757.

Wake turbulence can be extremely dangerous to airplanes of all sizes. Every year, these horizontal tornados catch some pilot by surprise—usually with fatal results. All aircraft generate wake turbulence—some more than others. It results from the dynamics of generating lift: with low pressure on top of the aircraft's wing and high pressure underneath, the differential triggers the roll-up of airflow at the wingtips which results in twin counter-rotating vortices trailing downstream (*see* AIM 7-3-2).

Most of the energy is within a few feet of the centers of the vortices. Their strength is governed by the aircraft's gross weight, airspeed, and the design of its wing. Although the extension of flaps or other lift-altering devices, or a change in airspeed, can alter their characteristics, the aircraft's weight is the primary factor. Consequently, with the vortices from heavy aircraft being a by-product of lift, their wake turbulence is stronger, with peak speeds of 300 feet per second recorded in wake vortices. Their strength is greatest when the generating aircraft is heavy, clean, and slow, which can cause rolling moments that exceed an encountering airplane's roll-control authority (*see* Figure 6-12).

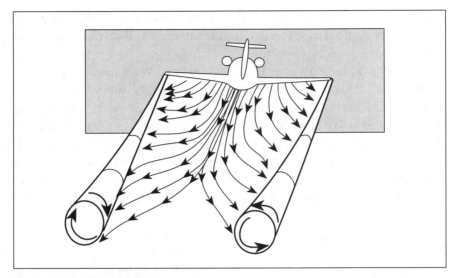

Figure 6-11. Wake turbulence.

The invisible nature of the wake vortex combined with the rush to get the aircraft on the ground by both ATC and arriving pilots, often accounts for the continuing series of wake turbulence related accidents. The point here is that all types of aircraft are vulnerable to the ferocity of wake turbulence, even large aircraft. After the Westwind accident, the FAA established new separation standards. All aircraft had to be spaced at least five miles behind a "heavy." Pilots of light aircraft are instructed to:

1. Fly final approach *above* the visual approach-slope guidance system or ILS glideslope;
2. Land *beyond* the touchdown point of the heavier aircraft; and
3. When in doubt as to the spacing interval, request updates from ATC concerning separation interval and groundspeed.

When departing behind a heavy, allow at least three minutes, or the recommended five-mile radar separation. Make certain you can rotate and lift off prior to the heavy's rotation point, since that is where the wake turbulence begins. When the tower controller sounds rushed and says, "cleared for *immediate* takeoff, caution wake turbulence, departing jet," he has covered himself legally, but you have been left dangerously exposed to the wake-turbulence hazard. Therefore, your reply should be simply, "I'll need a three-minute hold for wake turbulence."

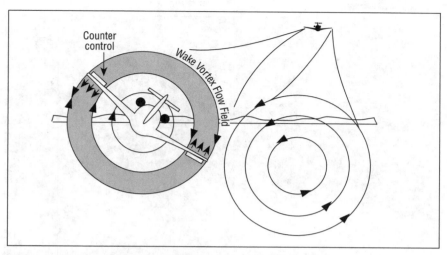

Figure 6-12. Vortex strength, and counter-control. (AIM Figure 7-3-2)

Microburst

No discussion of accidents on approach and landing would be complete without addressing wind shear. Over the years, low-level wind shear has caused several landing and departure accidents in all types of aircraft. While friction turbulence from strong winds over uneven terrain can be a player, here we are talking about an unexpected change in wind direction and velocity as a result of frontal passage, thunderstorms over or near the airport, or downburst and microburst winds.

Thunderstorms in the terminal area can produce vicious and unpredictable winds—the most dangerous involving the microburst. This short meteorological event usually occurs with young, building storm cells. Downdrafts in a microburst can reach vertical speeds of 6,000 fpm (60 knots!). Maximum horizontal winds, can exceed 80 knots, and occur about 75 feet above the ground. The life cycle of a microburst is about two minutes, with the event completely finished in five minutes. A microburst typically has a diameter of about 12,000 feet at the surface. Anything larger is classed as a *downburst*.

While some think this phenomenon is characteristic of a large, fully developed storm, just the opposite is true. Two recognized authorities in the field, Ph.D.'s Ted Fujita and Fernando Caracena, have both emphasized that microbursts are frequently generated in storm cells that appear

Figure 6-13. The National Center for Atmospheric Research documents a Colorado microburst in progress. (Photo courtesy of NCAR)

benign. They describe the phenomenon as occurring in a new, building storm cell which generates a catastrophic microburst, while a nearby old cell dissipates. The new cell builds from the outflow of an older, mature cell, and has very strong updrafts. These updrafts carry moisture higher than could normally be supported, then the large mass of moisture-laden air begins to fall.

Dr. Caracena identified what he calls the *vortex ring* (Figure 6-14), which concentrates the wind at ground level, expanding rapidly after touchdown while restricting outward flow and accelerating the wind. Its destructive effect resembles that of a tornado.

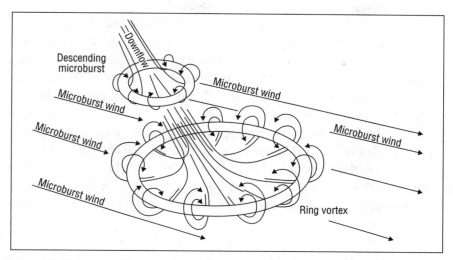

Figure 6-14. Vortex ring. (From "The Microburst as a Vortex Ring," Caracena, NOAA 1982)

The insidious danger of the microburst is that its effects can be encountered in clear air, well in front of or behind a thunderstorm. In fact, a microburst can be dry, with its effects being shown only by the telltale ring of dust (the vortex ring) it kicks up on the ground. Because it most often develops from a small, rapidly building cell lacking significant moisture it is unlikely to be detected by radar.

A microburst is typically about two miles wide, and produces a stream of cold air that falls rapidly to the ground and then spreads out and curls back up. It resembles water spouting from a garden hose pointed straight down. Its horizontal winds increase in intensity during the first five minutes with the maximum velocity lasting approximately two to three minutes. An airplane flying through it will encounter a stiff headwind from the outward flow, then a severe downdraft, and finally a tailwind. Sometimes microbursts concentrate in a line, and their activity may continue for up to an hour. Once they start, multiple microbursts in the same general area are common and should be expected.

Over the years, microbursts have caused numerous airline and general aviation crashes. One spectacular accident occurred some years ago before the phenomenon was well recognized. The flight crew of an L-1011 landing at Dallas-Fort Worth International Airport continued their approach into the rain shaft of a cumulonimbus cloud. According to the NTSB, at low altitude they encountered severe wind shear from a microburst produced by rapidly developing thunderstorm. The airplane crashed about 6,300 feet north of the approach end of runway 17L, hitting a car on a highway north of the runway and killing the driver. Finally, it struck two water tanks on the airport and broke apart. Of the 163 people aboard, only 26 passengers and three flight attendants survived. The potential for catastrophe in a light GA aircraft is obvious.

Thunderstorms represent a large turbulent, system of churning, up-and-downdrafts. The AIM warns of severe turbulence up to 20 to 30 miles from a severe thunderstorm, and 10 miles in less-severe storms: "*No flight path through an area of strong or very strong radar echoes separated by 20–30 miles or less may be considered free of severe turbulence*" (*see* AIM 7-1-28(c)).

Dust Devils

Hardly anything is written about dust devils yet they continue to cause occasional accidents. Resembling a mini-tornado, this pesky phenomenon can create windshear problems entirely unrelated to thunderstorms and bad weather. While they are most likely to affect a landing aircraft, they can upset an aircraft on departure too. Although seen at times all over the country, they are most problematic in arid areas, such as the desert southwest—Texas, Colorado, Utah, Arizona, Nevada, New Mexico, and other mid-western states. On a hot summer day, the dust devil evolves from thermals and uneven heating of the ground. When taxiing for departure in the heat of the day you may see the windsock or smoke indicating a wind from the east, while the tetrahedron at the other end points south or west. Interwoven with this odd wind pattern you'll likely see dust devils, visible because of the soil and debris they vacuum from the surface. Encountering one on final approach causes extreme turbulence followed by a sudden, rapid ballooning well above the desired glide path; or worse, a strong sink rate.

A high sink rate typically follows an encounter *with* the direction of the dust devil's rotation. Together with loss of airspeed and possibly a stall, these factors can precipitate a landing dangerously short of the runway. An encounter *against* the direction of rotation results in ballooning well above the glide path and a rapid increase in airspeed.

While accidents involving dust devils are rare during takeoff, at Bishop Field near Decatur, Texas, a highly experienced pilot was departing in a turbine-powered de Havilland Otter carrying seven skydivers. At about 300 feet the airplane encountered heavy turbulence. First it pitched up and then rolled hard right to about a 90-degree angle. The pilot countered the roll and pitch, but the aircraft hit ground during recovery. Five of the skydivers survived and were flown to a local hospital, one in serious condition. While this devil contained no dust, the presence of the whirlwind was confirmed by at least one eyewitness. One skydiver said, "We hit one two weeks ago in the same spot. That only gave us a scare." The hazard can be avoided by flying in early morning cool or at dusk when the sun is setting.

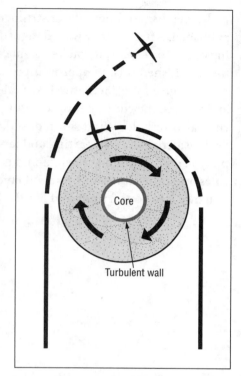

Figure 6-15. Dust devil diagram.

Summary

The thing to remember is that 60 percent of GA accidents occur during approach and landing. The rule of thumb is that a bad approach usually leads to a bad landing. Remember too, the facts that must be considered in calculating your effective runway length. Don't try to rationalize an excessive tailwind or contaminated runway, as you'll be flirting with disaster. One of the most important lessons is that following any major deviation from a normal approach and landing, be prepared to go-around. It appears that many GA pilots fail to practice and maintain proficiency of the go-around procedure.

Crosswinds continue to cause accidents year after year. While that demonstrated crosswind found in most POHs is not officially limiting, you have no way of knowing at what crosswind velocity you run out of control authority. Therefore, it should be treated as a limitation.

Remember to follow the instrument approach procedures exactly as published. After all, they were designed to ensure your safety. After breaking out of the clouds, if you lose sight of the runway for any reason, follow the established missed approach procedure exactly as published, unless ATC has given you alternative instructions. If it's a non-precision approach, and you see the runway early, carefully follow the VASI glide slope to the runway threshold. Wind shear, dust devils, and wake turbulence all must be considered when departing and landing. Any one of these factors can put you on the ground unceremoniously. In essence, fly by the established rules and procedures and you will enjoy a long, productive flying career. You owe it to your friends and family.

CHAPTER 7

Unique IFR Considerations

When flying cross-country, an IFR clearance is the safest way to go—especially when visibility is down to three miles or perhaps a bit less. Air traffic controllers do an outstanding job of keeping us separated and helping us get to our destination, but there are certain areas of IFR operations, that year after year, continue to be troublesome. The following are some examples of problematic areas.

Takeoff Visibility Minimums

14 CFR §91.175(f), "Civil airport takeoff minimums," restricts *commercial flights* to the IFR takeoff minimums published in the U.S. Terminal Procedures. If no minimums are published, the *standard* takeoff visibility minimums for singles and twins are one mile visibility, while airplanes with three or more engines need one-half mile visibility. These limitations apply in the absence of specified minimums for a specific airfield, e.g., at non-IFR airports—those lacking an instrument approach procedure and/or appropriate runway markings. Although the visibility limitations apply only to commercial flights, in reality they are based on past accidents and are there to protect all of us, not just paying passengers.

If by chance your aircraft is climb-limited and can't make the minimum specified climb requirement, then the airport's published departure procedure will show higher takeoff minimums. The higher minimums allow the pilot to visually avoid any charted obstructions. The restriction ends once the aircraft crosses the obstruction at or above the required altitude. Thereafter, obstacle protection is provided for the standard climb of 200 feet per nautical mile, unless otherwise specified.

Instrument Takeoff

The instrument takeoff (ITO) demands flawless piloting skill. Yet because of a misunderstanding of the criteria for an ITO, each year a few pilots attempt departure with little or no forward visibility and come to grief in the effort.

Conceptually, an ITO is a composite visual and instrument maneuver. Its composite nature is why the FAA requires takeoff visibility minimums for commercial aircraft. This provides the pilot with some physical references during the takeoff roll, so that, initially, visual-cues can be used in maintaining runway alignment. These include the runway centerline stripe, combined with runway edge lights. Without these special departure aids, our accident history shows that you need the "standard" one-mile visibility.

Besides the visual cues on the runway, with conventional (round dial) instrumentation the pilot (hopefully) has the additional benefit of the HSI/ HI and FD system. By setting the HSI heading bug to the surveyed runway heading, the V-bars or cross-pointers in the ADI offer major assistance in maintaining runway alignment. (An EFIS of course provides even better information.) During the early part of takeoff roll, when snow or rain can suddenly obstruct all forward visibility through the windscreen, the FD can be used to keep you aligned with the runway. Then, upon liftoff, either system—V-bars or cross-pointers in the ADI—can provide the minimum pitch attitude need for a safe climb to altitude.

The mindset for departing with zero visibility develops during training for the instrument rating. Every instrument pilot is taught that "your competency in instrument takeoffs will provide the proficiency and confidence necessary for use of the flight instruments during departures under conditions of low visibility, rain, low ceilings, or disorientation at night." Your instructor will align the aircraft with the runway heading and you will make the takeoff under the hood using only the flight instruments. While this maneuver *is* good training, when combined with the lack of mandated takeoff minimums for the non-commercial operator, the student is led to believe that once obtaining an instrument rating, a departure with less than the established takeoff minimums—even zero-zero visibility and ceiling—is a routine procedure.

In addition, §135.217 tells the commercial operator that if the weather is at or above takeoff minimums, but below IFR landing minimums, a takeoff alternate is required "within one hour's flying time (at normal cruising speed, in still air)." When you think about it, this too is only common sense for all of us. Yet, despite the inherent logic of these rules, the private pilot has no such requirements. This unfortunate dichotomy continues to cause accidents and fatalities year after year. The following examples illustrate the problem.

Instrument Takeoff Accidents

On June 13, 2014, 65 year-old philanthropist Dr. Richard Rockefeller was killed when he appears to have fallen victim to minimum takeoff visibility confusion. The accident occurred as he was departing Westchester County Airport (HPN) at White Plains, New York, in his single-engine turbo-prop Piper PA-46-500TP Meridian. The official weather report showed a 200-foot ceiling and one-quarter mile visibility in fog—below ILS landing minimums. Had his flight been commercial in nature, he would have been required to wait until visibility improved, and have a takeoff alternate too. But the confusing wording of the regulations combined with the ITO training requirements apparently gave him the self-confidence to depart.

At 08:06 AM he lifted-off from HPN and shortly thereafter control tower personnel were contacted by New York Terminal Radar Approach Control, to inquire as to whether the flight had departed. The local controller responded that the flight should have departed but *visibility was so low he couldn't tell*. The NTSB preliminary report stated that radar returns showed he had climbed to about 600 feet above the ground and was in a shallow right turn when radar contact was lost. One witness near the crash site reported hearing the engine before the aircraft came into view in a wings level attitude, then striking some trees. Two other witnesses watched as the plane began striking the trees, then crashed behind a house and in front of some horse stables. Fortunately, no one on the ground was injured.

Several years ago, six people were killed in a similar accident. It occurred when a Cessna 210 crashed during a dark, foggy predawn takeoff from what was then Bakersfield Airpark—since renamed Bakersfield Municipal Airport. The private pilot had been instrument-rated for less than a month when he attempted an ITO from the dark, unmarked runway in pre-dawn fog with zero visibility. According to witnesses, the area was covered by a seasonal night-time fog that every winter plagues California's San Joaquin valley. In his preflight weather briefing at 4:52 AM, the pilot was told that there was zero runway visibility due to the very dense fog.

Employed as crew boss for an oilfield construction company, the pilot, along with five fellow employees, commuted daily to their job in Currant, Nevada. With six men, round-trip fuel, and some drilling equipment, investigators found the aircraft was overloaded. At the time, Bakersfield Airpark consisted of an un-striped 3,150 by 30 foot asphalt runway, and its low intensity runway edge lights were hardly suitable for a night, zero-visibility ITO.

Yet reportedly, this new instrument pilot had done it successfully before. In fact, on at least one occasion the fog was so thick that his passengers had to walk ahead to help guide the airplane to the departure runway.

Witnesses heard the aircraft taxi at 5:44 AM. One said he could see its navigation and taxi lights from about 200 feet. After run-up the aircraft departed on runway 30. One bystander said, "the takeoff sounded good, but I couldn't see the aircraft until it was over the departure end, about 100 to 150 feet high, in a slight left bank." Suddenly all engine noise ceased, followed by sounds described as "what seemed like a prolonged fender bender." At impact the aircraft was at full power in a 25-degree right bank, and a nose down attitude estimated in excess of 22 degrees. The aircraft crashed in a school yard one-and-a-quarter miles from the airport—25 degrees right of the runway heading.

There are several things that could have contributed to this accident. Malfunctions such as a vacuum pump or alternator failure are fairly common. A vacuum pump failure would have caused a gross error in the attitude and heading indicators. An alternator failure would have distracted the pilot from his instrument flying. Hence the requirements for *commercially operated* single-engine airplanes under Part 135 to have double sources of vacuum and electrical power before being used in IMC.

Spatial disorientation is another possibility. The Air Force *Instrument Flying Manual* (AFM 11-217) states that spatial disorientation is most likely during takeoff and departure. "During this phase the inner ear's motion sensing is affected not only by changes in roll and pitch, yaw, and acceleration, but also by the motion of the pilot's head and body." The hazard after liftoff increases at night because of the swiftly changing pattern of illumination. This is created by the aircraft lights, runway centerline, and edge lights, along with buildings, followed by sudden total blackness off the end of the runway.

According to the Air Force *Physiological Technician's Training Manual* (AFM 160-5), another likely cause of this mishap is called *oculogravic illu-*

sion. (In the FAA's *Instrument Flying Handbook,* it's called *somatogravic illusion.*) This is a "false sensation of change of attitude that occurs when an inertial force concomitant with a linear acceleration, combines with the force of gravity to form a resultant force vector which is not aligned with true vertical." This kind of illusion occurs when a high performance aircraft accelerates forward in a relatively level attitude—as in takeoff roll. Then, after liftoff, as the visual cues disappear the pilot senses a false feeling of a nose-high attitude. This could explain the Cessna 210's rather steep nose down attitude at impact.

Coriolis illusion is still another possibility. This involves overpowering sensations of roll or yaw caused by abrupt head movement. For example, if after liftoff, a map fell from the glare shield, the pilot's instinctive reaction would be to look down and reach for it. When the pilot tilts his head down to look for the map and then returns to an upright posture, the change to his sensory system causes a strong illusion of turning or accelerating on an entirely different axis. This can be so overwhelming that it is difficult to follow the flight instruments. You may have seen this demonstrated to aviation groups in the FAA's vertigo training chair.

The point here is that without a runway equipped with special equipment—runway lighting, visibility measuring equipment—combined with frequent retraining to maintain proficiency, it's unlikely that most pilots can accomplish a *safe* zero-visibility takeoff. As stated previously, commercial pilots who are authorized reduced takeoff minimums have had specialized training, along with periodic checks of their competency, and even then the authorization *is not* for zero-visibility conditions.

Because Bakersfield was home base for the six occupants, they must have known that with a 30 to 45 minute drive they could have based the airplane at Mojave Airport. From Mojave's expansive desert airfield they could have departed each morning in "clear and 50."

Another case involved an instrument-rated private pilot flying a single-engine Bellanca Super Viking. It was January 1, 2004, when the aircraft departed Addison Airport (ADS) near Dallas, Texas, on runway 15. It was 9:57 AM when the aircraft lifted off. The weather was grim, with the ceiling reported as 100 feet overcast and seven-eights of a mile visibility. Four minutes later, the pilot reported having "lost my panel." The aircraft crashed into a private residence and came to rest in the garage of a second residence. Both houses were destroyed by the ensuing fire, and both occupants of the aircraft were killed.

Because everything had worked perfectly in the past, the pilot had not considered that, when flying in IMC conditions, loss of the ship's single vacuum pump, which supports the primary flight instruments, or that loss of the engine-driven generator could be as hazardous as engine failure. Consequently, he departed in very marginal weather with only a turn coordinator as a backup option if an emergency developed. (Ever practiced flying in IMC with only a turn coordinator for attitude information?) In addition, his over-confidence in his equipment was probably accompanied by compulsion, which unfairly placed his passenger and residents of the community below in great jeopardy.

Departure Procedures

When planning an IFR flight, many pilots either ignore the departure procedure or become too rushed or too complacent to even determine if one exists for the airport. The typical attitude is, "I usually just file for the first fix on my route of flight and ATC gives me vectors." But if it's an IFR capable airport, most likely it has a DP. The lack of a DP means the runway passes the *diverse departure assessment*, meaning no obstructions protrude into the departure airspace (*see* AIM 5-2-8).

While some GA pilots think that DPs are only for the commercial operators, in reality they are provided to protect everyone, private or commercial. In fact, the Terminal Procedures book clearly states, "*ALL USERS: Airports that have Departure Procedures (DPs) designed specifically to assist pilots in avoiding obstacles during the climb to the minimum en route altitude, and/or airports that have civil IFR takeoff minimums other than standard, are listed below. Takeoff Minimums and Departure Procedures apply to all runways unless otherwise specified.*" They are called takeoff minimums and (obstacle) departure procedures, but the keyword is *obstacle*. The following accident, which took the life of Frank Sinatra's mother, provides a tragic example of pilots failing to know and understand the departure procedure.

Palm Springs Departure

A Learjet had been cleared from the Palm Springs Airport (PSP), "*to the Las Vegas Airport, as filed, via Palm Springs (VOR) direct Twentynine Palms (VOR): Climb and maintain one seven thousand.*" While not stated in the clearance, this was the Palm Springs Cathedral Two Departure; a so-called *pilot nav DP*, current at the time. While the controller should have named the DP, pilots departing IFR are expected to be familiar with the appropriate published procedure.

Palm Springs VORTAC is located 4.5 miles northeast of the field. At the time of the accident the Cathedral Two Departure read: "*Rwy 30: turn right, climb direct PSP VORTAC.*" Crossing the PSP VOR at or above 4,400 feet, for the Little Mountain transition, you were expected to turn directly onto the 051 degree radial for the 36 NM leg to Twentynine Palms (TNP).

In essence, the Learjet was expected to follow the runway 30 departure and Little Mountain transition to TNP. The clearance assumed a right turn after takeoff from runway 30, which was depicted on the DP plate.

The MSAs were shown on the approach chart as 13,000 feet in the northwest quadrant, and 6,900 feet in the northeast quadrant. Obviously, maintaining the runway 30 heading would take the flight into some very high terrain within 25 miles. In addition, both pilots had flown in and out of Palm Springs on numerous occasions and should have been aware of the mountainous area.

As the aircraft taxied to runway 30 (now shown as runway 31), their clearance was revised to "*maintain niner thousand, cleared for takeoff.*" Unaccountably, the crew failed to question this new clearance. And despite the published MSAs and their acknowledged clearance, the flight failed to turn right after takeoff. Instead, because of the confused clearance, they continued on runway heading and dutifully climbed to 9,000 feet.

Of special significance is that the airport had no local departure control, so they were working with a very busy controller in Los Angeles Center. It appears, too, that neither pilot had studied the published departure procedure. This shows a casual attitude, combined with critically inadequate cockpit resource management. It's obvious, however, that the ATC controller's instructions were confusing.

The accident report failed to address the second-in-command (SIC). Typically, he or she is there to assist and takeover if the captain becomes incapacitated. This means that the copilot must also understand the clearance and departure procedure—also an integral part of cockpit/crew resource management. While the SIC is subservient to the captain, as this case shows, he or she suffers the consequences if the captain is allowed to make a fatal mistake.

After climbing to 9,000 feet—and already more than 10 miles straight out on runway heading—the pilot asked, "*are we cleared the zero five one*

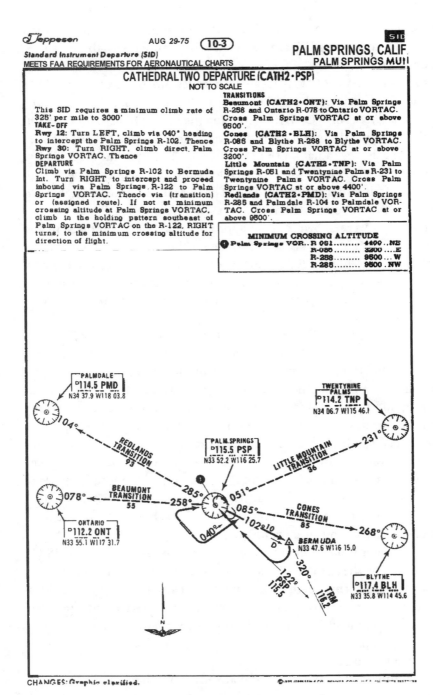

Figure 7-1. Palm Springs DP. (From NTSB Report NTSB/AAR-77/08)

to *Twentynine Palms?*" The controller replied, "*that's affirmative, sir; I had a change of route there...maintain nine thousand, I'll keep you advised.*" The flightcrew responded, "*okay, maintain nine straight ahead, right?*" The controller replied, "*affirmative.*" The controller thought they had made the turn and were following the DP. It appears also the controller was distracted by either traffic or other duties. He certainly wasn't watching their transponder on his radar scope.

Shortly thereafter the pilot asked, "we're maintaining nine on a heading of three one zero. What's our clearance from here?" The controller replied that they could expect further clearance after crossing the 20-mile DME fix. Again, this indicates the controller thought the Learjet had made the turn to PSP VOR and was proceeding eastbound. He then cleared the flight to "*climb and maintain 17,000 feet.*" But, unfortunately, there was no reply.

The wreckage was found three days later on the south slope of a mountain at 9,700 feet, 22 miles from Palm Springs, on a bearing of 306 degrees—virtually the extended centerline of the runway. There were just two passengers, one of whom was Frank Sinatra's mother.

This was a classic case of grossly inadequate resource management—confused communications, spatial disorientation due to inadequate preflight preparation, and a lack of command authority by the flight crew. Both the captain and SIC failed to study and use the DP. In addition, they had been in to PSP in clear weather and were aware of the mountainous terrain in their direction of flight. It is obvious that, despite the published MSAs which were critical to their departure, they had psychologically relinquished command to the ATC controller, who appears to have been overloaded with other traffic.

This accident shows why, during an IFR departure, you simply must be familiar with the published departure procedure for your direction of flight. Actually, the FAA strongly recommends you file a departure procedure for all flights at night and in marginal IFR conditions. But as §91.3 implies, you—the pilot-in-command—are expected to know the MSA and DP, *and continuously maintain situational awareness.*

Single-Engine IFR

For a commercially operated aircraft lacking the special modifications required for single-engine IFR operations, the air taxi regulation wisely limits single-engine IFR flights to VFR-on-top of broken conditions. Then, if the engine should fail, the pilot is expected to descend while remaining in VFR conditions (*see* §135.211(b)(2)). The following example shows how this rule makes good sense for all of us.

An accident occurred when a Cessna 210L departed at 7:00 AM from Hammond Northshore Regional Airport (HDC), Louisiana, on an IFR flight plan in IMC conditions to Grider Field Airport (PBF) at Pine Bluff, Arkansas. Fifteen minutes later, the pilot declared an emergency with Houston Air Route Traffic Control Center, and reported a loss of both oil pressure and engine power. Because he was in IMC, the ARTCC controller attempted to vector the pilot to Hurst Landing Strip near Kentwood. But unfortunately, the aircraft crashed into a line of trees. Witnesses who heard the crash told investigators that visibility at the time was 400 to 500 yards in haze.

The NTSB report stated: "The main wreckage, which included the engine and fuselage, from the cockpit aft to the vertical stabilizer, was intact and came to rest on the opposite side of the tree line." Although the pilot survived with serious injuries, his passenger was killed.

Of special importance too is that failure of the single generator, vacuum pump, or attitude gyro in solid weather also puts you in great jeopardy. In light airplanes certified to operate up to 25,000 feet, the battery must last 30 minutes "to power those loads that are essential to continued safe flight and landing." For aircraft certified to operate above 25,000 feet, battery life must be 60 minutes (*see* §23.1353(h)). At night with the lights on, it could be a lot less if you don't immediately shutdown all nonessential equipment. In transport category airplanes, the electrical system automatically "load-sheds" nonessential items and the battery must last at least 30 minutes.

The change in Part 135 rules to allow flying single-engine airplanes for hire in IMC was primarily intended to help reduce accidents in Alaska. The new rules limit single-engine airplane operations in IMC "to those equipped with dual generators and a standby battery or alternate source of electric power, capable of supplying 150% of the electrical loads of all required instruments and equipment necessary for safe emergency operation...for at least one hour" (*see* §135.163(f)). This includes "a power failure warning device or vacuum indicator to show the power available for gyroscopic instruments from each power source," i.e., main and standby vacuum pumps. While this increases aircraft investment costs, it makes the single-engine aircraft more useful and IFR flying infinitely safer.

As the accident record shows, flying a single-engine aircraft in continuous IMC without the backup required of commercial flights is a game of "bet your empennage." (Ever tried to make an instrument approach using the turn coordinator and magnetic compass with the ADI showing a 60 degree bank and the HI spinning?)

Position Awareness

A pilot's lack of position awareness caused the death of all four occupants in the crash of a Beechcraft A36 in the Rocky Mountains. He was flying on a VFR flight plan along an established airway, but in IMC over mountainous terrain. Because he lacked an instrument rating, he presumably didn't know about minimum enroute altitudes (MEA).The accident report stated that the airplane was in cruising flight at 10,500 feet, about 15 miles southeast of Jackson, Wyoming. Earlier, near Pinedale, the pilot had canceled flight following with Salt Lake Center. About 15 miles southeast of Jackson, while flying in the clouds, he hit Pinnacle Peak at 10,400 feet MSL.

Every IFR En Route Low Altitude Chart provides information on high terrain in the form of MEA and *minimum obstruction clearance altitudes* (MOCAs) along the airways; while each grid square depicts off-route obstruction clearance altitudes. Sectional charts use *maximum elevation figures* (MEFs) in each grid square. This is especially important information for pilots flying point-to-point using GPS.

The Expedited Departure

When departing from nontowered airfields and using the telephone to get your IFR clearance, the pilot is often given a *clearance void time* to get airborne. After that void time, your IFR flight plan is cancelled, so you must hustle to make the takeoff. Sometimes, with good weather, to avoid a departure delay, the pilot takes off VFR and picks up his IFR clearance while climbing on course. But as mentioned in Chapter 3, regarding midair collisions, unless you have a copilot to either fly the airplane or copy the clearance and look around, it is simply impossible to watch for other traffic and maintain separation from obstructions or high terrain. The MU-2/Saratoga mid-air collision documents that statement. But there are other considerations too.

Reba's Band

Under some conditions, such as in whiteout conditions due to glare over snow covered terrain or at night in clear weather with 50 miles visibility, the absence of visual cues requires IFR procedures and reference to the flight instruments. A high profile case in point involved the death of all the members of Reba McEntire's band in a corporate jet during a dark, early morning VFR departure from Brown Field near San Diego. The aircraft was a Hawker Siddeley DH 125-1A, which the captain had repositioned from San Diego International during daylight hours. In addition, having been on duty for almost 24 hours, investigators speculated that fatigue may have played a part; although he had the option for crew rest in several nearby motels.

The captain's personality and flying background are interesting too. The majority of his flight time was reportedly acquired in agricultural crop dusting. Others who had flown with him in corporate jets described him as "unprofessional." In fact, one experienced pilot who had flown copilot for him on another trip refused to fly with him a second time.

Investigators found the ship's copilot totally unqualified. There was no record of any training or experience in the Hawker. According to the accident report, he was switched to the DH-125 from the accompanying Sabreliner 40 carrying Reba, simply because of his stated desire to log flight-time in the Hawker. Despite §61.55, which requires training in type, this change was effected simply to gratify the copilot's whim. In essence, this two-crew airplane was being flown single pilot, with a pilot-rated passenger in the right seat (the legal aspects are sealed). With an untrained copilot, the Hawker captain was both flying the airplane and making all the radio calls.

Worse yet, the flight was an illegal Part 135 charter. The operator claimed it was a "sales demonstration." However, contractual documents and a letter sent to the FAA by the passengers' attorney documented the flight as a "revenue flight being paid for by the contracting passengers' company."

While awaiting his passengers, the captain had three telephone conversations with a flight service specialist. At 11:15 PM, he filed an IFR plan with a proposed departure of midnight. The flight service specialist suggested they depart VFR and pick up an IFR clearance once getting airborne. Then he asked the captain if he was familiar with the Brown Field DP. The 15,000 plus hour captain replied, "no, not really."

Near midnight, the captain phoned the FSS again. This time he told the briefer that he had looked at the approach plates but could find "absolutely nothing about some sort of special [standard instrument departure] out of here." In fact, there was no standard instrument departure (SID). But there was a *textural* departure procedure printed on the back of the Jeppesen plate; or using FAA charts, in the front of the book.

The flight service specialist then read the departure procedure for both runways 08 and 26. The captain replied, "okay, all right; that'll do me," then ended the call.

At 12:30 AM the captain made his third and final call to the FSS. He asked if the departure procedure would take him into Class B airspace. The FSS specialist replied, "yeah, that's right." The pilot continued, "so I'd be better off if I headed northeast and stayed down; say down around 3,000 feet?" Yet the Brown Field Municipal Approach Chart showed a minimum safe altitude of 7,600 feet in the northeast quadrant.

The FSS replied, "uh huh." The captain persisted, "do you agree?" The FSS specialist replied, "yeah, sure. That'll be fine." Keep in mind the FSS specialist is not a dispatcher, nor is he or she required to be a pilot. And the Jeppesen approach plate shows clearly the obstructions and the textural departure procedure. The procedure requires climbing westbound on a 280 degree heading, away from the mountains until attaining adequate altitude to proceed en route.

Interestingly, the San Diego Terminal Area Chart shows that on a northeasterly heading the bottom of Class B airspace is 5,800 feet rather than 3,000 feet. In addition, Brown Field and the area directly east, *is not within* the Class B airspace. The area chart shows he could have climbed on the runway heading—runway 08—to 17,500 feet without violating San Diego Class B airspace. Thus it is obvious that, despite his extensive flying experience, this captain lacked knowledge and understanding of his navigation publications.

At 1:40 AM, the Hawker lifted off from runway 08 at Brown Field. One minute later the captain contacted San Diego TRACON stating he was standing by for an IFR clearance. The fact he was making the radio calls shows that the flight was being conducted single pilot. But he had forgotten to update his flight plan, and it had clocked out. However, the TRACON controller kindly volunteered to "put it right back in."

The controller then assigned a transponder code of 0306, which the captain repeated. The controller then asked for the flight's position, but there was no reply. The Hawker had departed on runway 08, then made a 30 degree left turn to the northeast. The aircraft impacted about 172 feet from the summit of 3,566 foot Otay Mountain, killing all aboard.

Citation II Mishap

A Cessna Citation II accident was caused by the pilot/owner—described as a very busy, strong-willed, aggressive businessman—rushing to make good on a specific departure time. While he always flew the Citation himself, he had hired a chief pilot, who for unknown reasons was not flying that day. Although the airplane was considered airworthy, the chief pilot told investigators the captain's ADI was exceptionally slow erecting, "On occasion we've had to sit for almost two minutes waiting for the artificial horizon to reach the normal flight position." Further, he told investigators that during the last 10 flight hours, the pilot's heading indicator also required more time than normal to come on line. Consequently, the owner would occasionally use the copilot's heading indicator during departure until the pilot's side instrument became usable.

On the morning of the fatal accident, the Citation owner called Vichy FSS for an IFR clearance. It was 9:09 AM and a very dense fog blanketed the area. He told the briefer he could reach the Mountain View Airport, Missouri (MNF) in 15 minutes. The FSS briefer gave him his IFR clearance with a clearance void time of 9:30 AM. The telephone conversation ended at 9:14 and at 9:25 the pilot reached the airport.

Quickly, he loaded the baggage and two passengers and then started the engines. Following engine start, there was a pause while someone handed him some company material through the cockpit window, then the Citation taxied the short distance to runway 28. After taking the runway the pilot spooled up both engines to full power, and after a 60-second delay, at 9:30 he released the brakes. The chief pilot estimated a two-minute interval between engine start and takeoff roll. (It is curious that the chief pilot failed to have the airplane ready to go. He could have had the battery cart or battery power spooling-up the gyros; or better yet, had the checklist complete and the right engine running while awaiting the imminent arrival of the owner/pilot.)

The Citation lifted off and disappeared into the fog. At 1.75 miles north of the airport, the aircraft crashed at high speed, in a 90-degree left bank, and a 30-degree nose down attitude. The wreckage and three occupants were scattered over a 400 square yard area.

The Citation owner/pilot hated to wait or waste time. Although his chief pilot should have helped, the pilot/owner was consistently too rushed to be safe—a personality factor. The moral of this story is that being in a big hurry sets the stage for a major mistake. As someone once said, "death is nature's way of telling you to slow down."

Busting Minimums

Each year without fail, several accidents occur when the pilot goes below the published IFR minimums. A case in point occurred on March 29, 2001, when the captain of a Gulfstream III pressed his luck at night into Aspen, Colorado. They had been 45 minutes late departing Los Angeles and the captain was attempting to deliver 15 VIP passengers for a weekend of skiing. However, he not only ignored the prohibition against Category D aircraft, such as the Gulfstream III, from executing the VOR circling approach, but also the airport's established 2,000-foot ceiling and 15-miles visibility for VFR arrivals. (*Note:* aircraft category does not vary with a gross weight decrease due to fuel burn. Rather it's based on a speed of 1.3 stall in landing configuration at the maximum certified landing gross weight.)

Arriving just minutes after the 7 PM curfew, he compounded his sin by ignoring a newly issued NOTAM that banned all night-time IFR circling approaches into Aspen. (The tower controller told investigators he was not aware of the newly issued NOTAM. They didn't receive the NOTAM until the next day.)

By the time of their arrival, the visibility was less than the published VOR minimums for even a Category C aircraft to have initiated the approach. In the 20 minutes prior to their arrival, visibility had deteriorated from 10 to less than two miles. At the time of the crash, visibility was 1.75 miles in light snow and mist. Just before impact, the crew had acknowledged having the runway in sight. However, as the aircraft turned final, it dragged a wing-tip and then smashed into high terrain a half mile short of the runway. Because they hit short of the runway, it seems apparent that the crew had failed to monitor the visual approach slope indicator—in this case a PAPI—which would have provided a normal three-degree glide slope to the landing zone.

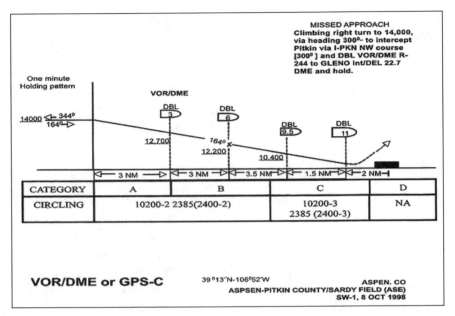

Figure 7-2. Aspen Approach Chart.

Especially noteworthy is that preceding the G-III's arrival, three aircraft had missed the approach. Two diverted to their alternate, one after missing two approaches. The third finally found the runway and landed. This fact alone shows that the airfield was below IFR minimums, and was reason enough for the G-III crew to divert to their alternate. Interestingly, the Governor of Colorado landed at Aspen just over an hour *after* the accident. This too was in violation of the FAA's new night-time restriction.

Diverting the G-III to an alternate airport would have required the passengers to drive several hours from an alternate such as Rifle, Grand Junction, Colorado Springs, or Pueblo to Aspen. Besides, it was after 7 PM, and with snow and drizzle falling, the roads were likely closed. Thus, the captain's desire to please the passengers *and* management was likely involved.

The NTSB found the captain took liberties with the rules and paid dearly for his transgression. Even though the tower was unfamiliar with the NOTAM, the G-III crew had seen it. The captain had to have known that Category D aircraft were not authorized the VOR Circling approach since it was printed on the approach chart.

By apparently ignoring the PAPI glideslope, this crew exposed themselves to several illusion-causing factors that make you perceive the aircraft is higher than actual. These include the featureless blackness of the high terrain in the approach zone, or black-hole effect, runway lights on full bright making the approach look higher than actual, and snow and mist on the windscreen giving the illusion of being high on final. With snow blanketing the runway and surrounding area, the contrasts needed for depth perception were essentially missing. Any or all of these would contribute to faulty altitude awareness, or the illusion of being high on final approach. Still, it is incomprehensible why the captain and SIC ignored the PAPI glide slope in such dangerous terrain.

The SIC's role in this mishap needs discussing too. Although modern crew resource management training encourages a committee approach to flying multi-crew airplanes, ultimately there can be only one final decision-maker. Yet, as this case shows, if the captain's decision appears hazardous the first officer must be assertive and voice his or her objection forcefully—or in extreme cases the SIC may need to take control.

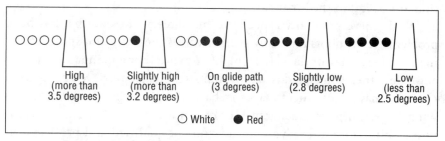

Figure 7-3. PAPI diagram. (AIM Figure 2-1-5)

Cessna Caravan 208B

Another accident in below minimums weather involved the pilot of a cargo Cessna Caravan 208B that was cleared to land at Bessemer Airport in Alabama The automated weather observing system (AWOS-3) was reporting an overcast at 100 feet and one-quarter SM visibility in heavy fog. A visibility this bad is obviously below ILS minimums. And since this was a Part 135 cargo flight, the pilot was prohibited from initiating the approach. Still, the Caravan was cleared for an ILS approach to runway 05. Subsequently, the aircraft crashed into trees .34 NM from the approach end of the landing runway.

The point here is that the weather minimums are established with operational safety in mind. And while the GA pilot *can legally* initiate the approach and "take a look," the fatal Caravan accident, flown by a carefully trained and supervised pilot, shows how unwise this can be.

The four or five miles from the FAF to the MAP are the most critical of the entire flight. Flying the aircraft and monitoring the instruments requires your absolutely undivided attention. If you have the luxury of an autopilot or a copilot, the workload is greatly reduced; and at minimums, it increases the time the pilot has to visually acquire the runway.

Spatial Disorientation

Spatial disorientation is best described as the inability of a pilot to orient his or her actual body position, motion, or attitude to the true horizon. The illusions in flight are numerous and are categorized as resulting primarily from visual misperceptions and those caused by the balance organ (vestibular system) in the inner ear.

While there are many aspects to this subject, the one that has been problematic for pilots for many years involves the *graveyard spiral*. Imagine it's a foggy day or dark, hazy night. You are flying manually (without autopilot), then you look down into your flight bag to retrieve a navigation chart, or maybe you turn to talk to a back seat passenger. In the process a wing drops slowly, producing little or no sensation of a turn. This develops into a spiral, and unless you are instrument qualified and proficient in unusual attitude recoveries, you and your passengers are in great jeopardy.

The John F. Kennedy Jr. mishap provides a classic case in point, when he *apparently* encountered the graveyard spiral. It was the dark and hazy night of July 16, 1999, when this talented young man, accompanied by two passengers, departed for Martha's Vineyard. He was flying a Piper Saratoga II and the weather was good VFR, but with reduced visibility over the dark, featureless ocean—reported variously by other pilots as two to five miles. With an estimated total of 310 hours of flight time, of which 55 hours were at night, Kennedy had made the trip about 35 times in the 15 months preceding the accident. Seventeen of these trips were without a CFI aboard.

Three months prior to the accident, he had started training for his instrument rating and had completed 12 of the 25 lesson plans. In the process he had accumulated 16.9 hours in the simulator and 13.3 hours of in-flight instrument training. His basic instrument skills were described as excellent, however, he reportedly had the usual beginners' problem of managing multiple tasks while flying.

When the accident sequence began, radar data showed that about 34 miles west of Martha's Vineyard Airport the airplane began a descent from an altitude of 5,500 feet. Initial speed was calculated at 160 KIAS. Rate of descent varied between 400 and 800 fpm. While still descending, the airplane began a right turn in a southerly direction. Thirty seconds later, the airplane stopped its descent and leveled off at 2,200 feet, then began a climb lasting another 30 seconds. The airspeed decreased to 153 KIAS. Then it leveled at 2,500 feet and flew in a southeasterly direction. But 50 seconds later, the aircraft entered a left turn and climbed to 2,600 feet.

Then, while still in a left turn, it began a descent that reached 900 fpm. Upon reaching an easterly heading the turn stopped, but the descent rate continued at 900 fpm. The aircraft then entered a right turn, with the rate of turn, descent rate and airspeed continuing to increase—with the rate of descent ultimately exceeding 4,700 fpm.

The last radar return was at 9:40 PM, at an altitude of 1,100 feet. The aircraft crashed into the Atlantic Ocean approximately 7.5 miles southwest of Gay Head, Martha's Vineyard, Massachusetts. The wreckage was subsequently located in 120 feet of water, a quarter mile north of the last recorded radar position.

Ironically, his salvation was as close as the autopilot button. Records show he had received some training in use of his Bendix/King 150 Series Automatic Flight Control System (autopilot). In fact, one instructor flying with Kennedy on a VFR trip to Martha's Vineyard, told of having to obtain an IFR clearance due to low clouds at their destination. He then demonstrated an autopilot coupled ILS approach through the un-forecast 300-foot ceiling.

Most new instrument-rated pilots fly manually in an effort to enhance their control skills, which is commendable. Unfortunately, they forget about the autopilot, and it becomes a neglected accessory. Then too, as a student in training for an instrument rating, without special instruction in spatial disorientation and unusual attitude recovery (including partial panel in case of a gyro failure), it probably never occurred to John Kennedy that the autopilot was available to relieve his spatial disorientation.

Typically the various uses of the autopilot are something you begin learning and using *after* obtaining the instrument rating. In this case it would have not only leveled the wings but he could have used it to climb back to cruise altitude.

The textbooks describe the graveyard spiral as beginning after a subtle wing drop. It may be so gentle it is imperceptible to the pilot. Even if he or she feels the turn begin, if it's allowed to continue, any sensation of the turn subsides after a few seconds and the pilot will again perceive being straight and level. However, a look at the instruments will show the established bank. When the pilot levels the wings, there will be the feeling of turning in the opposite direction. Confused by this false turning sensation, pilots will typically roll back into the original bank. This stops the turning sensation, but the altimeter and VSI will show a continuing and accelerating rate of descent.

The HI too will show the airplane still turning. Instinctively the pilot will add power and pull back on the control column to arrest the descent. Yet with the wing down, this only tightens the spiraling turn. And unless the pilot ignores his perceived "seat of the pants" attitude, and relies solely on his flight instruments, the descent will continue in an ever-tightening spiral.

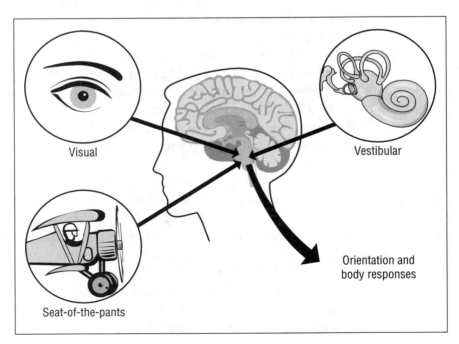

Figure 7-4. Sense of balance.

There is much more to learn about spatial disorientation. Suffice it to say, if you fly at night, as the John Kennedy Jr. accident shows, you need to be a proficient instrument-rated pilot. All of us, at some time or other, have experienced spatial disorientation, or *vertigo* as it's sometime called. The brief training you get in a private pilot course is woefully inadequate—especially for flying at night.

Resource Management

During an instrument approach to minimums, the pilot not flying (PNF) normally makes the standard altitude callouts, such as "1,000 above minimums," "500 feet above minimums," "200 feet above minimums," then, "100 feet." The PF does not look up until the PNF calls "minimums, runway in sight." If the runway is not sighted, the PNF calls "minimums, no runway. Missed approach!" The PF never looks up, but simply initiates the missed approach procedure. (The PNF must have an individual copy of the approach plate. Otherwise, with only one copy available to the PF, you lose half the safety of having a two-person crew, or crew resource management.)

If flying alone and your destination weather is at minimums, with an autopilot available the safest procedure is to fly a *coupled* ILS approach. Your only instrument task then is to keep the airspeed right with power. (More sophisticated airplanes have auto-throttles, which reduces the workload even more.) Even though you may be alone, make the standard callouts to keep yourself aware of your ever-diminishing altitude.

With the autopilot flying, you'll have the luxury of comfortably watching for visual clues to the runway environment, then returning to monitoring the instruments. With a talking altimeter (a ground proximity system) it's even better. Because now you'll be continuously reminded of the altitude leaving, and of arriving at minimums.

For those with glass cockpits, such as the Garmin systems, you have the WAAS enabled GPS-based aviation instrument approach procedure called localizer performance with vertical guidance (LPV). This system has the same basic minimums as an ILS—or 200 feet and half a mile visibility. As of January 15, 2009, the FAA had published 1,445 LPV approaches at 793 airports, a greater number than the published ILS procedures.

Attempting to use an untrained copilot can be counterproductive, if specific cockpit duties and procedures have not been pre-established and rehearsed. A copilot must be familiar with the aircraft systems—especially the radio and navigation equipment. In addition he/she must be capable of flying the aircraft. (*See* §61.55). Then, a specific protocol must be established as to exactly how the copilot is to assist you. It's not as simple as "you operate the radios and I'll tell you what I want." Over the years, this specific problem has contributed to numerous accidents.

Circling Approaches

The *circling approach* is simply an IFR procedure to get the airplane into VMC for a visual pattern to the landing runway. Yet, despite their simplicity, over the years circling approaches have proven statistically hazardous. NTSB data from 1983 to the year 2000 documented 577 accidents involving circling approaches—mostly fatal. When these mishaps are studied three causes stand out:

1. The pilot attempted the procedure with weather below circling minimums.
2. To keep the airport in sight, the pilot maneuvered too close to the landing runway and used an excessively steep bank in the final turn. This led to a stall.
3. The pilot descended from circling minimums on downwind, or he began descending when starting the base turn, and prior to acquiring the VASI glide slope, or descent began prior to reaching the point where "the aircraft is continuously in a position from which a descent to a landing on the intended runway can be made at a normal rate of descent using normal maneuvers" (*see* §91.175(c)(1)).

Below Circling Minimums

The following provide examples of some of the problems involved. It was a dark overcast night when the pilot of a Piper Lance missed the approach on his first try with an NDB circling approach. Then he returned and attempted a second NDB circling approach.

Shortly before the Lance's approach, the airport manager, who had just landed, advised the Lance pilot on UNICOM of a 700 to 800 foot ragged ceiling, with one mile visibility in fog. Immediately thereafter, the Lance pilot began his second approach. However, by the time the Lance reached

Figure 7-5. Attempting to circle-to-land in weather below minimums or beginning descent to land before reaching the normal descent point is a major cause of circling accidents.

circling minimums, the fog had intensified and visibility had diminished to a quarter mile. Why the airport manager failed to relay this information was not covered in the report; especially after he had witnessed the Lance's first missed approach in the rapidly deteriorating visibility.

Although the landing runway was equipped with a PAPI, the pilot apparently ignored it. While turning from base to final, he began descending and then dragged a wing-tip and crashed. Both the pilot and his passenger were killed.

Steep Bank Angle

The pilot of a Baron 58P had completed a successful VOR/DME-A circling approach to runway 22 into Brookhaven, Mississippi. The weather consisted of a 500 to 600 foot ceiling and three miles visibility. In this case the pilot's father and brother—both pilots themselves—were awaiting the Baron's arrival. When five miles south of the VOR, the Baron pilot communicated with his father on UNICOM. His father advised that winds were easterly at seven knots.

The pilot's brother told investigators that he first saw the airplane when it was south of the airport, paralleling runway 04/22. The report shows the pilot established a pattern for landing on runway 22. The seven-knot quartering tailwind should not have been a problem on the 5,000 foot runway. Witnesses noted the Baron's landing gear was extended, with flaps in the approach setting. When the airplane was about halfway down the runway on downwind, the brother noted it was "close-in; closer than normal."

When the Baron was about 20 degrees past the approach end of the runway, it began banking left for the base to final turn. But the pilot had maneuvered too close to the runway, and his spacing combined with the quartering tailwind caused the aircraft to over-shoot the runway center-line. Then, as the turn progressed, instead of "S" turning to realign, the bank angle increased to 70 to 75 degrees. Suddenly the nose pitched down and the airplane crashed, killing both the pilot and his wife.

Assuming the Baron's gross weight was about 4,000 pounds, with an airspeed of 90 to 100 knots during the turn, a 60 degree bank would have increased its stall speed to around 93 knots. A bank angle of 75 degrees would have essentially doubled the airplane's 65-knot stall speed.

It happened also to a Cessna T337G Skymaster. The pilot was complet-ing a circling approach at Fullerton, California. Witnesses reported the airplane's bank angle as around 80 degrees. This would have doubled the airplane's stall speed to around 120 knots. Predictably, it too stalled and crashed.

There were others too. A Piper 602P Aerostar at Georgetown, Dela-ware, and a Learjet 35A at Aspen-Pitkin Airport crashed because the pilots banked their aircraft too steeply during the final turn. Fortunately, in the Skymaster mishap, both the pilot and his son survived. The other accident was fatal.

Therefore, for emphasis, *it is never correct to use more than a 30-degree angle of bank in the traffic pattern*. Because, as the bank angle increases, so too does stall speed. And with an inadvertent stall in the traffic pattern, there's no room to recover.

Premature Descent

At Durango, Colorado, a Baron 58P was cleared for an "ILS/DME to run-way 02, circle to land runway 20." The circle to land was necessitated by a gusty 12-knot southwest wind. A few minutes later the pilot told ATC he had the runway in sight.

Witnesses told investigators of seeing the aircraft on downwind for runway 20. As it passed abeam the runway 20 threshold, it disappeared in clouds. Approximately five seconds later, it broke out of the overcast, whereupon witnesses saw a large green fireball. With an airport elevation of 6,685 feet, the circling MDA was 7,100 feet. The airplane struck power lines on downwind at 35 feet AGL.

There are two significant lessons here. First, you never descend below circling minimums prior to acquiring the visual glide slope on final, or, lacking a VASI system, you must delay the descent until reaching the point where a normal three degree glide path will put you in the touchdown zone—and this accident shows why. The second very important lesson from the Baron 58P accident is that when you encounter IMC during the approach—no matter where you are in this visual procedure—you must apply full power and turn toward the missed approach point and begin the missed approach procedure *for the instrument approach you utilized*, or as previously instructed by ATC.

In another, almost carbon copy accident—again on a dark, moonless night—a Comanche pilot completed the VOR approach and was circling to land at Sidney Municipal Airport, New York (N23). Weather was relatively good, with 1,500 foot scattered clouds and a 5,500-foot overcast. Visibility was seven miles, with winds from the southeast at five knots. With an airport elevation of 1,027 feet, the airplane crashed and burned on the downwind leg for runway 07. Impact with trees occurred at 1,550 feet—523 feet above airport elevation.

During IFR training for a circling approach, you probably were taught to descend to circling minimums and fly the pattern at roughly half the normal pattern altitude. However, a little known rule in circling approaches is that if the weather will permit a traffic pattern higher than the published MDA, there is no reason to continue to minimums. Ideally, fly at the regular traffic pattern altitude. After all, the circling instrument approach is simply to get you into VFR conditions. Yet despite the 5,500-foot ceiling, the Comanche pilot continued to descend below minimums on the downwind leg. (He was probably relying solely on visual cues and encountered black-hole effect over the dark terrain.)

Limitations to Icing Certification

Many of us fly well-equipped aircraft, such as the Piper's PA-46 Malibu, the Cheyenne 400LS, Cessna 337 Skymaster, or Cessna 421. Each of these aircraft is usually equipped with either an anti-ice or deice system. In the POH/AFM Limitations or Supplements section, you'll find that your airplane is approved "for day-night IFR conditions and flights into icing conditions if the proper optional equipment is installed and operational." But it doesn't say what kind of icing conditions or how long you can remain in icing conditions. For light general aviation aircraft, Part 91 does not provide the icing limitations as it does for large aircraft. The limitations for light aircraft are found in the respective airplane's POH/AFM. One POH states: "cleared for flight in icing conditions as defined by the FAA." What does that mean? Well, in the past we simply didn't know. (*Note:* Beechcraft is a notable exception. Their *Safety Information* manual regarding their icing certified models, has for years stated: "These aircraft are not approved for extended flight in moderate icing conditions or flights in any severe icing conditions. Flights in these conditions must be avoided.")

Adding to the confusion over the years is §91.527 (dated April 10, 2014) which outlines the icing limitations for "Large and Turbine-Powered Multi-Engine Airplanes." Sub-paragraph (c) seems to authorize flight into severe icing "if properly equipped." Yet the AIM has consistently defined severe icing as greater than the deice or anti-ice systems can control (*see* paragraph 7-1-21). This dichotomy has led to numerous fatal accidents. In fact, no U.S. certificated aircraft is approved for flight in severe icing conditions, such as freezing rain and drizzle, or so-called mixed-conditions. They are all composed of a moisture droplet sizes that constitute severe icing.

The FAA wisely clarified this problem by publishing Advisory Circular 91-74A (dated December 31, 2007), which resolved the icing definition problem for both general aviation and airlines. This was followed by a Safety Alert for Operators (SAFO) 08006 (dated January 25, 2008). Both documents directly address the regulation wording problem. The Advisory Circular specifically states: "Severe Icing: The rate of accumulation is such that ice protection systems fail to remove the accumulation of ice and ice accumulates in locations not normally prone to icing." This AC and SAFO should be part of every pilot's library.

Just for emphasis, remember that *no U.S. certificated aircraft is authorized to fly in severe icing conditions, such as freezing rain and drizzle.* In moderate icing, AC 91-74A advises, "The pilot should consider exiting the condition as soon as possible." The requirements for icing certification changed in 1973 and again in 1993. The earlier certification did not allow the aircraft *to remain continuously in* moderate or any severe icing conditions.

The following is a heartbreaking example of the confusion generated by all the fuzzy definitions and heretofore unpublicized certification criteria. It involved the pilot/owner of a Cessna 421C, N100KC, with a total flying time of 786 flight hours, of which 236 hours were in a Cessna 337 Skymaster. He had recently acquired a Cessna 421C, and at the time of this accident had logged 30 hours in the airplane. One January evening, the pilot, his wife, and five children, departed Savannah, Georgia, on an IFR flight plan to Pontiac, Michigan. Locally, severe icing was forecast with moderate mixed or rime icing in clouds and in precipitation above the freezing level. Cumulonimbus clouds with thunderstorms along the route were also in the forecast.

Several AIRMETS and SIGMETs warned of low ceilings, restricted visibility, snow, rain, and moderate to locally severe clear or mixed icing in

Figure 7-6. Tail-plane ice resulted in the horizontal stabilizers stalling when full flaps were selected. Note too, the stabilizer had no anti-icing protection.

clouds. The aircraft was well equipped for deicing and the radar would help the pilot/owner avoid the reported thunderstorms. Despite this grim weather report, the pilot had just finished extensive training in his new aircraft and felt confident with the "all-weather" equipment the aircraft had installed. Finally, he departed, seemingly filled with confidence in the airplane's capabilities.

Yet, as subsequent events showed, there was reason to doubt how well the pilot had mastered all this new equipment. In one transmission he stated, "I'm new with radar here." Throughout the flight his contacts with ATC revealed his uncertainties. Repeatedly, he asked for vectors to airways and around areas of precipitation. As the situation deteriorated and the stress increased, he appealed for more and more help from the controller. Finally, the controller was essentially managing the flight for him.

At 11,000 feet, and two-and-a-half hours into the flight, the pilot reported, "100KC is starting to pick up some ice." Two minutes later, while climbing to maintain 15,000 feet, he transmitted, "100KC having a problem-engine here, sir," and a few minutes after that, "extreme vibration...you had better lead me to an airport."

Here again, his understanding and proficiency with all that new equipment is obviously questionable. Was the propeller heat ON? Prop ice could certainly cause an imbalance and vibration. As for the engine, did he select "Alternate Air"? With induction system ice the engine could be literally choking for air. These mechanically operated two-position controls are located on the instrument panel, just below the pilot's control wheel. But he didn't seem to have been trained use them. And in his panicked state, was he using *any* of his deicing equipment? The ATC controller never asked because it wasn't his job. Besides, by now the pilot was in a state of panic and obsessed with finding the nearest airport.

During the next half-hour, the pilot badly botched a VOR approach into Lonesome Pine Airport. During this approach he requested: "tell me when I can go down to two six eight oh, will ya?" This was the field elevation at Lonesome Pine—2,680 feet—so the question was startling. When ATC radar showed the aircraft three-quarters of a mile from the airport, the pilot was asked if he had ground contact. Despite an MDA of 3,360 feet he reported being at 3,000 feet and did not see the runway. While no weather reporting was available at Lonesome Pine, a witness later recalled a 200-foot overcast, with one mile visibility, and freezing rain. The ground and trees, he said, were covered with clear ice about one-quarter inch thick.

After executing a missed approach, the pilot of N100KC was given a vector to Tri-City Airport, at Bristol, Tennessee, which was only 25 miles away. He was instructed to climb and maintain 6,000 feet. Weather at Tri-City was 1,600 broken, 4,000 overcast, with seven miles visibility in light rain. This airport had both an ILS and a radar approach control facility.

Next, the pilot reports level at 3,300 feet, and "we're trying to climb, sir." But now the airplane could barely maintain altitude, so further climbing was out of the question. Simultaneously, due to ice accretion on the antennas, communications began to deteriorate. The low altitude and mountainous terrain also contributed to the communications difficulty. Witnesses reported the engines sounded normal as the aircraft lights passed 100 feet overhead. Later investigation showed that both engines were developing power at impact. The Cessna 421 had three hours of fuel remaining when it crashed, killing all aboard.

The pilot's inexperience and personality traits were more significant than aircraft capability. The NTSB said that "had the pilot assessed the weather properly in conjunction with his capabilities and those of his aircraft, he would not have attempted the flight." He allowed his compulsion to return home with his large family, along with a false sense of security based on of his "all-weather" equipment, to blur his judgment. And too, he was badly misinformed as to the capability of the airplane's certification for flight in known icing.

By using alternate induction air, propeller heaters, and wing and elevator deice boots, the pilot could likely have climbed out of the icing conditions. NASA research shows that most of the time an altitude change of 2,500 feet will get you out of the ice. In addition, icing conditions seldom extend more than 50 miles. Certainly, prudence says he should have checked weather for various enroute airports. Once you're in desperate trouble, it is hardly the time to begin looking for alternates. This tragedy is a classic example of an accident that could and should have been prevented during pre-flight planning.

The FAA has established definitions to, "ensure that this icing terminology…is used consistently and clearly by the Flight Standards Service, pilots, dispatchers, the National Weather Service, the Aviation Weather Center, the Aircraft Certification Service and ATC." The agency defines moderate icing as, "The rate of ice accretion requires frequent cycling of manual deicing systems to minimize ice accretions on the airframe…The pilot should consider exiting the condition as soon as possible"; heavy icing as, "The rate of accumulation requires maximum use of the ice protection systems to minimize ice accretions on the airframe…Immediate exit from the conditions should be considered"; and severe icing as, "The rate of ice accumulation is such that ice protection systems fail to remove the accumulation…Immediate exit from the condition is necessary." (*See* AC 91-74A, section 5-3.)

Lightning Hazards

Modern airplanes are designed with built-in protection from catastrophic lightning strikes. They occasionally, however, still incur serious damage. Some years ago, lightning struck a Boeing 707 over Maryland which exploded, killing 81 people. And in Spain, a USAF C-141 was struck and it too exploded, killing all aboard. A military King Air 200 (C-12C) was struck while flying in clear air at 25,000 feet, some 25 miles from a large thunderstorm. After the strike, nothing unusual was noted in the aircraft systems or instruments. However, after landing an inspection showed a break in the radome, with burn marks on a glide-slope antenna, the propeller blades, and right outboard static eliminator. This "bolt from the blue" cost $40,000 to repair. In a two year period, the U.S. Army had 14 accidents due to lightning. Twelve involved their King Air 200 types (C-12Cs), along with two helicopters.

Studies of lightning frequency, as a function of temperature and altitude, show a strong tendency for strikes to occur in the 0°C zone. Thus, it is best to avoid flight through precipitation when the temperature is between 8°C and -8°C. The preponderance of strikes near the freezing level are thought related to the fact that the negatively charged cell center is also found near this temperature and altitude. Another important reason is that the negative charge is not located at a single point, but is spread out with varying densities over a large volume. It appears that lightning strikes do not follow a simple straight-line vertical path from the negative region to the ground or between the negative and positive areas. Instead, the discharge travels more or less horizontally through much of the negatively charged region, before turning up or down.

Thus, an airplane flying near the freezing level would be more likely to intercept a stroke than one operating well above or below the 0°C isotherm. Strikes occur most frequently within a cloud having rain and light turbulence. However, strikes can occur under many combinations of circumstances.

Aircraft damage from lightning has caused both direct and indirect effects. Direct effects resulted when the lightning current attaches to and flows through the aircraft skin. Indirect effects result from transient electrical and magnetic fields due to the lightening current. Unless avionics and other systems are properly shielded, they can be damaged by indirect lightning-effects.

Out of 773 lightning strikes studied by the USAF, the most commonly caused damage included:

1. Pilot disorientation/blinding;
2. Flight control failure;
3. Fuel tank burnout and explosions;
4. Engine flame-out and electrical failure;
5. Failure of non-metallic helicopter rotor blades;
6. Deformation and burnout of aircraft structures;
7. Acoustic shock/magnetic forces;
8. Damage to non-metallic aircraft surface components.

As mentioned briefly in Chapter 5, a corporate jet Sabreliner 80 was struck by lightning and lost both engines. Apparently, the electrical system was damaged, as the crew was unable to restart either engine. It was late in the afternoon, and the airplane was about seven nautical miles north of Ashland, Wisconsin, climbing through FL320 headed for Flint, Michigan. Convective SIGMET 59C was current for "severe thunderstorms moving from 290 degrees at 35 knots, with tops above 45,000 feet." The advisory warned of tornados and two-inch hail, with wind gusts to 70 knots. There was also the possibility of "severe or greater turbulence, severe icing, and low level wind shear."

When the lightning hit, both of the Sabreliner 80's CF700 fan-jet engines flamed out and refused to re-start. The captain broadcast a Mayday and was gliding towards Gogebic-Iron County Airport (IWD) at Ironwood, Michigan. As they were descending through 17,500 feet, the pilot reported loss of all navigation equipment only 12 miles west of IWD. The airplane missed the airport and crashed in a densely wooded area 3.5 NM northeast of IWD. Both pilots were killed and the two passengers seriously injured.

An Army study reported that lightning strikes to their aircraft have occurred as high as 37,000 feet, with most occurring below 20,000 feet. In that study, helicopters predominated in the data, showing strikes at from 9,000 feet to as low as 100 feet, with the majority occurring below 6,000 feet. Because of the low altitudes they fly, helicopters run the risk of a cloud to ground stroke, which can be deadly. Once again, the lesson is clear: avoid thunderstorms by 20 to 30 miles.

Summary

Despite VMC conditions, flying cross-country at night under IFR is infinitely safer than flying VFR. Remember, there are situations where the weather is VMC but you simply still must fly by reference to the flight instruments. Flight instruments protect you from the threat of spatial disorientation in reduced visibility or over featureless terrain, day or night; or with a snow covered landscape during white-out conditions.

Remember too, that year in and year out, those last six miles to the runway are the most critical of the entire flight and require your undivided attention. The highest number of accidents occur during approach and landing, thus, in reality, the so-called sterile cockpit rule applies to all levels of aviation, not just commercial pilots. In addition, distractions (such as looking up frequencies while on approach or in the traffic pattern) must be avoided by thorough, advanced planning. And when flying single pilot with marginal destination weather, couple the autopilot and let it fly the approach while you maintain airspeed and watch for the runway. You'll find it a very comfortable procedure.

Concerning in-flight ice, it's important to remember that despite the fact that your aircraft is certified for flight in known icing, it is actually only approved to *fly through* icing conditions, but not *continuously in* this hazardous environment. Remember NASA's recommendation to change altitude at least 2,500 feet up or down, or make a quick 180-degree turn to get out of the icing conditions.

Thunderstorms produce severe turbulence, lightning, and hail within 20 to 30 miles of the storm cell. For the utmost in operational safety, having both a Stormscope and radar should be considered life insurance. Remember the admonishment of AC 00-6A: "Any cloud connected to a severe thunderstorm carries the threat of violence." Think of a thunderstorm as nature's way of showing you "there's no such thing as an all-weather airplane."

CHAPTER 8
Maintenance Error and Material Failure

A study of one year's accidents by AOPA showed that in airplanes having a gross takeoff weight (GTOW) of 12,500 lbs or less mechanical or maintenance factors were involved in 15.5 percent of the accidents. The report noted that the largest percentage of these—109 mishaps, or 47.2 percent—involved engine or propeller problems, with 67 of the accidents classed as "power malfunction/loss for unknown reasons." The following accidents provide classic examples.

Cessna P210 Centurion

This fatal accident was the result of negligent FBO management operations and oversight, since it involved both inadequate initial training of the Cessna P210 pilots and grossly negligent engine maintenance and supervision. The first link in the accident chain that set the stage for this tragedy had occurred during engine maintenance ten months earlier. At that time, a mechanic applied inadequate torque to one of the through-bolts that provided the clamping force holding the engine's crankcase halves together.

The second link in the chain was the inept troubleshooting of a long series of engine problems by the FBO's mechanic and the maintenance supervisor. A third link was that the airplane was not on an engine oil analysis program. Although in this case it was not an FAA requirement, the program would have allowed them to foresee the problem developing and take steps that would have prevented the engine failure altogether.

The fourth link involved the inadequate training of the pilots in this complex single reciprocating engine Cessna P210. While the two U.S. Navy pilots were well qualified, their Navy training had been in turbo-prop and jet airplanes. This turbine powered aircraft background, combined with incomplete training in the P210, led to their failure to select a suitable area to crash land, which ultimately led to their deaths.

For six years prior to the accident, the FBO had been leasing various aircraft under contract to the U.S. Navy, including this Cessna P210. The PF had 370 hours total flight time, which included 42 hours in the P210—22 hours of which had been flown in the last 30 days. In the right seat, the PNF had 1,424 total flying hours, with 22 hours in the P210. He had not, however, flown the aircraft in the last 90 days which made him non-current.

The Navy's contract did not require any specific training, but, as a normal course of business, the FBO provided both ground and flight instruction using its Part 135 commercial training syllabus. This included both instrument flying and in-flight emergencies.

FBO records showed that three months prior to the accident, the PF had received two hours of ground school on the P210's systems, and normal and emergency procedures, along with emergency landing techniques. This also included two hours of dual flight instruction. However, his instructor acknowledged that they omitted any practice of emergency landings. Instead they simply discussed emergency glide speed.

One of the primary reasons for skipping simulated engine failure in the P210 could have been the threat of thermal shock due to long periods of cooling with the Continental TSIO-520-R engine at idle power. Yet the techniques could have been practiced in a Cessna 172—which the Navy also had under contract.

The PF had recently completed his biennial flight review (BFR) in a single-engine Beechcraft T-34B. This should have been an excellent vehicle for teaching or demonstrating engine failure in flight procedures—including the necessity of maintaining best glide speed and the critical necessity of selecting suitable terrain for an emergency landing. Unfortunately, the content of the pilot's BFR was not addressed in the NTSB report, but, as the record shows, his subsequent actions were contrary to a safe forced landing.

On their fatal flight, the two P210 pilots departed Point Mugu Naval Air Station near Ventura, California, in clear weather on an IFR flight plan. Their destination was Naval Weapons Center China Lake, located in the Mojave Desert. The flight had been carefully planned, as the navigation form found in the wreckage showed. Their initial track was northeast, direct to the Lake Hughes (LHS) VOR.

As any well-trained pilot knows, in a single-engine airplane you *always* plan your flight over areas of the least hostile terrain. In addition, you plan a cruise altitude that will allow you to glide to an area suitable for a successful forced landing from any point along the route. While these Cessna 210 pilots filed for an altitude of 9,000 feet, which provided a more than adequate safety margin, their later actions showed they did not adequately consider the moonscape terrain over which they would be flying.

The aircraft had just passed the Lake Hughes VOR when the engine failed. At that point, they were in easy gliding distance of flat terrain northeast of their position in the high desert, or southwest back into the valley. In addition, at the very moment the engine failed they were within gliding distance of at least two large bodies of water. Both lakes offered an excellent opportunity for a successful ditching. Meanwhile, the rocky, mountainous terrain visible ahead was clearly an unlikely area for a survivable forced landing.

Their subsequent actions showed a mind-set to find an airport and save the airplane, rather than locate an area offering the best chance of a survivable crash landing. Instead of looking for suitable terrain, the PF followed the lead of the PNF, who had quickly declared an emergency and requested clearance from ATC to the nearest airfield at this point.

The controller advised that Lancaster Fox Field (WJF) was "12 o'clock at about 20 miles." The PNF responded, "Okay, that's where we're headed." At the time their altitude was 8,950 feet.

While most light planes can glide about two miles for every 1,000 feet of altitude, the P210, with a relatively heavier wing loading, does so slightly less. The POH maximum glide chart shows a no-wind glide distance from 9,000 feet of about 14 miles—assuming that the correct glide speed for the gross weight is maintained. Unfortunately, they were gliding into a 30-knot headwind. By heading for Lancaster's Fox Field they had extended their track over some of the most hostile terrain in the state of California.

In the final moments of flight they found themselves over sharply upsloping scrub covered granite canyon walls, with a gradient estimated to exceed 30 percent. At around 100 feet above the brush, the PF failed to maintain glide speed—apparently anticipating impact with terrain. The airplane stalled and crashed out of control on the steep canyon slope in a nose down attitude, killing both pilots.

Neglected Clues

At the time of the crash the Centurion's Continental 310-hp turbo-charged engine had accumulated 618 hours since major overhaul. During this time it had developed several oil leaks, accompanied by low oil pressure indications. Each of the low oil pressure incidents was corrected by adjusting the pressure relief valve. In fact, on the evening preceding the accident the valve had been adjusted following yet another complaint of excessive oil consumption. Despite the high oil consumption on his flight, the pilot who made the report had found no oil streaks underneath the airplane. Hence, the oil was consumed internally, which meant the problem required careful troubleshooting.

On the night preceding the accident, the mechanic performing the maintenance also found that, for the seventh time, the right-hand vacuum pump had failed. The service manager told investigators they found the components inside the pump "shattered." Rather than troubleshoot these persistent problems, the service manager instructed the mechanic to simply "cap off the pump mounting flange and tubing." That left only the left pump available for operating the vacuum system. The repeated vacuum pump failures were major, yet unheeded clues to the serious internal engine problems.

Ten months prior to the accident, the number three cylinder had been removed to repair a Rosan stud. In removing the cylinder it was also necessary to remove the number two crankcase through-bolt. As noted earlier, the through-bolts are especially important because they hold the engine crankcase halves together.

The mechanic who performed the work told investigators that after the repair he re-torqued the cylinder hold-down nuts and the number two crankcase through-bolt in accordance with the Continental overhaul manual. In order to obtain the required torque on the through-bolts, Continental's engine manual required lubrication of the threads to reduce drag friction. But the mechanic could not recall whether he re-lubricated the threads. The report noted, however, that he believed the threads "did not require lubing as they contained lubricant after he removed the nuts."

The post accident investigation disclosed numerous engine discrepancies. For one, the torque on the cylinder hold-down nuts was found less than required. In fact, the number one cylinder hold-down nuts at the two and four o'clock positions were found finger tight. Only two bearings in the crankcase were found to be functional. The others showed major damage due to long term scoring and fretting (deformation and transfer of material from one surface to the other). Bearing saddles were broken, with the number one main bearing insert showing axial load damage. The number two main bearing insert in the right case half was fretted on its outer surface and worn to the copper material on its inner surface. Metallurgical examination of the engine showed in part that "the crankcase exhibited varying levels of fretting on bearing support bosses and damage to bearing saddles."

The NTSB report stated, "Fretting is a condition caused by relative movement of the crankcase halves due to inadequate clamping forces provided by through-bolts...The damage was centered around the No. two bearing support...the Nos. two and three bearings exhibited polishing on the back of the shells, indicating movement of the bearing shells within the bearing supports, due to inadequate clamping of the case."

The report noted further, "This condition occurs when through-bolts and nuts, which provide the clamping for the cases, are not properly torqued. Once the bearing support becomes damaged...the crankshaft is subjected to large bending stresses during operation." Ultimately, the board found that crankshaft failure was the cause of this engine failure.

Although not mentioned in the investigator's factual report, it is noteworthy that a *spectrometric oil analysis program* (SOAP) would have identified the internal problems as far back as 10 months prior to the mishap. The abnormal wear of the bearing saddles would have immediately started a trend of high metal content in the oil. And during the annual inspection only 22 days prior to the accident, the mechanic and his IA supervisor should have questioned the low oil pressure and high oil consumption problems. At the very least, an oil sample would have identified the copper wearing from the number two bearing insert. This would have positively shown that bearing failure was in progress.

Emergency Landings

An NTSB emergency landing study, *Emergency Landing Techniques in Small Fixed-Winged Aircraft* (NTSB AAS-72-3), states, "A pilot who has been conditioned during training to find a relatively safe landing area whenever his instructor closed the throttle for a simulated forced landing may ignore all the basic rules of airmanship to avoid touchdown in terrain where damage is unavoidable...a pilot should be more interested in sacrificing the aircraft so that he or she and passengers can safely walk away from it. Success of an emergency landing under adverse conditions is as much a matter of mind as of skills."

The actions of the Cessna P210 pilots immediately after the engine failure illustrate their inadequate training in the Centurion. Instead of looking around for a suitable forced landing site, the PF followed the lead of the PNF who had quickly declared an emergency with ATC and requested clearance to "the nearest airfield at this point." Yet, as pilots of a single-engine airplane in VFR conditions, it was *their responsibility* to have, not only the closest airfield continuously located, but a running idea of the closest and best area for an emergency landing. Unfortunately, their 9,000-foot altitude and a 30-knot headwind made gliding to Fox Field impossible.

The NTSB emergency landing study also highlights considerations that were routinely taught some years back. These included the recommendation that following engine failure the first priority is to lower the nose to maintain best glide speed and change the fuel tank selector to a different tank.

For the pilot who has flown for many hours without any problems, a sudden engine failure can lead to a psychological reluctance to accept the inevitability of a forced landing. And while immediately changing fuel tanks is always recommended, almost invariably the sudden engine stoppage is accompanied by a frantic but usually futile attempt to troubleshoot and restart the engine, instead of concentrating on holding best glide speed and identifying an area suitable for a *survivable* crash-landing.

In reality, it's only *after* you've established best glide speed and identified an acceptable crash-landing site that you can afford the luxury of attempting to troubleshoot or restart the engine. Even then, your primary task is to establish a proper landing pattern for the touchdown area, while maintaining the best glide speed.

The manufacturer has established the glide speed that provides the optimum lift/drag ratio. To reach your selected forced landing area it is critically important to get the maximum range possible out of your altitude. (Remember, as a "glider," you are now exchanging altitude for energy, i.e., airspeed.) To do this you must hold the best glide speed for your gross weight. (Some light aircraft have only one published speed, but the POH for the Cessna's P210 publishes speeds for various gross weights. Let your airspeed get five to ten knots slow and you may double your descent rate

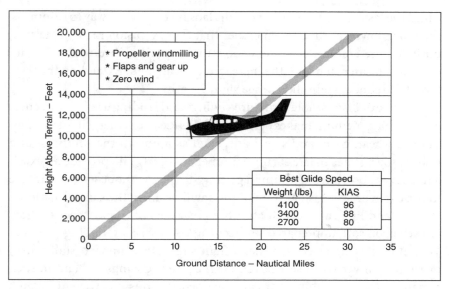

Figure 8-1. Cessna P210 glide chart.

and grossly shorten your glide distance. Glide 10 knots fast and this too shortens your gliding distance. Load your aircraft over the certificated gross weight limitation and you're really in trouble, because now you have an unknown glide capability. The point of emphasis is that you must know and use the correct glide speed.

In selecting a touchdown area your goal should be to keep vital cabin and cockpit structure intact and use dispensable structure, such as the wings and landing gear, to absorb the energy of a crash landing. The severity of the deceleration is governed by your ground speed and the stopping distance involved. Based on typical light airplane touchdown speeds, one can surmise that the shorter the stopping distance, the more severe the deceleration forces. Thus, you can say that the slower an airplane stalls, the more likely you and your passengers are to survive a crash landing. This single factor is yet another reason why the STOL (short takeoff and landing) modification, available for many light aircraft, is well worth the investment, since your touchdown speed is the most critical factor in survivability.

The rule is that kinetic energy is directly proportional to the square of velocity. Therefore, an impact at 85 knots is twice as hazardous as one at 60 knots. A crash landing is three-times safer at 60 knots than at 104 knots.

Thus, the last-minute extension of full flaps is yet another way to minimize the touchdown speed. But remember that flap extension must be delayed until you are committed to touchdown in a specific area, which you are certain you can reach with the increased drag applied. Extending the flaps too early reduces your glide range significantly.

The use of dispensable structure—wings and landing gear—as an energy absorbing medium makes cultivated fields ideal for emergency landings. Mature wheat, corn, and sugarcane, such as found in the southeast and mid-western states in late spring, summer, and early fall, provide an excellent energy absorbing medium in getting stopped without serious damage to the cabin area. Brush and small trees will perform the same function.

The landing gear too will absorb a great deal of impact deceleration. However, on soft, unprepared surfaces there's the risk of flipping inverted. With a high-wing aircraft, either a high sink rate at impact (stall-mush) or flipping inverted in soft terrain, can cause the wings to bend in such a manner that the cabin door can't be opened. Thus it is wise to unlatch the door(s) before touchdown so it can't be jammed in the closed position.

With a retractable landing gear, your configuration for a crash landing—gear-up or gear-down—should be based on the terrain involved. A smooth grass-covered pasture in mid-summer would make a gear-down landing feasible. A marshy area would call for gear up. A low-wing airplane has the additional consideration of fire potential if the wing fuel cells are ruptured when the landing gear is ripped out. This is especially true in light twins, wherein the proximity of the engine exhaust pipes can ignite the spilt fuel.

There is no hard and fast rule concerning landing gear position in retractable gear aircraft. In rough terrain and in trees, or with a high sink rate impact, the extended landing gear will absorb much of the impact and help protect the cabin structure. The gear's shock-absorbing characteristic has been found also to reduce spinal injuries to the occupants.

Remember, too, that a gear-up landing will cause the aircraft to float much farther than expected in the flare, even if flaps are used. This is due both to the loss of aerodynamic drag from the landing gear and ground effect, which also reduces drag. Consequently, excess floating can result in overshooting the planned touchdown area.

The lessons from this Cessna P210 accident show the critical need for thorough training in emergency landing techniques, so that the pilot develops a proper forced landing mindset. But perhaps the most critical lesson is the need for a professional approach to aircraft maintenance. Some mechanics don't really understand how to properly use a torque wrench; haste is often involved because the airplane is scheduled to fly. (The rule is "you want it bad, you get it bad.") The engine oil analysis program will forecast a wear-trend that predicts internal engine failure. Had it been used on this engine, the impending bearing and crankshaft failure would have been detected months earlier, thus breaking the accident chain.

Citation Jet

In this accident, a Cessna Model 525 Citation Jet was lost, simply because a maintenance technician improperly removed and/or installed the printed circuit board (PCB) that controlled the autopilot and trim system. Instead of using his fingers to handle the PCB, he used pliers. Under microscopic examination, investigators found the PCB board clearly marked by the jaws of the technician's pliers. This caused a runaway elevator trim to the full nose-down position. Only the timing of the event—in climb to a higher cruise altitude—averted a tragic accident.

The pilot told investigators he was climbing at 200 knots using the autopilot and had been cleared en route to FL330. But before reaching 18,000, feet he noted the aircraft was having difficulty climbing, so he disconnected the autopilot with the yoke disconnect button and attempted to hold level flight and the course heading by hand flying.

The electric trim control on the yoke did not respond to his inputs, and he was unable to relieve a rapidly building nose down pressure. Within seconds it was apparent that level flight was not possible. Despite the pilot's continued heavy back pressure on the control yoke, he reported the nose of the aircraft was still down about 10 degrees. With the airspeed rapidly building toward the over-speed point (V_{MO}), the pilot brought power to idle and asked his right seat passenger to assist in applying back pressure. The pilot's statement said, "At this juncture I estimate we were descending at about 2,000 FPM [with the nose of the aircraft] about 40 degrees below the horizon." Meanwhile, with engine power in idle and both the pilot and his passenger exerting maximum control yoke backpressure, the pilot related, "If we released any backpressure at this time I feel the aircraft would have gone to a vertical position...I advised SEA (Seattle) Center of the emergency and began to look for a place to land." At around 10,000 feet, the pilot spotted a Navy Auxiliary airfield with a north-south runway.

Meanwhile, he experimented to see if full power would help relieve some of the downward pitch force. It didn't, so he set the power at idle where it remained until touchdown.

"At this point I turned north over the water, leaving Whidbey Island to the west, and proceeded on a wide downwind leg with the possibility of a dead stick south landing at the auxiliary field. The yoke pressure was still terrific and required our combined strength to keep the nose from rapidly returning to an extreme (nose-down) angle. I quickly glanced at the white trim indicator; it was in the full forward (nose-down) position and I tried to use the manual trim wheel next to my right leg." Yet all of the pilot's efforts were futile. He simply could not make the trim system function electrically or manually.

Then he attempted to locate the pitch-trim circuit breaker, but with the extreme nose-down pressure to fight he was unable to find it. Finally, with the airspeed indicating 160K and passing through 1,500 feet, they were still descending with the nose down about 10 degrees below the horizon. The pilot told investigators that he made a left turn for a base leg and noted the airspeed at 140 knots. But then he changed his mind and aborted the landing approach, opting instead to ditch into the wind about 200 yards from shore into Penn Cove near the Coupeville dock, on Whidbey Island, near Seattle, Washington.

After a long three mile final, he planned their touchdown—gear up but flaps down—200 yards off shore near a small marina. With his airspeed now at 100 knots and a 500 fpm sink rate, the pilot estimated the aircraft's pitch angle at five degrees nose down. "The touchdown at about 10:15 local time was gentle...The impact did not drive us into the shoulder harness very hard and our heads moved forward about six inches. The water gushed completely over the windshield." Then the completely undamaged, but still pressurized aircraft, rocked back and floated. Only the exceptional aeronautical skill, physical strength, and judgment of the highly experienced 80 year-old pilot/owner explained their survival.

When the pilot opened the cabin door the now depressurized aircraft immediately began to sink. But the three occupants—the pilot, passenger, and an uninjured yellow lab—began swimming to shore. Shortly, a small boat came out from the nearby marina and took them aboard—and the aircraft sank.

Figure 8-2. The pilot was forced to ditch this Citation Jet when the elevator trim ran-away to the full nose-down position.

Cessna took immediate steps to prevent a reoccurrence by issuing an Alert Service Letter (ASL525-27-02). (The FAA followed later with an Airworthiness Directive, docket number 2003-CE-46-AD.) The ASL action immediately suspended the Citation Jet's single-pilot certification. If the condition occurs, both the pitch trim and autopilot servos circuit breakers are to be pulled rendering both systems inoperative—leaving the pilot only manual trim. All operators were warned that without the autopilot they must avoid reduced vertical separation minimums (RVSM) airspace.

The ASL does allow a series of single-pilot flights to get the airplane back to its home base, but any further flying must be with a second-in-command. The letter also emphasizes the necessity for pilots to review the AFM's abnormal procedures for Electric Elevator Trim Runaway. In addition, an extension collar was to be installed on the pitch trim circuit breaker to enhance circuit breaker recognition and to prevent it from being engaged. Meanwhile, the salvaged saltwater-corroded Citation Jet was junked, and the pilot/owner took delivery of a new Citation.

Figure 8-3. Although relatively undamaged, the salvaged Citation Jet was junked due to potential corrosion from having been ditched in salt water.

Cessna 337 Oxygen Supply

An incredible series of both maintenance and pilot errors resulted in the incapacitation and subsequent death from hypoxia of a pilot flying an unpressurized Cessna 337D Skymaster. He was on a high-altitude photographic mission, with an assigned cruise altitude of FL250. However, the ATC controller noticed the Skymaster's altitude begin varying, then subsequently level at 27,700 feet. Then it began an uncontrolled descent and broke apart.

The fuselage ended up suspended 30 feet above the ground in a hickory tree. Miraculously, the female passenger, who was unconscious throughout the ordeal, survived with only minor injuries. The pilot was found to have died from hypoxia.

The accident was caused by the local FBO's line service attendant who filled the Skymaster's two oxygen bottles with compressed air instead of oxygen. The FBO manager told investigators he had been purchasing oxygen from a local gas company for the past nine years, and that his current supply had been purchased seven months earlier. Still, the invoice showed delivery of "Breathing Air—Grade D (K)." A check of the FBO servicing cart showed four *yellow cylinders*. The manager told investigators that to his knowledge the cylinders had always been yellow. Unfortunately, oxygen cylinders are color-coded green.

The labeling, too, was confusing. Each cylinder was stenciled "AIR COMPRESSED UN1002 BREATHING AIR." Oxygen bottles are typically labeled "BREATHING OXYGEN." The FBO had been receiving and selling compressed air instead of oxygen to aircraft for a very long time without any of the pilots catching the error.

Compressed breathing air is used by scuba divers and consists of only 20 percent oxygen, 79 percent nitrogen, and one percent other gasses. If a scuba diver were to use pure oxygen rather than compressed air, oxygen poisoning would occur at a depth of 24 to 33 feet, resulting in convulsions. Conversely, pure oxygen is required at high altitude to keep the pilot's *blood oxygen partial pressure* at 98 percent or greater. Yet for nine years, no one had paid attention and caught this potentially lethal error.

Propeller Failure

A fatal MU-2B-60 accident was caused by lack of action by the FAA and the propeller hub manufacturer. As recently as a month before this accident, the FAA had declined to pursue the NTSB's recommendation for a fleet-wide inspection of the prop hubs in another almost identical mishap. Had the NTSB's recommendations been followed in that accident, the accident chain would have been broken and the following tragic accident would not have occurred. Among the two crewmembers and six passengers killed was the Governor of South Dakota.

The accident was precipitated by fatigue cracking and fracture of the left propeller hub arm, resulting in separation of both the hub arm and propeller blade. This in turn damaged the engine nacelle, wing and fuselage. At their cruise altitude of FL240, the fuselage damage from the prop blade caused a rapid decompression of the cabin.

The NTSB report stated, "The cause of the propeller hub arm fracture was a reduction in the fatigue strength of the material because of manufacturing and time-related factors (decarburization, residual stress, corrosion, mixed microstructure, and machine/scoring marks) which reduced the fatigue resistance of the material, probably combined with higher-than-normal cyclic loads...which was not appropriately considered during the airplane/propeller certification process." The fatal flight in N86SD was a return trip from a high level business meeting in Cincinnati. Three passengers were scheduled to be dropped off at Sioux Falls, then home to Pierre, South Dakota. At 3:37 PM, the flight had just received clearance to deviate around thunderstorms, when three minutes later the crew reported, "Chicago, Sierra Delta, we had a decompression." Then, "Mayday, Mayday, Mayday: Six Sierra Delta, we're going down here." Then they requested steers to the "closest airport we can get to here." They were informed that Dubuque (DBQ), Iowa, was 25 miles distant at their two-o'clock position, then cleared down to 8,000 feet. Unfortunately DBQ's weather was 300 feet overcast with 1.5 miles visibility in rain and fog.

At 3:44 PM the controller asked, "can you hold altitude?" To which the crew responded, "well, standby." Then they were cleared down to 6,000 feet. A minute later the crew reported difficulty holding altitude, whereupon the controller cleared the flight to 4,000 feet. At 23 miles southeast of the airport, the crew requested vectors to the ILS, and the controller informed N86SD they were joining the approach course. Minutes later the controller gave the aircraft's altitude as 2,700 feet and asked, "can you hold...there?" A crewmember responded, "I don't think so." At 1,900 feet and 10 miles southeast of Dubuque, ATC lost radar contact with the airplane. The controller advised of the loss of radar contact and handed the flight off to Dubuque tower.

At 3:51 the crew contacted Dubuque's tower and their first question was "how far out are we?" But the tower couldn't tell them since they weren't equipped to determine range. At 3:52 PM the flight crew acknowledged and that was their last transmission. The aircraft crashed 8.5 miles south of Dubuque, hitting a farm silo, a barn, several pieces of farm equipment, and several animals. Both the wreckage and the occupants were consumed by the post-crash fire.

Some two years earlier, another MU-2B-60 had experienced the same failure of the Hartzell model HC-B4 propeller hub in the right engine. However, in this case, the engine mount did not fail completely and the engine remained aligned with the relative wind. The hub failure released one propeller blade, which also punctured the fuselage. The airplane was climbing through 19,000 feet and it too experienced a rapid decompression. Even though the propeller's negative torque sensing auto-feathered the prop, the pilot still could not arrest the descent and was just barely able to reach the runway at Utica, New York.

Metallurgical examination of the fractured hub showed fatigue cracking that originated from multiple sites on the surface of the hole for a pilot tube. Origin of the crack was identical to the Dubuque accident—near the inboard end of the pilot tube. The prop hub in the Utica incident had accumulated 4,460 hours. The prop hub on the Dubuque accident had accumulated 4,346 hours.

In the Utica mishap, the NTSB had asked the FAA to, "Develop, with the assistance of Hartzell Propeller Incorporated, a nondestructive inspection technique capable of detecting hub arm cracks stemming from *inside* the diameter surface of the hub arm; at the approximate location of the inserted end of the pilot tubes on the Hartzell model HC-B4 propeller hubs, and issue an airworthiness directive requiring that HC-B4 propeller hubs with 3,000 hours or more be inspected using this technique the

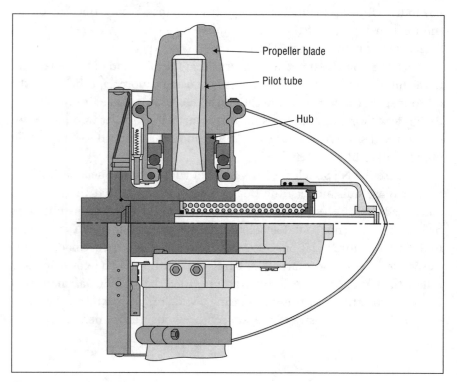

Figure 8-4. Propeller hub.

next time the propeller assembly is overhauled for any reason, or the next annual inspection (or equivalent), whichever is first." Two additional recommendations buffered this one.

The FAA first responded to these recommendations in letters dated October 26, 1992, and January 4, 1993. Their first letter stated that a review of the propeller's service history was being made to determine the magnitude of the problem. Then, in their January 4, 1993, response—about three months before the accident that killed the governor—the FAA said a review of the propeller's service history showed only one other failure. Further, "the stress levels in the crack initiation area are acceptable...no additional action was planned [by the FAA], but Hartzell would continue to monitor the service history of propeller."

The Board responded strongly in letters dated January 6, 1993, and March 4, 1993—the latter just a month before the governor's fatal accident—stating that regardless of the FAA's findings, the service history of the HC-B4 hubs contained no other examples of cracking or fractures similar to the Utica accident. The Board was convinced that a once-through-the-fleet inspection of the subject hubs was necessary, as requested in Safety Recommendation A-92-81.

Then the Board restated its concern "that the FAA had not taken action in the interim to examine the possibility of using a more appropriate method to inspect the hub arms; and that the FAA saw no need to review the design and fabrication process of other Hartzell propeller hub models to determine if similarities in design might indicate the need for inspection of these other hub models."

Because the NTSB felt the FAA had not addressed the need for inspection of these hub models, the Board "did not believe that the FAA had addressed these recommendations in sufficient detail." And just 45 days before the Governor's fatal accident, the Board listed the FAA's response to Safety Recommendations A-92-81 through 83 as "Open-Unacceptable Response." Yet on May 21, 1993, barely a month *after* the governor was killed, the FAA's Acting Administrator notified the NTSB Chairman "that it had taken actions, or was considering a wide range of actions, that were designed to be responsive to the subject (previous) recommendations."

Mechanical Failure

A sticking angle-of-attack vane caused the loss of first prototype of the popular Challenger CL-600 corporate jet, serial number 1001. It was a routine development test flight of Canadair Limited's new prototype corporate jet. The date was April 3, 1980, and the mission of the three-man crew was to check the aircraft's stall behavior in various configurations. Flying out of California's Mojave Air and Space Port, the aircraft was being flown by company engineering test pilot Norm Ronaasen, with fellow test pilot David Gollings serving as copilot. In the cabin, positioned at a large console monitoring aircraft systems and performance was veteran flight test engineer William B. (Bill) Scott. Because the flight involved a series of potentially hazardous stall tests, all three crewmembers were equipped with helmets and GQ Security 250 integral seat-type parachutes.

To keep airflow over the empennage clear of the two aft-fuselage mounted Avro Lycoming ALF-502L turbofan engines, the design had the horizontal stabilizers and elevators mounted atop the tall vertical tail-fin—euphemistically called a "T-Tail." However, wind tunnel tests showed that at high angles of attack the T-tailed aircraft was vulnerable to a so-called "locked-in deep stall"; wherein the stalled wake of the wing and flaps blocked airflow over the entire empennage. The aircraft would then assume a relatively flat attitude and drop vertically with an uncontrollable high rate of descent.

For a design vulnerable to this phenomenon, the U.S. Federal Aviation Administration typically allowed an artificial stall-barrier system. This included a stall warning light and horn, combined with a stick shaker that activated as the aircraft got to within about eight to ten percent of a stall angle of attack. Then if the pilot persisted, to prevent a deep stall, a "stick-pusher" forcefully moved the control column forward to reduce the aircraft's angle of attack. However, a senior member of Transport Canada had unilaterally decreed that the ship's natural stall characteristics had to be fully explored and that no artificial stall-prevention system could be used, and the aircraft would only be certified using "natural" aerodynamic stall control measures.

In earlier tests, as they approached a stall angle of attack they had heard loud metallic "banging sounds." Thus, despite completing 12 planned stall tests at 15,000 feet, Ronaasen decided to make an additional stall test in an effort to positively identify the source of the banging noise. As a safety precaution, he then climbed 2,000 feet higher. And as he had done in previous tests, with the airplane in a left turn and holding an indicated 14-units angle of attack with a constant one-knot per second bleed rate, he slowly pulled the aircraft into heavy pre-stall buffet. But, unknown to the crew, the ship's angle of attack vane was stuck at 14 units, and its actual angle of attack had continued to increase.

Then, just as the loud banging noise began, the airframe buffet became very heavy and the angle of attack vane broke loose and pegged at 34 units. Ronaasen quickly rolled wings level, but even with both pilots pushing forward on the controls, the aircraft remained in a slight nose up attitude and failed to recover. Gollings reported, "None of the flight controls responded, and one engine flamed out, as the airplane entered what is known as a 'deep stall' or 'super stall.'"

As a precaution against just such an event, the prototype was equipped with an anti-spin recovery parachute in the tail, which Ronaasen promptly deployed. The aircraft immediately pitched nose-down and recovered, and at this point it should have been a simple matter to jettison the chute and return to Mojave airport. But despite repeatedly activating the redundant jettison system, via two hydraulic releases and finally explosive bolts, the chute failed to release.

Theoretically, with 7,500 foot-pounds of thrust from each of the two turbofan engines, it should have been possible to overpower the chute's drag. However, with one engine inoperative and the other at full power, they were unable to sustain flight.

With the aircraft descending in a wings-level attitude and about a 30-degree-nose-down pitch attitude, their rate of descent was tracked by radar at an astounding 17,000 feet-per-minute—a figure Gollings later described as "beyond [human] comprehension." With the two pilots preoccupied with getting rid of the anti-spin chute, it was flight test engineer Bill Scott who was monitoring the instruments that suddenly called out "6,000 feet!" This was about 4,000 feet above the desert floor.

Gollings relates, "[Bill Scott's] call of 6,000 feet brought us to our senses and Norm immediately called for bailout. His [Bill's] main duty then was to get to the rear baggage door, open it and jump out—which he did with great enthusiasm…I watched him disappear out the door and observed with some curiosity as he disappeared *upwards*."

Gollings then followed and dived head first through the hatch and began tumbling head over heels until assuming a spread-eagle position facing the ground. Quickly he pulled the parachute's ripcord, and just after he felt the opening shock he landed, "with a thump and crunching of bone, as my foot suddenly headed in a direction opposite the rest of me." As he lay on the desert floor, Gollings watched Bill Scott still floating down slowly in his parachute.

Scott landed uninjured and later radar analysis showed he had jumped from around 3,000 feet—about 1,000 feet AGL (above ground level), with Gollings exiting immediately thereafter at around 800 feet AGL. It was Dick Rutan (later of Voyager fame) flying a small aircraft out of Mojave airport, who spotted Challenger's impact and began circling the crash site. He alerted Edwards AFB control tower and within minutes both Gollings and Scott were in the capable hands of paramedics and the USAF chief medical officer, who at the time was participating in a local training mission.

Norm Ronaasen had remained at the controls until both his flight test engineer and copilot were safely out. And while Ronaasen did make it out, he was so low he didn't have enough time to pull the parachute's D-ring. His delay to assure the safe exit of his crewmembers cost him his life. Dave Gollings credits Bill Scott's prescient callout at 6,000 feet and Norm's immediate call to "*bail out!*" with preventing total tragedy. Gollings remembered, "To my horror, Challenger One appeared to slowly slide into the desert floor accompanied with a great fireball followed by billowing black smoke which rose swiftly above the dead aircraft." It impacted the desert near California City, California.

Conclusions

As these examples show, the owner/operator of an airplane must keep informed as to the service history of the aircraft type. In addition, the FAA keeps a complete database on its website of all Airworthiness Directives for aircraft, engines, propellers, rotor blades, and accessories. (This should be checked at least during the annual inspection.) And the FAA's Service Difficulty Reports (SDRs) are also very useful. The National Business Aircraft Association (NBAA), AOPA, and AOPA's Air Safety Foundation are also good sources of up-to-date information. But most important of all is to keep in close touch with the manufacturer, because each company is very protective of the reputation of its products where safety and reliability is concerned.

CHAPTER 9

Human Factors in Safe Flying

With over 80 percent of annual general aviation accidents laid to pilot error, the causes need further analysis. The apparent lack of good judgment in our aircraft accident history appears inextricably linked with *compulsion* (we all "hate-to-wait") and *complacency* ("we've done it before and it has always worked"). The late cowboy-philosopher Will Rogers once said, "Good judgment comes from experience, and a lot of that comes from bad judgment." Yet ironically, he himself was the unfortunate victim of bad judgment—actually compulsion and obsession—on the part of his famous pilot-friend, Wiley Post, with whom he was flying. Because of an oversized engine, Post's airplane was known to have had an excessively forward center of gravity (CG). Yet he needed the big engine's horse power for his world-circling record attempt; and after all, he hadn't had a problem with it thus far. But when the engine quit on takeoff from a remote Alaskan Arctic village, that nose-heavy CG cost both famous personalities their lives.

For starters, it appears to be much easier to develop good flying skills than sound judgment. In aviation, as in all endeavors, good judgment seems to be a combination of hereditary personality traits, competent training, and access to lots of good information—all combined with operational experience. Adding to the safety equation are the manufacturers' publications and Federal Aviation Regulations that provide pilots with excellent guidance in decision-making—if they'll just use them. After all, the AFM and POH were derived from extensive flight tests, and the regulations from almost a century of operational experience and accident history.

The commercial operator, e.g., an airline or air taxi pilot, has both the regulations and the additional guidance provided by the FAA-approved company operations manual. This document also helps standardize the operational decision-making process. For example, if the weather is below the published takeoff or landing minimums, then both the ops manual and regulations tell the commercial pilot that he or she simply can't file for takeoff or initiate the instrument landing approach to an airport that's below the specified weather minimums.

For the conscientious private pilot the same rules used by commercial operators can provide a great source of guidance in their decision-making process. The hazards of a zero-visibility departure can be eliminated simply by abiding by the published takeoff minimums—a rule required of commercial pilots (*see* §91.175(f)). Of course, this will force you to plan ahead to avoid extended delays. If your home field has fog and zero visibility forecast for your early morning departure, you can plan for a later takeoff when the visibility has improved, or possibly position the airplane at a higher-elevation airport the day prior and thus avoid the problem altogether.

The same reasoning applies when contemplating an instrument approach into your destination airfield. With weather below minimums the private pilot can legally make the approach to minimums and "take a look" (*see* §91.175(c)). Yet, for the safety of paying passengers, the regulation governing air-taxi pilots (§135.225(a)(2)) says, "*No pilot can begin an instrument approach procedure to an airport unless…the latest weather report issued by that weather-reporting facility indicates that weather conditions are at or above the authorized IFR landing minimums for that airport.*" This rule was designed to prevent accidents, yet only commercial operators are bound by it. And despite weather reported as well below minimums, each year one or more privately flown airplanes is wrecked and all aboard usually killed, because the pilot-in-command decided to perform the approach and take a look.

In some cases the professional pilot can be approved for the lower Category II or III minimums. This requires not only frequent training and checks of his or her proficiency, but the destination airport must have special lighting and RVR measuring equipment before a reduced minimums approach can be initiated.

Pilot Error Analyzed

A study of pilot-error accidents shows seven basic links in the accident-chain that are consistently involved: (1) personality profile, (2) training, (3) proficiency, (4) stress or emotional factor, (5) physical deficiency, (6) supervisory-management, or (7) maintenance factor—a mechanic's error, material failure, or human engineering design error. Often the "error" attributed to the pilot was simply the final link in a chain of errors that originated within his/her support team. While the pilot is in command of the aircraft, if the deck is stacked against him or her an accident becomes inevitable. Look at the following to see how they relate.

Starting with personality profile, despite arguments to the contrary, there are some personalities that are not meant to fly airplanes. This statement is not intended to imply that it takes a superman or woman to become a competent pilot. Like riding a bicycle, most people learn to do it competently, with a few who become exceptionally skillful. Still, there's an occasional personality who just can't seem to get the hang of it. So it is with flying: there are a few people who, for whatever reason, simply cannot put it all together and fly an airplane competently and safely. And in aviation, this characteristic can costs lives and money rather than scrapes and bruises.

My first exposure to this phenomenon came while working one summer between college semesters as line-boy for Leithold's Seaplane Base in Ely, Minnesota—at the time, a WWII GI Bill flight school. A young Army veteran who was about to enter his senior year in college signed up for the private pilot course. He began his instruction in the flight school's float-equipped J-3 Cubs. Despite flying daily, after 20 hours of dual, he had not yet soloed, and the assigned flight instructor was exasperated with his performance. Early one morning I overheard the instructor discussing with his boss how the situation should be handled. Simply put, the student didn't seem to absorb information. He kept making the same mistakes over and over. Finally, with 23 hours of dual, the instructor reluctantly allowed him to solo; and his first flight alone was successful. But the next day, on his second solo flight, he spun-in on go-around from a touch-and-go landing. Fortunately, the Cub crashed into Lake Saganaga, producing only bruises and scratches. But his flying career ended at that point.

Commuter Airline Accidents

In this case, a relatively new first officer for a commuter airline had a history of proficiency problems, particularly with instrument flying. While the final cause of this mishap was challenged, the NTSB report shows that one dark and rainy night AVAir Flight 3378 departed Raleigh-Durham International Airport's runway 23R on an instrument departure. The first officer was the pilot flying and was told to, "report established on 290-degree heading and make that turn as soon as feasible." With the captain acting as copilot and obviously not monitoring the departure, she became spatially disoriented; the aircraft crashed 100 feet from the shoreline of a nearby reservoir, killing the crew and all twelve of the passengers.

Her background was in light twins and singles. During training for the Metro II she had required additional dual and took three checkrides before qualifying as second-in-command. The first check airman had written, "Needs more work on landing, having trouble maintaining glide path and speed control and keeping torque matched on landing." The second check airman wrote, "Refuses to fly the aircraft...performance unsatisfactory... recommend termination." He later told the Director of Operations that to bring her up to standards "would take a long time." The third check airman qualified her as second-in-command on the Metro II. It took a tragedy entailing the loss of a dozen lives to prove which of the check pilots was right.

Then there was the tragedy of the Colgan Air, Inc., DHC-8-400, which crashed into a residence in Clarence Center, New York, about five miles east of Buffalo-Niagara International Airport (BUF). Operating as Continental Connection flight 3407, it was 10:17 PM and the night weather conditions were VFR. Although they had encountered some in-flight ice it was not considered a factor. As they began the ILS approach into BUF, and contrary to the sterile cockpit regulation (§121.542) and company procedures, the CVR documented the captain and first officer idly chatting about things unrelated to their cockpit duties.

With the landing gear down and before landing checklist mostly complete, at an airspeed of about 135 knots the CVR recorded autopilot disconnect, and simultaneously the stick shaker activated; a warning of impending stall. Now at 131 knots, the FDR showed that the captain *pulled the control column aft* and increased engine power to about 75 percent torque. With the control wheel pulled back, as the power increased the aircraft pitched-up and rolled left to about 45 degrees, then rolled right. As the airplane rolled right, the stick pusher activated and the FO brought the flaps up. By now, the airspeed was registering 100 knots and the aircraft rolled to about 105 degrees right wing down before rolling back to the left—whereupon the stick pusher again activated in a programmed effort to push the nose down.

The FO then asked if she should retract the landing gear and the captain responded with "Gear Up!" With the ship's attitude reaching 25 degrees nose-down pitch and 100 degrees right wing down, the airplane entered a steep descent. The stick pusher activated a third time and the CVR recorded the captain stating "we're down," then the sound of thump. They crashed into a single-family home, killing its occupant, and the airplane was consumed by the post-crash fire.

Throughout his flying career, the captain had a long pattern of training problems and flight check failures. First, he failed his initial checkride for his instrument rating. While this in itself is not necessarily significant, when combined with his later failures, it was essentially the start of a pattern. He was subsequently disapproved for his initial commercial single-engine land certificate. Two years later, he was disapproved for his initial commercial multi-engine land certificate. In this case, the entire checkride had to be repeated since he failed to perform *any* of the maneuvers well enough to receive credit for them.

The NTSB accident report states: "The captain's disapproval for a commercial multi-engine land certificate was his third successive failure to pass an initial attempt for an FAA certificate or rating, and it appeared that his performance was not improving as he gained experience." The report also noted the possibility that his training could have been inadequate or possibly due to the stress of "performing required skills while under the stress conditions associated with a checkride."

Nervousness and under-performing are common reactions to the apprehension of a pending checkride. However, the pattern of under-performing recurred when he attended an eight month training program at the Gulfstream Training Academy at Gulfstream International Airlines (GIA), presumably centered on the BE-1900D. (The NTSB report didn't specify the aircraft specifically.) His training records show continuing problems with aircraft control. "During two simulator periods, he was graded unsatisfactory in *'approach to stall-landing configuration.'* During a later simulator period he demonstrated unacceptable altitude and airspeed control. During the final planned simulator session the instructor noted basic attitude flying problems and repeated deviations. Because he needed additional training an extra simulator session was provided the next day, with all maneuvers graded satisfactory—with the final checkride accomplished later that same day."

The NTSB accident report reads: "The captain's GIA training records clearly showed that his flying skills needed improvement, but he apparently met the minimum standards for completion of the training. Thus, he began flying the BE-1900D as a fully qualified first officer. However, the captain's GIA training records should have raised concerns about his suitability for employment at a Part 121 air carrier." Instead four crewmembers, 45 passengers and one innocent person in their home perished because of this gross management error.

Air Force Experience

The accident files are full of similar stories involving this personality trait. Even the military services, with the ultimate in close supervision, have their share of these problems. During my time in service, a flying school classmate had a major accident in the T-33 during advanced pilot training. The first year after graduation he was involved in two more—both in jet fighters. After the third he was finally grounded.

A more tragic example occurred when the pilot of an Air Force KC-135A tanker killed himself and his six-man crew. While landing, he flared too high and along the left side of the runway and abruptly pulled the power to idle. The aircraft dropped like a stone and bounced down the runway, yet he failed to add power and go-around. Finally, the aircraft dragged a wingtip, then burst into flames and exploded. The 10 passengers escaped through a rear hatch, but the crewmembers were asphyxiated by the acrid smoke.

Investigators found that the pilot, with 1,300 hours total flight time and 926 in the KC-135, had a long history of landing problems. While proficiency flying in the T-38 trainer, he had been graded "unqualified" for landings. His instructor noted, "His landings are characterized by a sinking final, high flare, and early power reduction…characteristically lands left of centerline and many landings were firm (hard) with incomplete flares." At another base he again had landing problems, which his instructors tried to help remedy. His training records showed that his bad landings "were not an every-time occurrence."

General Aviation

The problem in general aviation poses yet another dilemma, because a pilot with an identified learning, and hence, a proficiency problem, cannot be easily thwarted. First, Parts 61 and 91 are quite lax for non-commercial pilots. And when a notable problem does surface, how does the flight instructor or professional learning center resolve it? After all, the trainee is a customer who can simply take his business elsewhere. The following accidents provide classic examples.

Shortly after he failed the Pilot Initial Course in a newly acquired Cessna 421C, a company president killed himself and five friends when he flew the aircraft into IFR conditions. According to the accident report he attended initial simulator-based training from November 6 through November 10. The course consisted of 20 hours of ground school and 10 hours of simulator instruction. His training records show an over-all grade of "Unsatisfactory Performance."

As the program progressed he showed serious cognitive weaknesses. His simulator instructor noted that his instrument scan was "extremely slow and insufficient to the extent that under IMC conditions he could not maintain altitude within 1,300 feet or heading within 40 degrees." On November 8, the student requested that "all remaining time in the simulator be given under VFR conditions with systems orientation." On the last day of training, the instructor noted the pilot's "continued poor aircraft control, coupled with a limited cockpit scan, awareness, and limited systems retention, prevented satisfactory completion of requirements even under VFR conditions." Further investigation revealed this pilot had previously owned a Cessna 340. With that aircraft too he had shown significant trouble during both the Cessna 340 initial course and a follow-up recurrency course. On the grade sheet for his initial course the instructor had written "Wonder as a sim instructor how he got an instrument rating or M.E. Flight training completed to VFR standards." After he completed the recurrent course the instructor wrote, "He can do only one thing at a time. It seems very difficult for him to fly and tune radios at the same time." When he completed the course his instructor wrote, "He met the very minimum standards for VFR operation. Not within IFR standards at all."

A month after essentially failing the Cessna 421 Pilot Initial Course, the pilot/owner organized a Christmas ski vacation to Aspen, Colorado, with five friends. At a refueling stop in Tulsa he checked the weather but did not file a flight plan. He was advised of an AIRMET in effect with instrument conditions along his entire route of flight. In addition he was told that VFR flight was not recommended from Ponca City through western Kansas. Further, a radar map showed icing conditions northwest of Tulsa. An employee at the Tulsa FBO helped the pilot use the weather machine in the flight planning room. As they discussed the weather the witness stated, "he seemed nervous." And while they talked, the pilot's hands would shake "like a much older person."

At 2:24 PM, the VFR flight was cleared for departure on Tulsa's runway 36L. Thirteen minutes later, Tulsa Radar West control advised the pilot that radar service was terminated. The pilot acknowledged and was not heard from again. Radar showed the airplane climbed from 2,500 feet to 9,800 feet. During the next one minute and 28 seconds the airplane descended to 5,400 feet and then climbed to 8,300 feet. It then entered yet another descent, with the last radar hit showing it passing through 3,200 feet. This was within one-tenth of a nautical mile where witnesses saw the aircraft come out of the clouds in a flat spin and crash. In addition, investigators found that with full fuel tanks and six people aboard, the aircraft was overloaded by 150 pounds.

A similar example involved a MU-300 Diamond 1A. The captain of this flight was very experienced, with over 17,600 hours—reportedly mostly crop dusting. At the time of the accident his total time in the MU-300 was estimated at about 80 hours. As with the pilots in the other examples, he too had great difficulty absorbing new information. Whether his learning problem resulted from deteriorating health or just a basic intelligence deficiency was not addressed by the NTSB. But certain heart, circulatory, and blood pressure problems are known to cause cognitive disability. Prior to his attending the MU-300 Initial Course, he had been flying a King Air 200. He also had been recently type rated in the Citation, though he had no significant experience in that airplane.

As with previous cases, his simulator records showed great frustration on the part of his instructor, with notations such as, "Can't retain information. Can be told procedures over and over and no help… Client can't remember most basic operations; put N_1 on airspeed bug…landing out of control…stalls marginal…busted altitude by 1,000 feet…ILS crashed on landing…five V_1 cuts and five crashes…can't do trim check even [while] reading the procedures." Despite the simplicity of the Diamond's systems, he barely passed the academic final exam, making a minimum acceptable score of 70%.

Upon finishing the prescribed syllabus and failing to progress in simulator training, the accident pilot was given another instructor who was thought to be more pragmatic. Yet after providing the student with an additional simulator session, he too found the pilot unqualified for his simulator checkride for the MU-300 type rating.

Because his instrument flying was unsatisfactory, he asked to be trained and checked in the airplane rather than the simulator, since he felt he could fly it with no problem. It should be noted that flying the simulator was all by reference to the flight instruments, since it had no visual capability built in. However, while flying the airplane the student could see out of the cockpit, especially via peripheral vision.

By mutual agreement, the subject pilot left for a period of flying the airplane with a type-rated pilot in the right seat. Upon returning several days later, there was a noticeable improvement in his knowledge. In his first simulator session after returning, he was found qualified in the limited number of items accomplished. However, he still remained unqualified in many of the required tasks. After a second training session he was recommended for the check, but still without qualifying in all the FAA-required tasks.

The record shows he passed the simulator check, although the tasks covered were not graded individually. Then, following an unusually long 3.3-hour flight-check, he was issued the type rating. (The length of this checkride indicates the check-pilot was conducting training instead of checking.)

Seven months later, the new MU-300 pilot was flying a 69 NM trip from Scott City, Kansas, to Goodland, Kansas. The weather at Goodland was IFR, with a 400-foot broken ceiling and 10 miles visibility. The last recorded radar plot showed the airplane at 9,400 feet and 16 NM southeast of the runway, tracking two miles east of the ILS centerline.

Unless you had read this pilot's simulator training records, what happens next can only be classed as bizarre. The flight was cleared for the ILS to Goodland's runway 30. As the aircraft headed for the compass locator, the CVR recorded sounds of the over-speed warning warbler. The copilot then asked "speed brakes?" Shortly thereafter, the over-speed warning ended. During the next three minutes the flaps were extended 10 degrees and the landing gear extended. There was cockpit conversation about intercepting the localizer, then a call to Goodland UNICOM concerning runway conditions, after which there was more conversation about intercepting the ILS.

Suddenly the copilot exclaimed, "That's a shaker…" Two seconds later he repeated, "Shaker, power, power." Four seconds after that, the CVR recorded the "sound of a horn similar to an altitude alert." This was followed by a frantic call from the copilot of, "Full Power!" then, "Get your nose down…get your nose down—Let's get it, get it to flying!" Five seconds later, the recording ended.

Worth mentioning regarding the copilot is that to save money for the owner, the captain had trained him generally in accordance with §61.55, "Second-in-Command Qualifications." However, since the training was not documented in any form, he was legally unqualified to act as SIC. (Another contract copilot also had been trained by this captain, and he told investigators of their training.) Consequently, the flight did not have a legal crew, and according to a major aviation publication, the insurance company refused to pay for loss of the aircraft.

Still, despite his lack of proper training, the copilot was the only one functioning rationally. The captain had reverted to the old habits noted during his simulator instruction, and proceeded to lose control of the airplane. The copilot's apparent failure to take control was perhaps the result of his comparatively low flying time and a lack of self-confidence due to his inadequate training and experience. After all, this was his first opportunity to fly a jet airplane—and the captain was so experienced.

Compulsion and Complacency

In some personalities, compulsion, or getting the job done—a.k.a., "mission accomplishment"—enters the safety equation to cause an accident. This factor, combined with obvious complacency, appears involved in a *very* tragic example that occurred on March 22, 2009. A chartered single-engine turbo-prop Pilatus PC-12 crashed in good weather as the pilot attempted what was actually an unannounced emergency landing at Butte,

Montana's Bert Mooney Airport (BTM). The trip was intended as a late season ski vacation for three families to a resort near Bozeman, Montana. Although the aircraft was equipped and certified with eight passenger seats, and two pilot seats, the accident killed the pilot and 13 passengers. Seven of those killed were children, the youngest being a one year old boy, with the others ages three to nine years old. The crash essentially destroyed three complete families.

The 65 year-old professional pilot was a former Air Force transport pilot, which company records showed had 8,840 flight hours, of which 1,760 hours were in Pilatus PC-12s. At the time of the accident, he had been employed for six years by Eagle Cap Leasing, an aircraft management company. All with whom he had flown described him as very professional.

His drift towards complacency seems to have originated in a previous job flying PC-12s for the Native American Air Ambulance Service. Although the AFM required the addition of a fuel system anti-ice inhibitor (FSII) when refueling the aircraft, at the ambulance service the FSII was intentionally omitted since their trips were short and not flown at high altitude. This also resulted in a slight savings in the hourly operating cost.

At Redlands Municipal Airport (REI), California, where Eagle Gap Leasing was based, refueling records for February and March 2009 showed the pilot refueled the PC-12 four times, but without adding the FSII to the fuel. On the day prior to the accident, he had serviced the aircraft for the trip with 222 gallons of Jet A—and again, without adding the FSII. After all, omitting the FSII requirement hadn't been problematic in the past.

On the morning of the trip, the pilot departed for a 1 hour 30 minute positioning flight to Nut Tree Airport (VCB) in Vacaville, California. The temperature at his cruise altitude was recorded as -32°C. While descending to land, the CAWS, which recorded illumination of all advisory lights, showed that the left and right fuel booster pumps had begun to cycle automatically. This indicated a drop in fuel pressure—a sign of fuel system icing. The Board felt it was likely that, "at least one of the fuel booster pumps provided adequate pressure to the fuel system, within 0.3 seconds of the low fuel pressure condition being sensed."

He landed the aircraft shortly thereafter with no indication of fuel level imbalance in the ship's wing fuel tanks. And since the automatic boost pump activation had kept the wing fuel tanks perfectly balanced, despite the earlier CAWS warning, the pilot seemed to have been satisfied with ignoring the AFM requirement for the fuel additive.

At Nut Tree Airport he refueled the turbo-prop aircraft to capacity, with 128 gallons of Jet A fuel. Surveillance photos and subsequent chemical analysis showed that, despite the earlier CAWS low fuel pressure warning (likely due to some fuel system icing) and the requirements of the AFM Section 8, "Handling, Servicing and Maintenance," he had again failed to add FSII to the fuel. This final act of complacency was obviously serious, since he would be cruising for 2 hours 30 minutes at FL250, where NTSB investigators determined the temperature to have been -40°C.

During his preflight before leaving Nut Tree Airport, he also failed to sample the under-wing fuel tank drains and fuel filter drain to check for water content in the fuel. Although all jet fuel contains some moisture, a milky-white appearance after refueling would have indicated excess water content. Perhaps his most serious failing was in not checking the fuel filter bypass indicator to see that it was flush with the filter housing assembly. Had this one check been made, he would have undoubtedly found the bypass indicator extended—a positive indication of ice crystals and water in the fuel which had caused the CAWS fuel boost pump advisories during his repositioning flight into Nut Tree Airport.

Although the PC-12's cabin was equipped with only eight passenger seats, because it was being flown by a single pilot, the extra cockpit seat was used by a passenger. Although his flight plan, pre-filed the previous day, showed only five passengers, as the flight departed Nut Tree Airport, there were nine passengers aboard—four adults and five children. With the aircraft having a full fuel load investigators determined he departed Nut Tree Airport 432 lbs over the airplane's gross weight limit, but still within the CG envelope. He landed 13 minutes later at nearby Oroville, where two more adults and two children were boarded, making a total of 13 passengers.

One of the three aircraft owners who had organized the trip told investigators they had done it before with the same number of passengers on a previous flight. Consequently, "he didn't feel they were pushing the envelope," because, "the trip was within the weight and balance limits...but there were just not enough seatbelts for every passenger." In other words, as one of the aircraft owners, he felt his judgment superseded that of the Pilatus engineers and test pilots as reflected in the AFM, not to mention seat belt requirements in the regulations.

The flight departed at 12:10 PM for Bozeman Yellowstone International Airport (BZN) in Bozeman, Montana, with 1,352 pounds of usable fuel in each of the ship's left and right wing tanks; enough for 3 hours 30 minutes of flight. The IFR flight plan showed 2 hour 30 minutes en route at FL250, with eight passengers plus the pilot aboard, it once again exceeded the aircraft's maximum takeoff and landing weight limitation of 9,921 pounds; but it was, "*within* the CG envelope."

According to the CAWS, 22 minutes into flight the right boost pump was on for 3 minutes 45 seconds, indicating a fuel imbalance of 70 lbs and a right wing heavy condition. After shutting off, it remained off for the next 48 minutes.

About 1 hour 18 minutes into the flight, the aircraft's left boost pump activated and remained on continuously. Then at 1:31 PM, the right boost pump resumed running. This indicated the left-side fuel pressure had degraded to less than 2 psi and the right boost pump was required to maintain adequate fuel pressure to the ship's 1,200-hp PT6A-67P turbo-prop engine. In this configuration, the relatively high right-side fuel pressure would have stopped any fuel flow to the engine from the left wing tank. Thus, the Board concluded, "about 1 hour 21 minutes into the flight, the fuel supplied to the airplane's engine was being drawn solely from the right [wing] fuel tank by the right fuel boost pump, and the left-wing-heavy fuel imbalance continued to increase."

The Pilatus PC-12 AFM states that the fuel balancing system was designed to automatically correct fuel imbalances "of up to 270 lbs, or about a six-bar differential on the fuel quantity gauge and then shut off." (One bar equals about 7.17 gallons, or 48.3 pounds.) A Pilatus Engineering Report (ER 12-28-00-001) states that if the fuel imbalance between both wing tanks exceeded 25 percent of the full tank load, "the resulting rolling moment cannot be corrected by trimming alone and the control [wheel] must be used." The addendum cautioned further, "that this would increase the pilot's workload and decrease the airplane's safety margin in the event of a maneuver requiring higher-than-normal-levels of piloting skill."

The Pilatus PC-12 AFM Section 2, Limitations, dated March 30, 2001, instructed pilots to monitor the fuel quantity gauges during normal operations (with the fuel boost pump switches in the AUTO position) to verify that the fuel was balanced laterally. The AFM stated further that the maximum fuel imbalance for the PC-12 was about 178 pounds (26.4 gallons)—*a three bar maximum* on the fuel quantity gauges.

After 1 hour 52 minutes of flight—around 2:02 PM—the left fuel boost pump was running continuously, with the right boost pump cycling. This

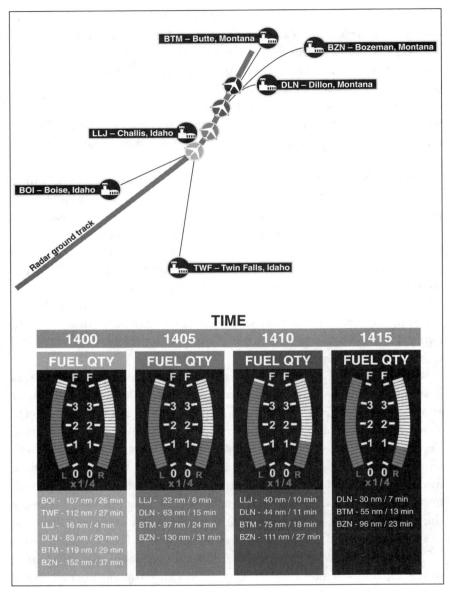

Figure 9-1. NTSB depiction of fuel gauges and available airports along the route of flight.
(From NTSB Report NTSB/AAR-11/05)

indicated the pilot had recognized the fuel system icing problem and manually selected the left boost pump to ON.

Investigators estimated that somewhere between 1:31 PM and 1:35 PM—about 1 hour 21 minutes to 1 hour 25 minutes into the flight—the maximum allowable fuel imbalance occurred. The PC-12 AFM states that when a fuel imbalance occurs the pilot should land the airplane *as soon as practical*. Yet, he failed to divert, even though three airports were available along his route of flight: Boise, Twin Falls, and Challis, Idaho. He seemed determined to get his passengers to within driving distance of their ski resort. After all, his complacency was the cause of the fuel icing problem.

About 2:00 PM to 2:05 PM, half an hour after exceeding the maximum fuel imbalance, the pilot finally began diverting to Butte, Montana, even though Challis, Idaho, was closest to the aircraft's position at that point. Once his route of flight changed, Dillon, Idaho, became the most suitable diversion airport. Yet still he pressed-on towards Butte, which would put the passengers within easy driving distance of the Bozeman area ski resort.

As the aircraft descended through 12,200 feet, the CAWS annunciated a R FUEL LOW caution. This indicated the right tank had only 133 pounds of usable fuel remaining and required an immediate landing. The aircraft now had a 1,219 pound imbalance—a 26-bar differential on the fuel quantity gauge.

Although assigned 13,000 feet, the pilot continued descending and finally reported the runway in sight and cancelled his IFR flight plan. The last recorded radar target showed the airplane at 9,100 feet (3,550 AGL) and about 1.8 miles from the runway 33 threshold at a speed of 189 knots. At this time he had 66 lbs of fuel in the right tank and 1,368 lbs in the left tank—a 1,302 lb imbalance, or 27-bar differential on the fuel gauges.

Clearly, he was too high and fast to land, so he began a turn to the left to downwind for runway 33 and supposedly began decelerating—although the accident report didn't say so. During what witnesses reported as a "sharp left turn" at about 300 feet AGL, the aircraft suddenly pitched down, impacted the ground and exploded.

The NTSB investigation disclosed no mechanical problems with the ship's engine or propeller. Instead, they found the probable cause was "(1) the pilot's failure to ensure that a fuel icing inhibitor was added to the fuel during refueling before the flights on the day of the accident; (2) his failure to take appropriate remedial actions after a low fuel pressure state (resulting from icing within the fuel system) and a lateral fuel imbalance developed, including diverting to a suitable airport before the fuel imbalance became extreme; and (3) a loss of control while the pilot was maneuvering the left-wing-heavy airplane near the approach end of the runway." Needless to say, there are close relatives of three families, including the pilot's, who will never get over the trauma of this needless loss of their loved ones.

Psychological Tests

While airline crews and military pilots receive pre-employment psychological screening, the GA pilots discussed certainly did not require this for their licenses or jobs. According to a guest editorial in August 1998 issue of *NBAA Digest*, by Doctors Diane Damos and Elizabeth Parker, both neuropsychological assessments and information-processing tests can detect subtle deterioration in cognitive capacity that can be caused by any number of different factors, such as use of medications, stroke, or just aging. "These tests can detect problems such as early Alzheimer's Disease, before brain imaging tests such as MRIs and CAT scans can detect abnormalities. Neuropsychological tests are particularly sensitive to changes in brain chemistry that may be undetectable using current brain imaging techniques... Testing may begin with a brief screening to identify possible problems."

The information-processing tests measure how fast certain cognitive processes are executed. Because these processes typically require only a few milliseconds, information processing tests are administered using a computer. Damos and Parker report, "The software usually flags an unusual result, so no specialist is needed to administer the tests. Information-processing tests have good characteristics for repeated testing and can be administered frequently, even on a daily basis, without biasing the results." In fact, the two doctors say that the more data available, the easier it is to detect subtle changes in cognition.

Some years back, the FAA made the EKG mandatory for a Class I physical for persons over a certain age—the aim being to prevent sudden in-flight incapacitation. Although heart condition is watched carefully in commercial and airline pilots, there has been a consistent and disturbing pattern of accidents stemming from subtle mental incapacitation. The incidents described in this chapter are but a sampling of some of the case histories. Yet despite the continuing accidents associated with mental dysfunction, there is still no FAA requirement for testing cognitive capacity.

In the Cessna 421 and MU-300 mishaps, both pilots were 66 years-old, and in both cases their simulator instructors had clearly identified serious cognitive problems based on their training performance. But the instructors lacked the legal authority to challenge their students' medical qualifications, and they risked a possible lawsuit if they took action to have their students' licenses revoked.

As for the military and airline pilots, their records were replete with evidence of serious cognitive (learning) problems. But there was reluctance by their supervisors to have them grounded, and instead they played "good guy" and kept ignoring the obvious. Yet in the real world of modern medical science, there are tests that can detect mental dysfunction and prevent these kinds of accidents.

Still, the problems with the GA pilots were more difficult in that they answered only to themselves—with the exception of the contract MU-300 pilot who was beholden to the aircraft owner. In this case, the first simulator instructor clearly and positively identified this pilot's serious learning problem. Yet a different instructor, who was known to be more "customer-friendly," was brought in to help the pilot through to his type rating. The check airman too was taken-in by the desire to help this affable old guy so he could continue to make a living in aviation. Common sense should have led to a discussion of the problem with the aircraft's owner, who after all, was paying the training bill.

The pity of this accident is that had the pilot been trained to use the autopilot (which his training records show was omitted), he could have coupled it up at cruising altitude and let the autopilot fly the entire ILS approach. Then his only function would have been to modulate the power levers to maintain airspeed.

In the case of the Cessna 421, the pilot's instructor in the C-340 had, two years earlier, highlighted the problem in a final summary statement found in the training records: "Wonder how he got an instrument rating and M.E.(multi engine)?" This is where action should have been taken to see that he never flew another airplane. This means reporting the problem to the insurance company and FAA.

The moral of these stories is that the flight instructor, the aviation manager, the designated pilot examiner, and the director of the training facility are the last links in the safety chain. (*Also see* Chapter 12.) You don't need a degree in psychology to spot a serious learning problem and take appropriate steps to prevent a future accident. This is where ethics must predominate over personal popularity; it's counter-productive to rely on product liability lawsuits to enhance the safety equation, because the damage is already done. If *your* loved ones were the victims, *nothing* is going to ease the emotional pain.

Emotional and Physical Factors

It doesn't happen often, but emotional or physical incapacitation of a pilot in flight usually results in a fatal accident. Inevitably, close friends or family members are killed. An eight-year NTSB study (1990–1998) documented 98 such incidents. However, not included were several accidents during the period from "unknown causes;" a few thought to have been suicide, or there was no obvious and logical explanation for the crash.

Although heart attacks predominated in the category of incapacitation, there were cases of strokes, epilepsy, hypoglycemia, food poisoning, fatigue, carbon-monoxide poisoning, and the fatal case of hypoxia in a Cessna 337 described in Chapter 8. Still, thanks to modern medical technology, most of these incidents of physical or emotional failure could have been prevented.

Stress

The FAA's Civil Aero-Medical Institute (CAMI) defines stress as "the sum of biological reactions to any adverse stimulus, be it physical, mental, emotional, internal or external, that tends to disturb the body's natural balance." Two forms of stress have been identified: acute and chronic. While acute stress can be beneficial and motivate you towards better performance at some moment in time, too much can leave you confused and unreliable. Chronic stress can destroy your personality, your ability to think and reason, your memory, as well as your physical health. Chronic stress results from seemingly irresolvable problems, such as financial, long-term medical ailments involving yourself or spouse and children, or continuous marital discord. The insidious nature of chronic stress is that you get used to it. Stress can be involved at all levels of experience in the pilot community. The following is an example.

After completing an ILS approach, a Boeing 727 carrying 77 passengers was seriously damaged during landing when the captain passed over the runway threshold 60 knots too fast. While still 40 knots too fast and almost halfway down the runway, instead of going around he forced the aircraft onto the runway, landing nose-wheel-first and bouncing badly. The aircraft overshot the runway and received major damage after hitting a ditch. Fortunately, no one was seriously injured. Both physical and psychiatric exams failed to explain the captain's strange performance.

The NTSB's investigation report did not mention that the captain was worried about his seriously ill wife; or that he had attempted to rearrange his schedule to be with her every night. He had also expressed inordinate concern about a forthcoming route check that would require his absence for at least two days. While not identified in the NTSB report, the captain's worry about his wife's medical problems offers a perfect example of possible "cognitive incapacitation" due to emotional distraction.

We all know how stressed-out a person can become when angry, undergoing a divorce, or mourning the loss of a relative or close friend. Under such circumstances, one can't think straight or concentrate. In an automobile for instance, when you're upset, you may drive too fast and recklessly. Or, if lost in thought, you might drive through a red traffic light, or rear-end someone who is stopped. In fact, almost two percent of auto accidents have been identified as suicide or an attempt to commit suicide. As with automobile accidents, emotions regularly play a part in aircraft mishaps. There have been three well-publicized incidents wherein the pilots obviously committed suicide by airplane; two occurred in foreign airliners and one in general aviation. Suicide is the ultimate enactment of emotional distress.

The first involved a Japan Airlines DC-8 on final approach into Tokyo, piloted by a captain with a history of mental illness. It crashed when the pilot put the two inboard engines into reverse thrust while the airplane was still airborne. Although the first officer and flight engineer tried to restrain him and salvage the approach, the aircraft crashed short of the runway, killing 24 of the 174 passengers.

Another case involved an Egypt Air Boeing 767 while at cruising altitude. The cockpit voice recorder documented that in cruise flight, while the captain was briefly out of the cockpit, the first officer intentionally put the aircraft into a vertical dive and crashed it into the Atlantic Ocean.

Seizures

I once watched as an Air Force colonel experienced an epileptic seizure just as he was exiting the cockpit of a Convair C-131 transport. Although this was his second episode, he vigorously denied having a problem. But the flight surgeon prevailed and he was mercifully retired.

Another case involved an Alaskan bush pilot who was attempting to land his overloaded Piper Super Cub. The aircraft crashed on landing, killing both occupants. Investigators discovered the pilot had lost his medical 20 years previously due to epileptic seizures. Yet by taking medication he had been able to control the problem and continued to fly passengers for his hunting operation.

Still another case involved a young pilot at an aviation safety seminar. He was talking to the FAA Chief Surgeon who had just finished a formal presentation. The pilot was bemoaning the fact that he had had a short seizure a couple of years earlier, but (he claimed) it had been due to fatigue and other things and he had since been unable to obtain a new medical certificate. As he stood telling his story, he suddenly collapsed with another seizure. While we may admire his interest and sprit, I feel certain he never again flew as a pilot.

Near Brookhaven, New York, the pilot of a Baron 58 was approaching to land and instructed by approach control to follow another airplane to the airport. He followed as instructed but then failed to turn onto final. The tower then told him to turn 180 degrees for re-sequencing. While he turned toward the airport, the aircraft began descending from 2,000 feet. At 1,600 feet he resumed climbing in a shallow left turn. He continued to ignore the tower, and as he climbed his airspeed decayed. Finally, when ATC radar showed the Baron's airspeed at 44 knots, the airplane entered a spin and crashed. The ATC tapes revealed that the pilot sometimes took almost a minute to change frequencies. His voice was reported as indecisive and hesitant. Investigators discovered that he had been treated for seizures since 1974, and anti-seizure medication was found in his toxicological samples. For almost two decades he had jeopardized the lives of his family, friends, and the general public.

Heart Attack

While the record shows improvement, heart disease remains one of the top health concerns in the United States. Genetics and life-style have been found to play a major role in maintaining physical fitness. According to an official with the Environmental Protection Agency, "Many diseases thought to be caused by external factors we know now have a genetic component." However, it is well known too that tobacco use, heavy drinking, a high-fat diet, obesity, chronic fatigue and lack of exercise, all play directly to any genetic proclivity.

For a number of years, our major airlines included an in-depth interview of pilot-candidates to check their family medical history. Their motive was to determine whether the odds were favorable for a full career as an airline pilot. Union contracts stipulated that if a pilot reached age 46 and became physically disabled, he went on medical leave, then loss of license insurance and workman's compensation until reaching age 50. At that point he could receive full airline medical retirement. In other words, if you reached age 46 employed, the airline owned you. But due to the Americans with Disabilities Act, the requirement for a persons' family medical history is now illegal.

While the FAA doesn't consider your family medical background in issuing your medical certificate, it is still an invaluable long-term health predictor. Properly considered, it allows you to avoid the lifestyle patterns likely to actualize a genetic proclivity.

In Alaska, a 44 year-old pilot was a licensed assistant hunting guide and head of his own drilling field supply business. Flying a Super Cub with a fellow pilot/guide, they were scouting a hunting area preparatory to the arrival of a client-hunter the next day. They flew south out of Delta, Alaska, then deviated west due to strong winds in the mountain pass. While flying at slow speed and reconnoitering the foothills at 200 feet, the back-seat passenger tapped the pilot on the shoulder. The pilot looked back and his passenger gestured for a right turn. The Cub's right wing dipped then the left wing "dropped off like a full stall."

The pilot then slumped over to the left forward part of the cockpit. Since the control stick in back had been removed, the passenger was helpless and the aircraft crashed almost vertically. Yet miraculously, both men survived the impact. The passenger, who never really lost consciousness, suffered a fractured vertebrae, which left his left hand numb and useless. In addition, a leg and two fingers on his right hand were broken—one finger essentially torn off. The pilot was awake and hollering since gas from a wing fuel tank was gushing onto his chest. He was trapped and had multiple fractures of both legs.

The temperature was about 28°F, with the ground covered by a couple feet of snow. Despite excruciating pain, the passenger managed to get out of the wreckage. By leaning against the airplane's fabric fuselage with his mutilated right hand, he helped the pilot extract himself from the wreckage. Then, using seat cushions from the airplane to preclude hypothermia, he made the pilot a makeshift bed.

He then began searching for the aircraft's ELT to make certain it was operating, but the pilot said the airplane didn't have one. Still, he eventually found it stowed under the front seat—in the OFF position. He activated it then wrapped up in his Filson double mackinaw. With flares and guns beside him, he laid back to await whatever fate had in store.

Thanks to a worried wife whose call to Rescue about an over-due husband helped explain the ELT signal they were hearing, the pair was rescued by early evening. While awaiting help, the pilot and passenger talked intermittently, but shortly before the rescue team arrived, the pilot died from a heart attack.

Although the pilot had no history of heart disease, he was aware of problematic symptoms. His wife told investigators that about two weeks prior to the accident, "he asked me to listen to his heartbeat. I put my ear on his chest and could hear what seemed to be his heart skipping a beat." He told her it was normal and nothing else was said about it. Yet, as this case shows, ignoring obvious symptoms—sometimes called denial—ultimately cost him his life. Worse yet, it jeopardized the life of a good friend and left him with *very* serious injuries, requiring a year of medical treatment and physical therapy.

Another mishap involved a 47 year-old pilot flying a Beech Baron. His passenger told investigators that before departing the pilot complained of "not feeling well." After departure the pilot's condition deteriorated and he complained of "tingling in his fingers and pressure on his chest." During his landing approach witnesses said the airplane was flying erratically, until the passenger finally assumed control. The aircraft missed airport buildings but the right wing struck a pole. While the passenger was uninjured, the pilot died during the process. The NTSB listed the accident cause as "pilot incapacitation due to ischemic heart disease."

On December 30, 2013, about 30 minutes after takeoff from Des Moines, Iowa, the captain of United Airlines Flight 1637 a Boeing 737 en route to Denver at 30,000 feet, suffered a major heart attack. Following a chilling announcement by a flight attendant, "Does anyone know how to fly a plane?" Captain Mike Gongol, an Air Force B-1B pilot, rushed to the cockpit and served as copilot for the First Officer who successfully landed the airliner at Omaha's Eppley Field. The captain's life was saved by quick-thinking nurses Linda Alweiss and Amy Sorenson who were passengers on the flight.

For all of us over age 40, there's the ever-present danger of heart attack. Once a person has experienced one and recovers he or she begins to feel better and usually wants to resume flying immediately. However, renewing a medical certificate following heart problems requires careful coordination with your Aero Medical Examiner (AME) and the FAA.

Improper diet can be physically incapacitating too. In one accident, a 27-year-old pilot flying a Cessna 150 was cleared to land on runway 18L, but instead he lined up on runway 17. The tower informed him of his error, but cleared him to continue and land on runway 17. The aircraft hit, flipped over, and was substantially damaged. Later the pilot told investigators that at about 200 to 300 feet he became dizzy and blacked out. Fortunately, the unconscious pilot was not injured. The NTSB found that he had lost consciousness due to *reactive hypoglycemia* compounded by his "improper dietary habits."

From these examples it should be obvious that it pays to practice good health habits and get regular, comprehensive physicals. Modern medical technology can spot many of the problems discussed *before* they occur. And as the examples show, the pilot is only kidding his or herself when attempting to beat the system.

Ethical Considerations

None of us enjoy admitting to physical infirmities. But when the lives of others are threatened, there is an ethical aspect involved. Some pilots erroneously believe that because they possess a current medical certificate they can "get away" with flying despite known physical problems. Yet §61.53, "Prohibition on Operations During Medical Deficiency," shows this is not the case. When you recognize a physical problem, you should consider yourself grounded until the problem is resolved. Another aspect involves taking medication or treatment that you suspect or know makes you ineligible to act as a flight crewmember. As the examples that follow will show, the risk of flying with a temporary medical problem could cost the lives of your best friend, your spouse, your children, or grandchildren—even innocent strangers on the ground.

An associated problem involves making false statements or omissions on your medical application. If false information is discovered, §67.403, "Medical Standards and Certification," allows the FAA to *suspend or revoke* "all airman, ground instructor, and medical certificates and ratings held by that person." In the early 1990s, a couple of student pilots in Florida were charged with falsifying their medical history and faced time in federal prison.

Equally important considerations are the airplane's and your own insurance policies. Typically such insurance is based on legal flight operations. Fly in violation of the regulations, such as an unairworthy airplane or when you're unqualified to hold a medical certificate, and both you and the airplane may be uninsured. The MU-300 accident described earlier which had an untrained copilot offers a classic example. The insurance company refused to pay for the loss.

A highly qualified 63 year-old ATP-rated pilot crashed during departure in a Piper Aerostar. When a line crewman told him of ice patches adhering to the left wing, the pilot waved him off and departed without deicing. Later investigation found horizontal stabilizer or elevator ice was a factor too. When he crashed on takeoff, the mishap was blamed on ice adhering to the airfoils. Weather at the time was 31°F with wet snow falling. Investigators found this pilot had also made false statements to obtain his first class medical certificate. Three prescription drugs were found in his briefcase: Valium, a tranquilizer, Reserpine, a drug used to treat high blood pressure, and EryTab, an antibiotic. All three were prescribed by the pilot's long-time AME.

Postmortem tests revealed a therapeutic level of Valium in the pilot's blood. This is one of a group of drugs known as benzodiazepines classed as *hypnotics* (or sedatives). A physician at FAA's CAMI said these drugs would affect a pilot's motor and mental performance.

Drowsiness, which may be accompanied by loss of muscular coordination and mental confusion, is a frequent side-effect. Amnesia too is a possibility. Thus the Board felt the pilot's judgment was impaired by illegal use of Valium.

For 23 years in a row, this pilot had also certified on his medical records he was free of eye problems, high blood pressure, or that he had taken any medication. In a letter to the Investigator-In-Charge (IIC), the AME explained that the antibiotic was for a severe pulmonary infection—pneumonia—which he had at the time of his latest first class physical examination. Yet the pilot's other medications were not noted on any of the pilot's FAA Medical Records.

For the past 20 years the AME, whose name appeared on all three prescriptions, had failed to note any abnormalities or disqualifying defects during the pilot's physicals. In describing the pilot's health history, the AME told investigators that his patient had experienced blurred vision in the left eye. Consequently, he was referred to the Johns Hopkins Medical Center, where a tumor was removed from the optic nerve. Yet this too had not been documented in the airman's medical records. In effect, this amounted to falsification under §67.403(a). And while the pilot was now dead, the AME was left holding the legal bag.

One final example involved a Beechcraft F33A Bonanza. The 36 year-old instrument-rated private pilot had no record of heart problems. However, his twin brother told investigators that while visiting in Reno some eight to ten years previously, the pilot "had some kind of heart issue." As a result, he had been told to avoid coffee and watch his cholesterol level.

One day, while departing VFR, the pilot told ATC, "I'm climbing ah now above the cloud layer, climbing through eleven thousand four hundred and the cloud layer seems to top at ten thousand." Later, after an in-flight weather briefing by Cedar City Flight Watch, the pilot responded, "okay, roger that, ah understand…"

During this eight second transmission the pilot was heard breathing heavily and forcefully. His rate of speech had slowed noticeably and investigators thought he sounded preoccupied or distracted. The mode C altitude readout then showed the aircraft transition from a shallow climb to a steep dive. Both the pilot and his passenger were killed in the subsequent crash.

Post mortem examination read, "Sections of coronary show severe sclerosis. The right artery shows over 60 percent occlusion. The left anterior descending branch shows over 90 percent occlusion as does the left circumflex branch." The pathologist reported compound fractures of both ankles, but no arm, wrist, hand, or finger injuries. The lack of hand injuries indicated he was not holding the control wheel and probably unconscious at impact.

Over-the-Counter Drugs

As noted already, flying while taking unauthorized drugs can prove fatal too—particularly when combined with fatigue. This is especially tempting with a common cold, and business reasons generate a compulsion to get going. A 23 year-old cargo pilot flying a Piper Saratoga reported for work at 2:00 AM and flew from Burbank, California, to Phoenix, Arizona. He managed about five hours sleep in the company apartment; then at 8:55 PM he departed on the return trip to Burbank.

After maintaining a constant airspeed, heading, and altitude for some time, at 10:30 PM he collided with a mountain that was 110 miles south of his usual course. Another company pilot found a new box of Dimetapp® decongestant with two tablets missing in the dead pilot's toiletries kit. He was inadequately rested, had a cold, and had taken unauthorized medication. While his effort to keep flying is commendable, he sealed his own fate by violating the rules.

Falsifying Medical Records

A heart-related incident involved a 57 year-old pilot who "intentionally omitted important medical history" on her medical certificate application. Investigators reported that she "had not complied with her physician's instructions regarding use of medication." The accident occurred when she blacked out while cruising near a lake in a Sea Ray amphibian. Rescuers found her experimental seaplane floating upside down in the water, but were fortunately able to get her out before she drowned.

A look at her medical records showed a 10-year history of *atrial fibrillation* (or, *arrhythmia*). The report stated the pilot's symptoms were consistent with transient ischemic attack, commonly called TIA, or mini-stroke. This involves blood clots that form during periods of atrial fibrillation, and are propelled to the brain when the heart resumes beating normally.

By acting as a pilot when you are aware of a medically disqualifying condition, you have intentionally violated §61.53. Disqualifying conditions include the common cold, which can be very debilitating. (If you've ever had an ear or sinus block during descent from altitude, you'll understand that statement.) In fact, as already discussed, merely taking medication, such as a decongestant, makes you ineligible to act as a flight crewmember.

Design Factors Leading to Pilot Error

Human engineering is the term used to describe design features and innovations meant to reduce *pilot error* accidents. Some years ago there was a major accident problem in general aviation involving the placement of the landing gear and flap switches by different manufacturers. To illustrate the problem, let's say the pilot of a Cessna or Piper twin is getting newly qualified in a Beechcraft twin. During touch-and-go landing practice, because of the different order or location of the flap switch and landing gear knob, the pilot inadvertently retracts the gear instead of the flaps.

The same problem involved the arrangement of the throttle, mixture, and propeller controls. Until they were standardized within the industry, you might sometimes attempt to adjust the prop pitch in a new aircraft, but because of a different arrangement of the throttles, props, and mixture levers, you would inadvertently get the mixture. As a result the engines would cough and sputter, or worse, shut down.

You may remember that country singer John Denver was killed because his newly purchased home-built had a non-standard fuel selector. Instead of being mounted on the floor between the pilot's legs, it had been mounted behind the pilot's head, making it almost impossible to reach while in flight. He ran out of fuel in one tank and stalled out trying to reach the badly misplaced fuel selector.

Summary

This chapter has covered some aspects of human factors that lead to aircraft accidents. Perhaps the most important factor covered is the necessity for ethical decisions regarding your personal health. For those of us who fly for hire, both an honest medical appraisal and the presence of exceptional stress in our lives can jeopardize innocent passengers. The FAA is overdue instituting the information processing tests that can detect a pilot's slow mental deterioration.

There is an old trite saying in aviation, that "flying consists of hours and hours of boredom, interrupted by moments of stark terror." But if that describes your flying experience, you're doing something wrong. By following good operational practices and abiding by the Federal Aviation Regulations and especially planning ahead to avoid compulsive decision making, there is no reason for you to ever experience those "moments of stark terror."

CHAPTER 10

Seaplane and Ski-plane Accidents

For those with an urge for outdoor adventure, a seaplane in summer or a ski-plane in winter is perhaps the ultimate vehicle. A floatplane allows you to reach that isolated lake where the fishing or hunting is exceptional. With skis attached, every snow covered field or frozen lake becomes a potential airfield. But, as the accident statistics show, with either pontoons or skis, there are unique and important safety considerations that must be observed.

Figure 10-1. Unloading a canoe from a C-185.

Seaplanes

Seaplane operations require a unique dimension to a pilot's knowledge-base because flying from water combines the skills of both boating and aviation. And while pontoons provide uncommon access to wilderness areas, because you are operating in a potentially hazardous off-airport environment, some on-the-job experience with a veteran of the lake country is recommended.

In some areas of the country, seaplanes can offer more safety advantages than found with wheel-equipped airplanes. For example, in our lake-dotted northern tier states and of course Canada and Alaska, or even in Florida's lake-country, if the engine fails there are almost unlimited places for an emergency landing. Or, if the weather deteriorates you can simply land on the nearest lake and await improving conditions. Run short on fuel because of un-forecast headwinds (or poor planning), and you simply land and call for assistance on your cell phone. Your alternative of course is to manually activate your personal locator beacon (PLB) or the ship's emergency locator transmitter (ELT).

Still, because of the potential for unplanned wilderness emergencies, our northern tier states along with Alaska and Canada require a basic survival kit, with several days food supply, insect repellent, and a tent and sleeping bags for the occupants. (A survival gun is no longer required, as your ELT or PLB provides emergency assistance or evacuation 24/7. Also, in Canada pistols are illegal and rifles may require registration.)

If you're really thinking ahead you'll wear your own customized survival vest, which includes a built-in personal floatation device (PFD), along with the basic necessities of shelter, fire-starting capability, and at least two means of signaling potential rescuers.

Of special importance is that all GA airplanes should have the 405 MHz ELT, that when activated manually provides your location via satellite to the Air Force Rescue Center. The older VHF/UHF models, which unfortunately are still legal, are no longer monitored and of very limited value.

An individual PLB is also strongly recommended. When the unit's 911 button is pressed it alerts the rescue center just the same as the aircraft's ELT. It provides rescuers with not only your location but with your registered unique identifying number (UIN). Your UIN includes personal data such as your next of kin, home telephone number, and basic medical information.

Taxiing

While this chapter is not meant to offer seaplane instruction, what follows includes some of the basics and a discussion of the more problematic safety areas. This includes taxiing, wind, and water surface conditions, along with takeoff and landing considerations.

As all seaplane-rated pilots know, there are three ways to taxi on the water: with the engine at idle power *in displacement*, wherein the float bottoms are fully wetted; *on-the-step*, at near takeoff speed; or in the *plow* position, halfway between the first two at near full power, with the nose reared-up. Meanwhile, to assist in taxiing, turning, or establishing and maintaining a desired track, the flight controls, sometimes even the cabin doors, are used in unique combinations.

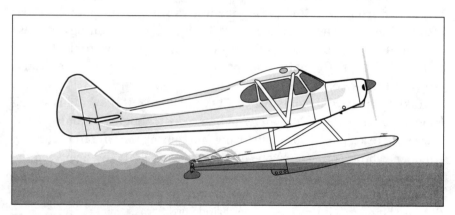

Figure 10-2. Plow taxiing.

The taxi technique you'll use in any given circumstance—whether departing or arriving, or simply repositioning the airplane—will be determined by the surface winds. With strong winds, in order to turn downwind and overcome the airplane's strong weather-cocking tendency, the plow position is used for short radius turns. It's unsuitable for long distances due to both engine heat buildup and propeller erosion from the rather significant water spray generated.

Harnessing The Wind

For seaplane operations, wind direction and velocity is especially important for several reasons—not just takeoff and landing. When taxiing on the water with a strong surface wind, the flight controls can be used to "sail" to a destination, using engine power, ailerons, elevators and rudder, sometimes even the doors to turn or maintain a heading or desired drift angle.

With strong surface winds the weather-cocking tendency of pontoon-equipped aircraft causes them to strongly resist turning downwind. In fact at some point the wind can become strong enough that the airplane simply will not turn downwind. Then you have two choices: (1) a high-speed *step turn*, or (2) you can simply sail backwards towards your destination with the engine idling, or in some cases with the engine shut down.

In flying seaplanes, rough water in strong winds is a major safety concern. With strong winds churning the water's surface, the pounding that results from bouncing across the waves during takeoff or landing can cause structural damage or failure of the engine mounts and forward float struts. In some relatively flat bottom amphibians, the rough surface can cause structural failure of the hull itself.

Taxiing crosswind can be especially challenging. If the wind is strong enough you may need a passenger out on a float, hanging onto the windward strut to keep the wing from lifting and causing the aircraft to capsize. An open cabin door also may be needed to act as a sail and help keep the nose pointed in the desired direction.

The point is, with a strong surface wind you must taxi prudently: Because being in a hurry can cause serious problems.

Rough Water

The rough water produced by strong surface winds is actually one of the seaplane pilot's most significant hazards. Water conditions are identified as being "rough" when the surface wind velocity reaches about 18 knots. And while the wind velocity provided by the FAA's Flight Service will not be available in remote areas, experienced seaplane pilots begin re-thinking their operations when the waves on the waters' surface are just beginning to whitecap. Flying from a river requires a special caution; if the wind direction is opposite the current flow, the wave pattern on the water's surface can be especially hazardous.

Because float planes lack built-in shock absorbers, the succession of bounces from wave to wave can cause structural failure of either or both the pontoon strut fittings and engine mounts. In addition, a churning, white-capped surface can conceal a variety of hazards, such as partially sunk soft drink cans, bottles, rocks, sand-bars, floating logs or lumber, even stumps. Hit any of these at high speed and you'll likely puncture a float.

If you are high speed taxiing on-the-step, a float puncture or pontoon leak will quickly flood the float compartments—like sticking a fire-hose inside. This is because with increasing speed, water pressure on the float bottoms increases significantly. Then shortly, the damaged float will begin sinking, leaving you vulnerable to capsizing.

If a noticeable list develops, it may be advisable to move all occupants onto the opposite pontoon to counterbalance the damaged float. Then hopefully it *may* be possible to *slowly* taxi to shore.

Glassy Water Hazard

Calm winds can also pose a unique hazard because the water's undisturbed mirror-like surface robs you of all depth perception; yet you will not realize it. This has caused more than one experienced pilot to come to grief by inadvertently flying into the mirror-like surface of a lake, bay or the ocean. You'll know that glassy water procedures are required when there is no surface wave pattern, or before taxiing, you can see the aircraft's reflection in the water.

In a heavily loaded airplane the glassy water may necessitate a wide, circular takeoff run on-the-step so you can hit your own wake and thus break the water's surface tension. Or, if the aircraft is slowly accelerating, to achieve takeoff speed more rapidly you can use a full roll input on the flight controls to lift a pontoon out of the water and thus reduce drag from the water's surface tension. While en route, you'll need to stay near the shoreline so that if the engine fails you'll have some way of judging the water's surface for a forced landing.

A glassy water landing is a carefully controlled, powered approach, holding a 150 to 200 fpm descent rate until touchdown occurs. Or, you can make a pass at tree-top height and drop out newspapers or spare inflated life vests, which you'll later retrieve. These floating objects will provide visual references on the mirror-calm surface. Otherwise you'll simply have no depth perception. (*See* §91.15 regarding dropped objects.)

My first encounter with the phenomenon was at age 19. With a private certificate and 16 hours in a float-equipped J-3 Cub, I had been working that summer between college semesters as lineman for Leithold's Seaplane Base on Lake Saganaga outside Ely, Minnesota. The experience was priceless—refueling the flight school's Cubs and Aeroncas, pumping the floats and loading 50-gallon drums of fuel-oil into the Noorduyn Norseman, and packing tourists' camping and fishing gear into the elderly but reliable Stinson SR-JR.

It was mid-September and the trees were ablaze with their fall colors. The flight was to be my last before returning to college. I was flying with my mentor and part owner of the operation, the late Jack Isaac (later Captain, Delta Airlines), who was showing me the duck concentrations on Basswood Lake, preparatory to their fall migration. At the time, the Superior-Quetico area of northeastern Minnesota and southern Ontario had not yet been designated a Wilderness Area.

We were flying over a finger of Basswood Lake where the ripening wild rice had attracted an awesome concentration of waterfowl. As I banked to watch the flocks taking off and landing, Jack said calmly, "John you're getting a bit low. Why don't you let me fly while you look at the ducks."

At the time I was trying to identify the species of a small flock in flight. But my concentration was broken when Jack took control, and upon looking up I was surprised to discover I had been watching their mirror-image reflected on the lake's surface, and was in fact, *very close* to the water. Close enough to have been startled by the discovery and to remember it all these years. Had I been alone, the flight would have become just another fatal accident statistic.

Floatplane Mishaps

Having discussed some of the basics, let's look at some floatplane accidents. The first case involves an Alaskan bush pilot flying a de Havilland Beaver (DHC-2). With four fishing lodge guests, he was caught by both a strong crosswind and river current at the confluence of the Alagnak and Kvichak rivers. The pilot told NTSB investigators that just as the aircraft got on the step he retracted the water rudder. (The water rudder remains down for a cross-wind departure, especially with a strong river current.) As the rudder retracted, the airplane veered sharply left into the wind and the pilot was unable to control it or get airborne before colliding with trees along the river bank.

In another rough water mishap, a Beaver pilot/fishing guide was departing a remote lake about two miles east of Iliamna, Alaska. While the wind velocity was not given in the accident report, the pilot told investigators that before departure he had noted two foot rolling swells. During the takeoff run, but before reaching liftoff speed, the airplane struck a large wave and became airborne prematurely—subsequently stalling, then hitting the water and tearing off the floats.

Downdrafts

Strong, gusty downdrafts during takeoff pose a threat too. Although we normally think of the downdraft problem occurring in mountainous terrain, it can happen when departing the smooth surface of a sheltered cove in rolling hill country. In this case, a Cessna 185 was departing a remote Alaskan lake with about 750 pounds of a hunting client's moose meat aboard. The lake, located about 18 miles southeast of Pilot Point, Alaska, is about 1,900 feet long and 800 feet wide. The pilot reported he lifted off about 300 feet from the end, but at about 50 AGL as he left the sheltered cove the aircraft encountered a strong downdraft, caused by a stiff wind blowing over the surrounding terrain. With the engine already at full power, there was nothing he could do but ride it into the soft marshy terrain, where it nosed over.

In yet another Alaskan mishap, the pilot of a de Havilland Beaver was landing in the choppy waters of Bell Island Narrows, about 34 miles north-northwest of Ketchikan. As he touched down, the floats struck what a passenger thought was probably a floating log. The pilot snatched the aircraft back into the air, but it stalled at about 75 feet, then plunged down steeply into the water. The passengers were okay, but the pilot was seriously injured.

Rough Water Landing

A rough water landing in a Lake Amphibian on Folsom Lake near Sacramento, California, resulted in structural failure of the amphibian's hull. It was a clear, sunny afternoon, but the surface winds were strong and gusty. A Forest Ranger stationed near the lake reported the winds were from the northwest at 10 to 20 knots, with gusts up to 30 knots. The swells, he said, were reaching one to two feet. While Folsom Lake's rolling-hill shoreline has many sheltered coves where smooth water could have been found, this pilot elected to land in the very middle of the turbulent lake. The amphibian's two passengers reported that the aircraft touched down, skipped twice, then nosed in and sank.

The pilot told investigators he made a normal landing, whereupon the aircraft settled, then nosed-over and sank. Because he saw light from a hole in the floor as they went down, he felt the aircraft had hit an obstruction. And this too is quite possible. When the wind is strong and the water is rough, Folsom Lake is plagued with floating debris. However, the pilot's story could not be verified as the airplane sank in 200 feet of water and was never recovered.

The Windward Turn

If you've had seaplane training you may remember that turning downwind is not usually dangerous because centrifugal force opposes the force of the wind. It's the turn *into* the wind that's a persistent cause of seaplanes capsizing. In fact it's one of the most perilous maneuvers in seaplane operations. This is why it's almost *always* done in displacement, at idle power. Here's why.

Pontoon-equipped airplanes typically have more fuselage side area exposed to the wind aft of the center of buoyancy. This is what gives them a strong weather-cocking tendency (some amphibians excepted). Thus, turning into the wind with *any* appreciable speed, e.g., a plow-taxi or step-turn, adds momentum to centrifugal force. At the apex of the turn, the lifting force of a crosswind under the upwind wing combines with centrifugal force and the weather-cocking momentum to lift the upwind wing. Consequently, the downwind wing digs the water and the aircraft capsizes.

Conversely, a downwind turn is not usually dangerous. In fact turning a float-plane downwind in a stiff breeze can necessitate a plow-turn

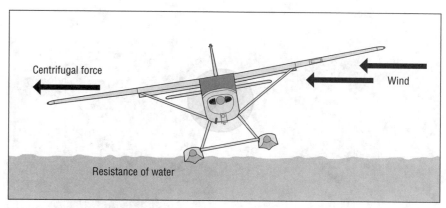

Figure 10-3. Windward turn.

to get it pointed in the right direction. Often, to keep it on a downwind track, you must step-taxi to keep it going on the desired downwind direction. However, when running downwind on-the-step, once you're ready to depart, you *must* decelerate to a slow taxi speed before turning into the wind. Then, with water-rudder retracted, it is standard procedure to simply sit in displacement, at idle power and let the airplane weathercock into the wind. This also provides the smallest radius of turn. The following mishap illustrates the potential problem.

Cessna 206

An accident occurred in Canada's northern Saskatchewan Province on Lake Athabaska, near the defunct Gunner Uranium mine. With a 15 to 20 knot breeze churning the water, the owner/pilot was taxiing downwind in his float-equipped Cessna 206. Although not on-the-step, he was described as clearly in a big hurry and taxiing much faster than normal displacement speed. Subsequently, with lots of power applied, he attempted a rapid plow-turn into the wind. Predictably, as the aircraft turned crosswind the relatively new aircraft promptly went bottoms-up.

In my first view of it, John Rodgers, owner of Great Shield Air, the local seaplane operation, was working in a wet-suit and scuba gear to get the airplane upright. It took a couple of days, but he soon had it flying again. Fortunately the owner/pilot survived uninjured, but it was an expensive way to learn a very basic lesson in seaplane flying: *you don't rush a windward turn.*

Figure 10-4. SCUBA diver John Rodgers evaluates the problem of salvaging a Cessna 206. The aircraft's owner just learned why you don't rush a turn into the wind.

Personal Flotation Device

When flying over water the mandatory wearing of a PFD is an FAA requirement only for passengers on commercial flights. But when private flying, it's just plain common sense. An NTSB investigator from Anchorage once told me that 90 percent of the state's seaplane fatalities resulted from drowning—simply because the occupants weren't wearing life vests. And typically, if PFDs are aboard the aircraft, they will be found oily and dirty in the baggage compartment, or perhaps still sealed in their original plastic bags in the aircraft's seatbacks or in the cargo compartment.

Some time back, while departing an Alaskan lake, I was one of three passengers when our float-equipped Beaver "water-looped" during a crosswind departure. Fortunately the aircraft was undamaged, but I noted afterwards that I was the only one wearing a PFD. In fact, despite my earlier suggestion, neither the pilot nor my two companions had chosen to wear theirs.

During the second departure everyone was now wearing their PFDs, but for some reason, they declined to hook-up the chest straps. Alas, they had not had the benefit of Air Force water survival training. I still remembered the instructor's demonstration, showing that with an unsecured harness, as the carbon dioxide cartridge rapidly inflated the bladders, the wearer was ejected from the straps.

Another instance involved a charter trip out of Kodiak, Alaska, with three of us hunters—once again in a float-equipped Beaver—headed for some deer hunting on Afognak Island. After getting airborne I noticed that no one was wearing their PFD. In addition, the required inflatable life vests were not in the seat-backs. Playing the devil's advocate, I asked our pilot for their location. (He was supposed to have pre-briefed his passengers on the wearing and use of the vest, along with several other items—such as how the doors and seatbelt buckles worked.) His response to my question was, "In the aft cargo compartment."

We were all professional pilots, so I guess he had felt a preflight briefing and the mandatory wearing of PFDs was unnecessary. But having anticipated this based on past experience, I was wearing my Sterns (CO_2) inflatable *survival vest*, which included the basic necessities plus a hand-held VHF survival radio. As for my friends, had we been forced to ditch in the cold waters of the Pacific Ocean, I could image the pandemonium and panic as they attempted to find and don their life vests—while upside down and submerged in 35° to 40°F water. (As mentioned in Chapter 5, the Coast Guard says that in 50 degree water the average person can hold his breath about 15 seconds—much less if it's colder.)

Missing Life Vests

A very sad tragedy occurred on a fishing trip in Alaska, when a complete lack of life vests or floatation devices (seat cushions) took the lives of a prominent Florida heart surgeon and his young son. The airplane was a float-equipped Cessna 206 used by a fishing lodge to service its clients. The lodge's pilot and a fishing guide had flown the pair to a coastal bay where the salmon were reportedly running. They had landed at high-tide and taxied up the confluence of a glacier-fed river.

After fishing for several hours, it began to get dark so they decided to leave. But by now the tide was out. While taxiing back to the expansive bay, apparently on-the-step with considerable speed, the floats went hard aground on a gravel bar. They quickly off-loaded the aircraft to lighten it and get it afloat again. Yet despite their best efforts the pontoons were solidly stuck. Consequently, they settled back to sit through the short Arctic night and await the next high tide.

Shortly before dawn, the tide crested and the airplane floated free. Without checking for damage or pumping the floats, the pilot awakened his passengers and started the engine, then taxied into the bay. It was still too dark to takeoff so the pilot began taxiing in circles while awaiting first light. After a while the airplane began listing to the right, and the pilot suddenly realized he had a major pontoon leak. In a desperate attempt to reach shoreline, he tried to plow-taxi at full power, but because of the increased water pressure on the float bottoms, this actually hastened the inevitable.

With a seaplane at rest, i.e., pontoons static in the water, the upward force of the water pressure on a float equals the weight of the water displaced by that float. But as speed increases, so too does the water pressure underneath. Under conditions of high power and in a plow attitude, even a relatively minor leak becomes a veritable high-pressure fountain. Consequently, with full power applied, the right float began to submerge and the Cessna 206 finally rolled inverted and began to sink.

In the cold pre-dawn blackness the occupants managed to evacuate the aircraft's cabin, then sat shivering atop the undamaged float. Unfortunately there was not a single life vest or floating seat cushion on board. To make matters worse, the tide had crested and was now going out.

Finally, as the airplane sank lower in the water, the doctor fashioned a rudimentary flotation device by inverting his hip boots. This trapped enough air to help keep the two of them afloat.

Figure 10-5. Using inverted hip boots as a rudimentary floatation device.

Complicating the problem, there were no boats or lights along the shore-line to give them a clue as to which way to swim toward land, nor offer any hope of assistance. Their world was just a very cold, wet, pitch-black void.

Finally, the pilot and fishing guide began swimming towards what they hoped was the shoreline. (Why the passengers didn't stay with the pilot and guide was not addressed in the accident report.) After a long and exhausting two hour struggle against the out-going tide—and despite the cold water temperature—somehow they managed to reach shore. They walked for over four hours before finding help.

The surgeon and his son were last seen holding onto their makeshift flotation device and slowly drifting out to sea. The NTSB report said that during rest periods, the pilot and guide reported hearing their clients' occasional plaintive cries of "help, help; somebody help!" But in the cold dark vastness of the expansive Alaska Bay there was no help available. Unfortunately, their bodies were never recovered.

There are several lessons in this senseless tragedy. First was the unspeakable negligence of the pilot and guide in not providing PFDs for each occupant and seeing that they wore them. Second, it is painfully obvious the pilot was lacking in knowledge and judgment. Like a boat's captain, being aware of the tides is a basic responsibility. It was the duty of both the pilot and guide to know of the hazards at low tide in the area. After all, they were being paid specifically for their skill, knowledge, and familiarity with the area. At the very least they should have departed with enough daylight to see the submerged hazards—in this case a large gravel bar.

Float punctures are common in wilderness operations, and smart pilots not only carry some minor repair capability, but also the required survival kit. Alaska State Law required a survival kit with specific items mandated for each occupant. Yet, in this case, the survival kit too was missing.

Had the pilot attempted to pump-out the floats before taxiing he would have discovered the leak in the right pontoon. Later investigation disclosed several punctures near the keel—which implies considerable speed when they went aground.

While enjoying the scenery, the fishing, the hunting, or maybe just the novelty of being many miles from the nearest human habitation, it is easy to get careless with the safety rules. Maybe it's over-familiarity, or the fact that nobody is watching. With everything going as planned, who needs all that survival gear? But when you need it, *you need it bad!*

Takeoff Technique

This case involved a stall/spin accident in an Air Force aero club's float-equipped Cessna 185. Piloted by a conscientious Army helicopter pilot, it was his first time to carry passengers in the airplane, and first time to make a heavy weight takeoff. With the airplane at near the maximum gross weight, he and three friends were departing for an afternoon of fishing. While his total fixed-wing time was only 55 hours—35 in the past year—the pilot had just that morning completed the club's mandatory five hours of flight training in the aircraft. This included his annual proficiency check flight. His instructors considered him a good pilot who obeyed the rules and did things by the book.

His training and checkride had consisted entirely of takeoffs and landings. There had been no instruction in stall-recovery, slow flight, or steep turns. Nor had he been required to experience a heavy-weight departure.

Normally, a float-plane pilot gets airborne at near stall speed, then remains in *water effect* (otherwise known as ground effect) while accelerating to climb speed; whereupon flaps are retracted incrementally. Then, once climb speed is established, engine power is reduced to the climb setting.

Unfortunately this pilot's instructor had taught him to liftoff at just above stall speed and climb steeply as in a maximum performance takeoff. Then, contrary to both the Cessna 185 POH and the aero club's operations manual, the instructor had him reduce engine power *prior to* beginning flap retraction.

With four people and fishing gear, combined with round-trip fuel, the airplane's gross weight was estimated at 3,220 pounds—about 100 pounds less than the maximum weight of 3,320 pounds and with an aft, but within limits, CG. They were departing in perfect weather from Six-Mile Lake near the Elmendorf Aero Club, with light winds to assist in the takeoff.

As the pilot taxied for takeoff, a pilot-friend in the right seat read him the checklist. With flaps set at 20 degrees and full power applied, the aircraft accelerated to around 55 knots then lifted off and began climbing. The pilot told investigators the aircraft surprised him by assuming a steeper than usual climb angle—likely the result of the aft tending CG.

He remembered lowering the nose somewhat, then reduced engine power to 25 inches manifold pressure, and began retracting the flaps. With a steep nose-up attitude and a heavy gross weight, either or both of these two actions—reducing engine power and retracting the flaps—increased the stall speed.

The pilot told investigators that the aircraft started to roll right, so he put in *left aileron* and the aircraft leveled for a second. Then it rolled left, and he applied *full right* aileron, and simultaneously re-applied full power. Adverse yaw from the fully downward-deflected left aileron then combined with P-Factor and engine torque to cause the aircraft to stall, then pitch nose-down to the left into a left-hand spin. It impacted Six-Mile Lake and was destroyed. Fortunately, none of the occupants were seriously injured.

Witness statements indicated the airplane stalled and recovered twice. But the pilot apparently failed to recognize the stall recovery. After all, he was a helicopter pilot and new to fixed-wing aircraft. All four occupants told investigators they did not hear the stall warning horn, which implies it was inoperative. Still, had he been properly trained, the Cessna 185's pre-stall buffet would have provided more than adequate stall warning. Investigators found that the pilot had been inadequately and inappropriately trained, which made the mishap inevitable.

Figure 10-6. Wreckage of Cessna 185 shows classic pattern of a spin to the left.

Ski-planes

For true outdoor freedom and adventure almost nothing compares to flying with skis. Handled with knowledge and good judgment, a ski-equipped airplane makes almost any snow-covered field or frozen lake an instant airfield. And while the FAA requires no special rating to fly with skis, the pilot who values his struts will get a thorough checkout with a knowledgeable instructor. Because, as with seaplanes, you are operating in an off-airport environment with all the attendant risks. And too, with American-made skis, you are working without brakes. (Russian-made skis for their bi-wing AN-2 single-engine aircraft have ingeniously designed hydraulically activated carbide-steel claws which function as brakes. When the pilot applies brakes, the claws extend underneath the ski to grip at the ice or snow and bring the airplane to a stop.)

For every departure and landing a ski-plane pilot must consider a number of relevant factors. On a slick ice or crusted-snow covered surface, the lack of any braking capability makes the wind an especially important consideration. Like a floatplane, an airplane on skis wants to weather-cock into the wind, and the effect is more pronounced with tricycle landing

Figure 10-7. Bellanca Scout ski-plane.

gear. This is because more fuselage side area is exposed to the wind aft of the center of rotation (the main landing gear). In addition, because there's no surface traction, a stiff crosswind can push the aircraft along sideways, especially on glaze ice, such as the surface of a frozen lake. Consequently, turns during taxi and when ready to stop must be thoughtfully planned and timed.

Taxiing cocked into the wind in a skid, or drifting sideways in a turn is normal on skis. Therefore your track must be carefully preplanned in order to miss obstructions, drifts, snow ridges, and perhaps other parked airplanes. It's quite awkward at first, and always requires lots of maneuvering room. In fact, just as with seaplanes, you'll frequently use the flight controls to sail.

Snow Conditions

As a general rule, lacking brakes on ice and crusted snow, you must taxi as slow as possible to remain under control. Following a long taxi, you don't stop for any length of time. Otherwise the bottoms of your skis, heated by friction against the snow, will cool and quickly freeze you in place.

Conversely, on deep, loose snow you'll need to step-taxi, keeping the taxi-speed just shy of takeoff. Otherwise, the airplane will sink down into the soft powder and stop moving.

Figure 10-8. Following a long taxi, don't stop for any length of time or the skis, heated by friction with the snow, will cool and freeze you in place. Otherwise park skis on pine boughs or burlap bags.

Landing On Ice

Frozen lakes offer excellent landing sites for ski-planes. However, as a few pilots discover each year, just because it's 0° to 15°F doesn't mean that every frozen surface is suitable. If not covered with snow, the color of the ice is important. For example, blue ice is usually quite thick. White ice is nearly always thin, especially on fast-flowing rivers. Muskeg lakes are often loaded with gas-producing vegetation. Thus they are inevitably covered with thin ice. On large lakes, if the ice appears cloudy or milky, it may have air pockets caused by trapped air or gas within the ice. Dark patches of ice indicate water near the surface.

River ice is not dependable because ice thickness varies. This is due to a variety of factors, such as river depth and water velocity, the existence of warm currents, along with local temperature variations. In addition, because of ice movement, the surface of river ice can be extremely rough.

Ice Thickness Check

Before committing to a full stop landing on snow-covered ice, the wise ski-plane pilot will touch down and remain at near takeoff speed and slide for a couple hundred yards: then go-around and return to check for discoloration in the ski-tracks. If the tracks turn dark, that indicates water beneath the snow and probably thin ice.

Figure 10-9 shows the result of a Cessna 185 pilot who broke through the ice. He obviously ignored evidence of thin ice, since there was a clearly visible large area of surface-slush indicated that melting was in progress, and broke through the ice.

Figure 10-9. With large patches of melting snow showing, the pilot of this Cessna 185 chose to ignore clear evidence of thin ice.

Cessna 185 Accident

Near Cripple, Alaska, a ski-equipped Cessna 185 was landing on a slough. (Cripple is approximately 42 miles on the 310-degree radial of the McGrath VOR.) The charter pilot was unable to find the usual landing area due to a fresh snowfall. Consequently he decided to land on the icy surface of the frozen slough.

The aircraft was equipped with *wheel-skis*. The pilot stated that he had the wheels protruding through the bottom of the skis because there was no snow cover on the frozen slough. This was a standard procedure used to provide some braking friction and thus shorten the landing slide.

The surface winds were not given in the NTSB's report, but apparently they were light. The airplane touched down hard and bounced and the pilot discovered there was no traction at all. He was unable to get stopped; and the aircraft was damaged when it slid into some scrub spruce trees at the end of the slough.

The Cessna 185 POH says that, "Under the most favorable conditions of smooth packed snow, at temperatures of approximately 0°C (32°F), the ski-plane landing distance is approximately 20 percent greater than that shown for the land plane." No mention is made of landing on ice. But we can logically assume that traction is virtually nil, and that the accident-pilot reported it as such. Thus, a headwind and aerodynamic drag from the fully extended flaps were this pilot's only means of decelerating. But the aerodynamic drag proved inadequate for getting stopped.

Crosswinds

Because of the slick surfaces from which ski-planes operate, a crosswind is especially hazardous. With little or no traction, the aircraft may be *crabbing* from the start of takeoff slide until liftoff.

Crosswinds were involved in a Cessna 185 mishap that occurred on a remote frozen Alaskan lake. The pilot told the NTSB Investigator that the sky was clear with 60 miles visibility. The temperature was 20°F, with the winds from 270 degrees at 10 knots gusting to 20 knots. Equipped with wheel-skis, she was landing to the north with a direct crosswind.

The Cessna 185 POH states, "Maximum demonstrated crosswind velocity is 15 knots," but as noted several times previously, it's not a limitation. Still, this figure is based on a wheel-equipped airplane with new tires, on a dry, paved runway. And while the demonstrated crosswind may not be an FAA-mandated limitation, the GA pilot has nothing better to gauge at what crosswind velocity the aircraft runs out of control authority. Thus, with a crosswind gusting to 20 knots, her attempt to land was a very bad gamble.

The NTSB report shows she was landing with the skis deployed—i.e., wheels fully retracted. During the slide-out she noticed, "the wind was stronger than anticipated, and the ground speed was faster than anticipated." This implies she landed with a quartering tailwind. During the landing slide a gust lifted the left wing and the airplane began to ground-loop. The tail swung around, and the right wing hit a snow bank. The airplane came to a stop with major damage to the right wing spar, right horizontal stabilizer, and the right side of the fuselage.

In another case, a Cessna 185 was landing at Fairbanks International on the airport's 3,978-foot ski strip 19. Once again there was a crosswind. The pilot said the wind was from 130 degrees at 11 knots with gusts to 22 knots. While this is only a 60-degree crosswind, the effective crosswind component was 18 knots, which exceeds the Cessna POH demonstrated crosswind of 15 knots. The airplane ground-looped to the left and the right ski broke off, then hit a snow berm on the side of the runway and nosed over. Once again, that demonstrated crosswind may not be legally limit-ing, but *you don't know* where the aerodynamic controllability ends. The manufacturers and insurance companies certainly do!

Ski Precautions

In some ways, landing with skis may seem easier than with wheels. In fact, when the snow melts you may find your wheel landing technique a bit sloppy. Still, for off-airport work, certain precautions are necessary. First, under very bright conditions quality sunglasses are an absolute necessity, otherwise you may lose depth perception and inadvertently fly into the snow-covered surface. Extreme brightness and snow powder can hide a multitude of hazards. For an open field landing, brush, small trees, stumps, or other such obstructions may be hidden by a blanket of snow. And a drift-covered fence can ruin your whole day.

Thus, when evaluating a prospective landing area, like a flight of mallards checking out a decoy set, several passes will be necessary. As described earlier, when landing on a frozen lake or river's surface, checking snow depth is the first order of business.

Whiteout

Whiteout is a phenomenon that occurs when a dense cloud layer overlies a snow or ice covered surface. This diffuses the light-rays so that they strike the snow from many angles. The diffused light reflects back and forth countless times between the snow and the cloud, thus eliminating the hori-zon and all shadows. Buildings, people, and dark-colored objects appear to float in the air. The result is a complete loss of spatial orientation.

As mentioned earlier, bright sun and an expansive snow-field will also precipitate loss of depth perception. Cautious Alaskan and Canadian bush pilots sometimes carry spruce or pine boughs to toss out and mark the snow for landing. At many northern airports, both spruce and/or pine boughs, along with spray paint, are used to mark snow-banks and runway thresholds and edges. This is needed for safe taxiing and for runway ori-entation during either bright sun or whiteout conditions.

A whiteout, or the extreme glare can blind you in a heartbeat, which is the reason good sunglasses are mandatory when flying from snow. In fact, a spare pair should be available in your survival kit too. A lost or broken

Figure 10-10. Canadian Twin Otter pilot John Rodgers demonstrates the problem of whiteout conditions in otherwise VFR weather.

pair of sunglasses can be very serious—even on a cloudy day. The following are some examples of whiteout accidents.

The date was May 1, 2000. A pilot had departed Kivalina, Alaska, at 5:30 AM in a ski-equipped Super Cub. The weather was down, with a 100-foot ceiling, light winds, and five miles visibility in mist. Despite the low ceiling, by Alaskan standards the five-miles visibility made the flight sound reasonable. But the combination of low ceiling combined with precipitation was the clue to possible white-out conditions.

En route to Kotzebue, the Super Cub pilot apparently encountered whiteout conditions. He was killed when he crashed in the snow-covered terrain, 33.5 miles west-northwest of his departure point. Villagers near the crash site reported a low ceiling with scattered snow showers in the area. Without a horizon to remain visually oriented, he had become spatially disoriented and crashed inverted about one mile east of the coastline.

Because he had not filed a VFR flight plan, the wreckage wasn't discovered until late in the day. Villagers traveling on snow machines found it along the coast near Cape Krusentern.

Another example involved a Cessna 207 on an air-taxi cargo flight. Once again, the aircraft departed with the weather less-than-VFR. It was foggy, with a light snow falling, and with lighting conditions reported as *flat*—no distinct horizon over the ice and snow covered terrain. The visibility of two to three miles reported at the remote, uncontrolled departure airport was ideal for whiteout conditions.

After takeoff the aircraft was seen to climb to about 500 feet and begin a turn to the right. Shortly thereafter, the bank angle increased to 90 degrees, and the airplane dived into the ground. The NTSB found the cause as spatial disorientation, due to the "lack of a distinct horizon over ice/snow covered terrain."

Conclusions

There are numerous other accidents in the NTSB files, but they are essentially carbon-copies of those just described. The point to remember is that you can have a report of five miles forward visibility, but that doesn't mean it's actually safe to fly using visual references, i.e., VFR. You simply must be proficient in flying by reference to the flight instruments and recovery from episodes of spatial disorientation—unusual attitudes.

As the accidents described again clearly show, the air, like the sea, is terribly unforgiving of inadequate knowledge and training, a compulsive nature, and poor judgment.

CHAPTER 11

Flying After Scuba Diving

It was late morning at Treasure Cay in the Bahamas when the happy bunch of scuba divers boarded the Sabreliner-80 Corporate Jet I was flying. In fact they were still wet from their morning outing and casually tossed their bulky equipment—masks, air tanks, and buoyancy control devices (diving vests)—into the forward baggage area. Although I was not yet a trained scuba diver, something seemed wrong. I vaguely recalled reading in the AIM about a required surface interval between diving and flying to prevent the *bends*—technically known as *decompression sickness* (DCS). Twenty-four hours came to mind. Or was that the alcohol rule? I simply couldn't remember. Complicating the problem was that the leader of this spirited pack of collegians was both their father and the aircraft owner. And his wet hair showed that he too had been diving that morning.

Normally the flight would have been conducted at 35,000 feet or higher to minimize fuel consumption and maximize true airspeed. But if we flew at high altitude directly to our destination of Columbia, South Carolina, the ship's cabin pressure would be 8,000 feet, and according to an Air Force physiological training course I had attended some years earlier, it's the first 8,000 feet of pressure change that's most hazardous.

To avoid the long, high altitude trip to South Carolina, I used the requirement to clear customs as an excuse to land first at Fort Lauderdale, Florida. Then, to keep from spoiling the happy occasion and yet try to protect them from their ignorance, and possibly my own, I set the ship's pressurization schedule at sea level. At this setting we could climb as high as 21,000 feet where the maximum 8.2 psi pressure differential would be reached without experiencing a cabin pressure change. This lower cruise altitude would prevent an unpopular delay and resolve any doubt in my mind as to the flight's safety. I was aware of the danger to my passengers of a sudden cabin pressurization failure. But the aircraft was in good mechanical shape, and under the circumstances, the risk seemed worth taking.

Later, I found a remote section of the AIM that included a couple of short paragraphs entitled, "Decompression Sickness After SCUBA Diving," (8-1-2, (d)). It recommends that after a dive not requiring a controlled ascent (non-decompression dive), the diver wait 12 hours before flying. For a dive that requires a decompression stop on the way back to the surface (decompression diving), the diver should allow a 24-hour wait before flying.

Figure 11-1. A diver surveys aircraft wreckage. (Photo ©2000, courtesy of Alese and Morton Pechter)

DCS Case Histories

One of the earliest recorded episodes of DCS involved an airline crew of a Boeing 727 on a layover in the Bahamas. All three cockpit crewmembers spent the day scuba diving, but no deeper than 30 feet. Less than four hours later, they departed as scheduled, flying with a typical cabin pressure altitude of 8,000 feet. Ironically, all three developed bends, with the captain and first officer becoming totally incapacitated. Fortunately, the flight engineer's symptoms were delayed 12 hours and he managed to land the airplane unassisted.

Two other cases required treatment in a hyperbaric chamber. The first involved a young woman, who during an outing completed two 32-foot dives. On her first dive she had a bottom time of 45 minutes. (*Bottom time* begins at the time of descent and ends at the time of direct assent to the surface.) After a surface interval of one hour, she returned to the 32-foot sea bed for another 45 minutes. Five hours later she flew home in a cabin pressurized to 8,000 feet—whereupon she promptly developed DCS.

The second case involved a pilot who dived to 80 feet. His bottom time was 35 minutes. He had apparently not studied the PADI Divers Manual, because four hours later he headed home in an un-pressurized airplane at 5,000 feet. In short order he developed the bends, with numbness and pain in one hand.

Most cases of DCS occur within 24 hours of surfacing from a dive. Yet occasionally, especially when flying is involved, there are cases where the DCS symptoms appear after a much longer interval. An example involved

Figure 11-2. A diver's *bottom time* is measured from the time of descent until the time of direct ascent to the surface.

a 30 year-old man who had been vacationing in Hawaii and spent two days diving. The first day he accomplished four dives, which included one evening and one night dive. The next morning, after a surface interval of 12 hours, he dived to 80 feet for 25 minutes. Then, after an hour and a half on the surface, he dived to 60 feet for 35 minutes.

Approximately 30 hours later, he flew back to the U.S. mainland. The following morning he awoke feeling somewhat fatigued and "with general soreness and aches and pain in his shoulders and elbows." Then he flew home at 5,000 feet in an un-pressurized private airplane. Five days after returning home, and six days after onset of symptoms, he consulted a physician. Subsequently, he required two treatments in a hyperbaric chamber before the symptoms were totally resolved.

A fatal case involving an *air embolism*, occurred when the diver remained underwater too long and ran out of air. This forced him into an *emergency swimming ascent*. But on the way up he committed the unpardonable sin of holding his breath. As the water pressure rapidly diminished, the air held in his lungs expanded enough to rupture a lung, and upon surfacing he became very ill.

Friends arranged air transportation in a pressurized aircraft to a hyperbaric chamber. Unfortunately, they failed to consider that at optimum cruise altitude the pressurized aircraft maintained a cabin altitude of 8,000 feet. And alas, as mentioned earlier, it's the first 5,000 to 8,000 feet that are the most critical. As a result, the patient died in flight.

DCS Background

DCS was first identified about 135 years ago when French tunnel workers, who breathed compressed air for long periods, began surfacing bent over in pain. Hence the illness became known as the bends. Subsequently, scientists theorized that excess nitrogen, absorbed by the workers' tissue in the depths, was coming out of solution and forming bubbles as they returned to the reduced atmospheric pressure on the surface. The small nitrogen bubbles then pressed on surrounding tissue and blocked blood vessels. This resulted in various levels of pain, or in some more serious cases affected the brain and nervous system.

The air we breathe consists of 79% nitrogen, 20% oxygen, and 1% other gases. During a dive, our body tissue absorbs nitrogen from the air we are breathing in proportion to the surrounding pressure. Time at depth is also a major factor in how much a person absorbs. As long as the diver remains under pressure, the absorbed nitrogen poses no problem. But if the surrounding pressure is reduced too quickly—as when rapidly returning to the surface—the nitrogen comes out of solution and forms bubbles which block the blood flow to certain tissues.

Decompression illness (DCI) is the medical term used to describe the physical problems that most people know as the bends. Yet in reality, DCI encompasses several manifestations, some of which are *very* dangerous.

In an article provided by the Divers Alert Network (DAN), Dr. E.D. Thalmann, DAN Assistant Medical Director, explains that DCI actually encompasses two diseases, DCS and arterial gas embolism (AGE). DCS results from nitrogen bubbles forming and enlarging as the surrounding water pressure is reduced. This causes pain and potentially tissue or nerve damage.

Dr. Thalmann describes AGE as the result of nitrogen bubbles "entering the lung circulation, traveling through the arteries and causing tissue damage at a distance by blocking blood flow at the small vessel level." This is potentially life-threatening. DCS and AGE comprise what is identified as DCI.

DAN reports that each year approximately 1,000 scuba divers experience some form of DCI. The known risk factors include long, deep dives, cold water, and rapid assents. Other factors thought to influence the onset of DCI, but not considered conclusive, include obesity, dehydration, pulmonary disease, or hard exercise immediately after surfacing. Rapid assents are closely linked to cases of AGE.

Dr. Thalmann warns that DCI is most common when the diver has violated the diving table limits, but it can also occur when the guidelines have been followed. The illness can be explained by Henry's Law, which states that the amount of gas that will dissolve in a solution (body fluids) and remains in solution, is directly related to the pressure of the gas (atmospheric or water pressure) surrounding that solution.

DCS evolves from the *rate* at which the human body adjusts to the changing ambient pressures around it. For example, to keep the partial pressure of nitrogen consistent with the surrounding pressure, blood is classed as a *fast phase tissue*. After it cycles through our body, it expels nitrogen rapidly into the lungs' alveoli where it is exhaled as we breathe. Muscle is classed as a *medium phase tissue*, which expels nitrogen moderately fast. Body fat is a *slow phase tissue,* which releases nitrogen slowly.

There are several forms of DCS, which is known primarily for the joint pain it produces. But it can also include lung problems (*the chokes*), central nervous system disturbances, and skin manifestations called *paresthesia*.

AGE—normally called *air embolism*—can occur if the diver holds his or her breath during ascent. As the water pressure diminishes, the expanding air pressure escapes from the alveoli directly into the pulmonary veins and the bubbles migrate throughout the arterial system.

The bends normally involves pain in the larger bony joints, such as shoulders, elbows, knees, and ankles, and may begin as a deep, dull pain. When the pain is first noted, an attempt to "work it out" by exercising will make it worse. Over time the pain may spread and involve the muscles. In a severe case the pain may become so unbearable that movement in the affected joint is impossible.

The chokes result from nitrogen bubbles in the smaller blood vessels of the lungs—usually around the alveolar capillaries. This involves a deep sharp pain, centrally located under the breastbone, combined with a dry progressive cough. Expansion of the lungs during ascent increases the pain and decreases the victim's ability to breathe.

Central nervous system disturbances involve the brain and spinal cord. Reportedly, no particular pattern is identifiable from case to case, but the most common symptoms are visual or vocal disturbances, dull and persistent headache, vertigo, and loss of orientation. Spinal cord injuries can be temporary or permanent, leaving the victim paralyzed.

Symptoms of paresthesia, which means literally "perverted sensations," include peculiar sensations such as *the creeps*, or tingling itchy spots on the skin. It can even cause a mottled, reddish or purplish rash to develop. This is due to very small subcutaneous gas bubbles which stimulate the many nerve receptors.

The earlier example of a fatal air embolism by the diver who held his breath during an emergency swimming assent ascent provides a classic example of AGE. By holding your breath as you rise to the surface the water pressure diminishes rapidly and the retained air in the lungs expands to the point of precipitating AGE; or as in the case described, a ruptured lung—called *pulmonary barotrauma*.

If air escapes from the alveoli directly into the pulmonary veins, the bubbles will find their way into the heart. From the heart they travel up to the carotid arteries in the neck and find their way into the small arteries and capillaries of the brain. Eventually the air bubbles get stuck in the small arteries and capillaries and plug the blood supply to brain tissue. This leads to unconsciousness and death.

Another hazard from an air embolism is *mediastinal emphysema*. In this case air from the alveoli escapes into the mediastinum—the space between the lungs near the heart—then travels up alongside the windpipe. The air pressure against the heart results in mediastinal emphysema, which causes chest pain, breathing difficulties, and faintness. Obviously, any additional reduction in ambient pressure by flying would be critical.

Subcutaneous emphysema also causes breathing difficulties as well as swelling and voice changes. This is due to the air bubbles that have traveled from the mediastinum area, along the windpipe and under the skin into the neck and upper chest region. There can even be swelling under the skin around the neck.

Pneumothorax refers to a rare but serious medical condition, wherein air that escaped from the alveoli gets into the pleural lining—the moist membrane between the lungs and ribcage. Expanding air in the plural space can not only collapse a lung, but also affect the heart and circulation. Symptoms include chest pain and breathing difficulties.

Dr. Thalmann's article specifies that when flying an AGE victim to a medical facility in an unpressurized helicopter or airplane, the cabin altitude must not exceed 800 feet (244 meters). Anything higher could be a ticket to sudden death.

Safety Considerations

Incidents of DCI don't happen often, but when they do both time and knowledge are critically important. Basically there are three things that every diver or aircrew member must know:

- First aid treatment for a diver with symptoms of DCI is 100% oxygen, while concurrently treating the victim for shock.
- Call the Diver Alert network for help. Not just any physician or hospital will know what to do. The phone number is 1-919-684-9111—call collect if necessary. Their web address is www.diversalertnetwork.org.
- When transporting a "bent" patient by air, make certain the pilot is aware of the passenger's problem and plans a cruise altitude that will keep the cabin pressure altitude at sea level.

Administering 100% oxygen accelerates the *denitrogenation* process and helps decrease the potential for permanent damage. Most corporate jets and turboprop airplanes have a portable emergency oxygen bottle which will provide for the victim's immediate needs. Some airplanes have an emergency medical mask in the cabin that works from the ship's oxygen system. Both the Super King Air 200 and KA300 have a first aid oxygen mask stowed in an overhead container in the toilet compartment. It must be manually opened, then the ON/OFF valve selected ON. In the cockpit, the ship's oxygen control system must also be ON.

The early oxygen first aid can sometimes reduce symptoms of DCI substantially, but they may reappear later, with the otherwise reversible damage becoming permanent. Consequently, even though the symptoms may seem resolved, it's important to always contact DAN and speak with the on-duty dive-qualified physician for additional first aid advice and for the location of the closest *available and operational* recompression chamber. Remember too, the new world-wide DAN emergency number is 1-919-684-9111.

With headquarters in Durham, North Carolina, DAN is a non-profit organization, which exists solely to provide expert medical information for diving related problems, and is available 24 hours a day, seven days a week. Either the diver or the attending physician can speak with a dive-qualified physician for advice on treatment. DAN maintains a continuous up-to-date status of all recompression chambers and will assign the nearest one based on its availability and operational status.

For a bent patient, air transportation to a recompression chamber is almost always required. But of utmost importance for the victim's survival is the aircraft's pressurization system—or the lack thereof. Except for a helicopter, which can stay at 800 feet or less over the surface while transporting the patient to a hyperbaric chamber—assuming one is nearby—you simply don't fly a patient with symptoms of DCI in an unpressurized airplane. Two popular bush planes in worldwide use are the Cessna Caravan and Quest Kodiak. But both are unpressurized and therefore unsuitable for transporting a bent patient. And too, as the previous accidents emphasized, for divers returning home without observing the recommended time delay interval between diving and flying, an unpressurized cabin will likely precipitate DCI.

It's important, too, that the pilot flying a bent patient is familiar with the aircraft's cabin pressurization capability. Sometimes the pilot may not really know the system thoroughly; you should refer to the POH or AFM, which is located in the aircraft, and check on the ship's pressurization schedule.

Aircraft with pressurized cabins are not all alike, and their differences can be very important. As mentioned earlier, a typical airliner flying at cruise altitude will likely have an 8,000- to 9,000-foot cabin pressure at altitude. Many pressurized single-engine aircraft, cabin class twins, corporate jets, and turboprop aircraft can maintain a sea level cabin to a reasonable cruise altitude. But you have to be certain the pilot realizes the seriousness of the bent patient's problem.

The popular Beechcraft King Air 200 can maintain a sea level cabin to 17,000 feet. Many corporate jets can cruise as high as 21,000 feet (FL210) to 26,000 feet (FL260) while maintaining a sea level cabin. However, landing at an airport with a higher elevation could be dangerous to the patient, so clear this with the DAN physician prior to departure.

As for pressurized light aircraft, the single-engine Cessna P210N will hold a sea level cabin up to an altitude of 7,000 feet. But because the aircraft usually cruises at a much higher altitude, the pilot must be aware of the patient's problem, since anything higher would seriously jeopardize the patient's life.

| Cabin Altitude vs. Airplane Altitude with 3.35 PSI Differential ||
Airplane Altitude in Feet	Cabin Altitude in Feet
7,000	Sea level
8,000	800
10,000	2,400
12,000	4,000
14,000	5,500
16,000	7,000
18,000	8,500
20,000	10,000
23,000	12,100

Figure 11-3. Cessna P210 pressurization schedule.

Pilots of either a twin-engine Cessna 414 or Cessna 421 departing and arriving at a sea level airport—like from the Bahamas to an airport in Florida—can select "sea level" on the cabin altitude selector and the cabin will remain at sea level up to a tolerable cruise altitude of 11,000 feet.

Airplane Altitude in Feet	Cabin Altitude in Feet
Sea level to 11,060	Sea level
13,910	2,000
16,850	4,000
19,920	6,000
23,120	8,000
26,500	10,000
30,000	11,950

Figure 11-4. C-414A pressurization schedule.

Conversely, the pressurization system on the twin-engine Cessna 340A doesn't begin pressurizing *until reaching 8,000 feet.* Then it maintains an 8,000 foot cabin to 20,100 feet MSL. This system would obviously jeopardize the bent patient's life.

Airplane Altitude in Feet	Cabin Altitude in Feet
Sea level to 8,000	Same as airplane altitude
8,000 to 20,100	8,000
23,500	10,200
26,300	12,000
28,000	13,000
30,000	14,200

Figure 11-5. C-340A pressurization schedule.

One word of caution to the novice diver/pilot who may be planning to dive but is unable to locate clean, uncontaminated air for his or her air tank: compressed air that tastes or smells odd should be considered as contaminated. Worse yet, the deeper you dive the more toxic it becomes. Of special importance is that if clean compressed air is not available, don't be tempted to fill your air tank with aviation oxygen, because when used underwater in scuba diving, oxygen can be dangerous.

In your high altitude physiology training you learned about denitroge-nating for 30 minutes before an unpressurized flight, to prevent high alti-tude DCS. But in scuba diving some things are just the opposite. Because breathing pure oxygen underwater can be deadly. For example, at 33 feet (two atmospheres) oxygen poisoning can occur. Symptoms include mus-cular twitching, nausea, vision and hearing problems, difficulty breathing, anxiety, confusion, unusual fatigue, and clumsiness. Yet, after completing a dive and back on the surface, breathing pure oxygen *will help* denitroge-nate a bent victim.

Studies by Richard D. Vann, Ph.D., Director of Research at Duke Uni-versity Medical Center, show that the AIM time intervals before flying may be too risky. Based on his tests, Dr. Vann recommends a preflight interval of at least 13 hours following a single non-decompression stop dive. For repetitive non-stop dives he recommends a 17-hour wait.

Summary

Several aspects of diving are exactly opposite to what a pilot learns about high-altitude physiology. For example, holding your breath at altitude is no problem, although not recommended. Conversely, when scuba diving, holding your breath while returning to the surface—especially during an emergency swimming ascent—can rupture a lung or make you vulnerable to a deadly air embolism.

When flying, you can denitrogenate before climbing to altitude unpres-surized by breathing pure oxygen for 30 minutes before departure. This lowers your body's partial pressure of nitrogen and helps prevent DCS at high altitude. But pure oxygen used when scuba diving becomes toxic in water as shallow as two atmospheres, or 33 feet.

Remember that your bottom time after diving is a *very* important con-sideration. After an hour of breathing compressed air at a depth of 60 feet, the nitrogen partial pressure in your body effectively doubles. During ascent to the surface you'll lose some of it, but only time at sea level will allow your system to totally expel the excess nitrogen. As mentioned ear-lier, this is where breathing pure oxygen helps expidite the process.

After non-decompression diving, the AIM recommends a 12-hour pre-flight interval before flying at flight altitudes up to 8,000 feet. However, for a single, non-decompression stop dive, Dr. Vann recommends a 13-hour wait, and for repetitive non-decompression stop dives he recommends a surface interval of 17 hours. After a dive requiring a *controlled ascent* (decompression stops), your pre-flight interval should be at least 24 hours.

Remember too, that when flying a bent diver with any type of DCI to a recompression chamber, the airplane's pressurization schedule is a critical consideration. Most can be programmed to maintain a sea level cabin pressure, even though fuel consumption will be increased at the lower cruise altitude. Keep in mind that some utility airplanes are unpressurized and a few have pressurization systems not suitable for transporting scuba divers or a bent patient.

One final point of emphasis: when anyone experiences DCI, contact a qualified dive-doctor. The location of the nearest operational and available recompression chamber is critical. This information is readily available 24/7 from the DAN. Their *worldwide emergency number* is 1-919-684-9111 (call collect if necessary); their web address is www.diversalertnetwork. org. The pilot carrying a bent patient should use the call-sign "Lifeguard" before the N-number so ATC will give the flight priority handling.

Both scuba diving and flying offer us interesting and challenging adventures. But remember that both undertakings can be terribly unforgiving of ignorance or carelessness.

CHAPTER 12

The Last Word in Safety

After taking a close look at GA accidents it should be evident that flight instructors, FAA inspectors, designated pilot examiners (DPE), and aero medical examiners (AME) have a major influence in accident prevention. The quality and depth of training and the thoroughness of the subsequent licensing flight check constitute the foundation of a pilot's flying career. The quality of your medical examination also represents part of that basic foundation. Get shortchanged in any area and it's the new pilot who ultimately pays the price. To further emphasize the point, the following are some additional examples.

The first involved a young pilot who was a high school senior and scheduled to graduate in the spring. Just the day before he had received his private pilot certificate at the small grass airport at Papillion, Nebraska, very near Omaha. It was about 11:00 AM when he attempted to depart with his mother and sister aboard the rented Grumman AA-5 Tiger. It was his first flight with passengers and first time to make a heavy-weight takeoff in the aircraft.

The grass runway was covered with about an inch and a half of wet, melting snow and the sod underneath was now soft. Still, he had become accustomed to the snow during his training, so a soft-field takeoff was not new to him. But it was late February, and in addition to the extra passenger weight, the ambient temperature had warmed up to an unseasonable 35°F instead of the usual 0° to -10°F to which he was accustomed.

He lined up for takeoff and at full power the aircraft rolled sluggishly down the sodden 3,000 foot grass airstrip. But on this occasion the aircraft refused to accelerate to takeoff airspeed. Whether he'd been trained in rejected takeoffs was not addressed in the short accident report, but he doggedly pressed on.

As he neared the end of the runway, still not at takeoff speed, in total disbelief and desperation he pulled back on the control stick forcefully. The aircraft roared into the air in an exaggerated nose-high attitude behind the power curve, wherein aerodynamic drag was greater than engine thrust. He managed to get the sleek, struggling airplane over the airport boundary fence, and across a paved perimeter road, whereupon it settled into a soft plowed field. Fortunately, no one was injured, but the kid's pride was severely hurt. His instructor apparently hadn't explained the hazards of slush-drag deceleration from a snow or rain soaked runway. Nor is there any FAA or manufacturers' information as to how soft a soft-field can be before becoming too soft to use.

Another case of inadequate training and checking involved a new private pilot who was flying passengers in a Cessna 172. His first landing attempt was long, so he went around for another attempt. During the process witnesses reported the airplane was performing strangely. On the second attempt, the pilot again landed too long and was forced to go around. With full flaps selected, he added maximum power, whereupon the aircraft pitched up, stalled, and crashed.

The two long landing attempts were bad enough, implying both inadequate training and substandard proficiency. In fact, the NTSB investigator found only two entries in the pilot's logbook regarding go-around training, both were pre-solo. Nor had the new pilot been required to perform a go-around from a landing approach on his flight check for a private pilot certificate.

In an interview with investigators the accident pilot's CFI could not satisfactorily explain the Cessna's full flap go-around procedure. Nor did he seem to understand the deleterious effect on climb performance of the drag from fully extended flaps; or why lots of forward nose-down control wheel pressure was required with the airplane trimmed for landing and with full power suddenly applied.

Another accident involved a pilot whose private certificate was only six months old, and who had recently purchased a Piper Lance. According to the NTSB accident report his reputation was that of a head-strong individualist, "who knew what he wanted and when he wanted it."

Investigators figured his CFI had been forced to train to the pilot's whims. They were told that when his instructor had attempted to teach him the rejected takeoff procedure, he had snapped that he already knew enough about it and to get on with the program. Despite training to the contrary and regardless of the wind direction, he insisted on departing from the nearest runway.

Unfortunately, this ultimately proved to be his downfall. One day he attempted to depart on a runway with a 40-knot quartering tailwind. Witnesses heard the tires squealing as the airplane skidded off the edge of the pavement. Yet he tenaciously continued with the attempt. Unfortunately he failed to get airborne and was killed in the subsequent crash.

The NTSB investigator theorized that his CFI had been intimidated into recommending this pilot for his private pilot flight check. In addition, the DPE who issued the accident pilot's private certificate was part owner of the FBO that had sold him the airplane. And too, they were known to be "drinking buddies."

In another example, I was the flight instructor and my student was a pilot who needed a Sabreliner type rating. He was 32 years-old and had been hired recently as the chief pilot for a cantankerous old man with a reputation for thriftiness that made Scrooge look like Santa Claus.

During training, he showed an excellent proficiency in instrument flying. Yet he seemed to have no sense of discipline, nor any concept of or respect for basic safety practices. In one instance I found him standing on the air-stair door smoking a cigarette while the fuel truck was pumping Jet A into the airplane. In addition, he confided that while living in a South American country with his airline pilot father, he had been involved in three major accidents; one in which he over-stressed a bi-wing aerobatic airplane and had to bail out.

After two weeks of training I was reluctant to recommend him for the type rating simply because his adolescent personality and flighty judgment worried me. In fact, his attitude was so flippant that I even talked to him in all seriousness about his demeanor and attitude. But his flying performance was faultless. Subsequently, I recommended him and he passed the type rating checkride with flying colors.

Thirteen months later, after desperately trying to find a copilot/mechanic who would tolerate the owner's overbearing personality, the inevitable occurred. They had managed to hire a pilot/mechanic with a newly minted ATP certificate—his flight check having been administered in a light twin.

With the aircraft's owner and eldest son as the only passengers, the fatal accident occurred during a night departure from New Orleans Lake Front Airport. It was a clear, moonless night, with two-miles visibility in smoke and haze as they departed over the black, featureless expanse of Lake Pontchartrain. Tower personnel told investigators that less than three minutes elapsed from engine start to liftoff, so they obviously ignored the aircraft's checklist. Upon getting airborne, the Sabreliner was seen by several witnesses to climb to about 400 feet, then began a slow descent to the water, where it exploded on impact.

Only the young captain survived and he called me from the hospital to tell the story. With the copilot flying to gain experience in his first jet airplane, they had lifted off normally. Shortly after getting airborne the copilot noticed that the captain's altimeter was stuck. With the captain's head down in the cockpit attempting to troubleshoot the altimeter and the copilot watching his effort, the airplane began a slow descent to the water. Later, investigators found the trim selector switch in the OFF position. They also suspected the captain's flight director was inoperative, since the selector switch was in the number two (copilot) position.

Despite this being his first jet aircraft, NTSB investigators determined the new copilot had never received any training in the aircraft. He was therefore found unqualified to act as second-in-command.

In retrospect, the captain should never have been recommended for the Sabreliner type rating. But how do you stop a man's career in mid-stream just because you *think* he has a personality or judgment problem, or that he may be accident-prone? He should never have been hired. My contract was simply to train him for his type rating, not analyze his qualifications and emotional maturity for the job.

Smart companies use careful pre-employment testing and evaluation of the pilot's personality, intelligence, and background. Psychological testing, too, is a very worthwhile tool in pre-employment screening. Any skilled interviewer would have spotted this pilot's personality flaws. His accident history alone was a key indicator of his unsuitability for employment. It's not bad karma that causes certain people to have multiple accidents in cars or in airplanes.

Santa Claus Factor

As these examples show, the flight instructor and DPE are key players in aviation safety and accident prevention, simply because they have the last word in verifying a person has the knowledge, skill and proficiency required for a pilot's certificate. When either or both fail in their task, the stage is set for a major accident. However, complicating the problem is that both the flight instructor and DPE live with the threat of economic retribution. Develop a reputation as a tough task-master as an instructor or examiner and watch business disappear. It gets around fast too if a DPE is a Santa Claus, i.e., gives easy or quick flight checks.

In the case of the Cessna 172 pilot who crashed during an attempted go-around, investigators found that on the day of the accident pilot's flight check for a private pilot certificate the DPE had flown a six-hour trip in a Citation. He then conducted a commercial certificate and three private certificate flight checks. The accident pilot's oral had lasted about 20 minutes and the flight check 25 minutes. Yet the entire *Practical Test Standards* table of contents had been checked off as accomplished. When interviewed by investigators, some of this DPE's applicants even complained about the short check rides. But at $200 per checkride, the DPE was realizing the American Dream. After a two-year investigation, the FAA finally revoked the DPE's credentials.

In another instance, a DPE in a corporate jet was issuing type ratings to pilots following only two or three days of training—"whatever it takes," he reportedly said. The cost of this "training" was $3,000. (At $1,000 per day, he too was realizing the American Dream.) His training program consisted predominantly of touch and go landings. Yet, with the three inch thick AFM, which contains the FAA approved normal and emergency procedures, as well as the FAA Approved performance charts, at least five to six days are required for the average person just to review it. He was also reported to have signed off copilots as qualified as second-in-command, without ground school or flight training. When this was reported to the designee's Flight Standards District Office (FSDO), their flaccid response was, "Do you know of one of his students who is non-proficient?"

In another case, a FSDO was contacted by a Congressman who demanded that a new flight school owner in his district immediately be made a DPE. Yet no one in the office had met the individual. After some strong resistance at the FSDO, and yet another demanding letter from the Congressman, the FSDO was ordered by management to comply.

At first the new DPE seemed to be a good examiner. Then his flight school began advertising in *Trade-A-Plane* a guaranteed 100% pass rate. The FAA office was mystified. The examiner was accomplishing a record number of flight checks and had a 27% failure rate. Thus, FAA's upper management felt he was beyond reproach. But a tenacious FSDO inspector kept checking.

The inspector noted that ATP flight checks were being accomplished at a relatively remote airfield, which lacked an ILS for the required approaches. The nearest facility was 45 minutes away. Yet the total flight time for each flight check was only half an hour.

The DPE was doing a brisk business and forwarding numerous temporary licenses through the FSDO each week. Consequently, the inspector decided to retain 10 per week and do a follow-up surveillance on the conduct of the flight check. Initially, he began with the pink slip failures which interestingly were followed closely by a successful retest.

Upon calling one of the recently qualified pilots he learned that there had been no flight on the day of the pink slip. In each case the applicant insisted he had passed the flight check on the first try. Thus it became clear that the 27 percent failure rate was bogus. The DPE was submitting phony pink slips to hide the advertised 100 percent pass rate.

This FAA inspector noted too that the flight school had an unusually large number of foreign students. Most were to be pilots for their respective national airline. Thanks to an informant, the inspector learned that the DPE—who by now was also a written test (FAA Knowledge Exam) examiner—was helping the applicants complete their written test. Then, if the student had in his hand an airline ticket home with a departure date within five days, for a $1,000 fee the DPE would write out an ATP certificate without a flight check. In fact, the FAA inspector quickly documented four ATP's that were supposedly given in one day with no flight time shown in the company aircraft logs.

With this information the FSDO immediately moved to suspend the DPE's designation. But the DPE sued the FAA to retain his designation. With unmitigated gall the DPE's lawyer argued in Federal Court—successfully—that the FAA would be depriving the individual of his livelihood. Due to either incompetent legal representation of the FAA or an irrational judge, the FAA was ordered to retain the DPE and continue processing the licenses he submitted. Worse yet, despite the fact that the DPE's actions were felonies, the FAA Regional Attorney refused to prosecute, because, as he told the inspector, "the process was too involved."

But the tenacious FSDO inspector was not finished. He noted that the DPE was getting his second class medical from an AME in a mid-western state. Upon further checking, the inspector discovered the DPE was taking medication for both a heart problem and high blood pressure, yet this was not reflected in his records. While never proven in court, the inspector felt the AME was simply mailing the medical certificate as needed to his boy-hood friend. Subsequently, the pilot's medical certificate was terminated and the physician's AME designation was revoked without argument.

Flight Instructor

In a case of flight instructor malpractice, a student pilot was dispatched for his multi-engine flight check in an un-airworthy airplane. The FAA inspector administering the flight check noted that during the pre-takeoff power check, the applicant checked the right magneto of the right engine twice, and skipped the left magneto. Just to be certain, he asked the applicant to repeat the mag check. Upon checking the left magneto the engine quit. Then the applicant admitted that his flight instructor had told him to fake the mag check, "because they didn't have time to fix it before the checkride."

The instructor couldn't explain what would have happened if the inspector had given the applicant a left engine failure after lift-off. Teaching a student to cheat the system showed a gross lack of ethics and moral character by the instructor. Needless to say, both the applicant and flight instructor were appropriately disciplined by the FAA inspector.

Bottom Line

When a person becomes a student pilot, he or she becomes part of the aviation industry. The safety record and profitability of that industry is directly related to the integrity, skill and knowledge of all those involved.

When you look at the regulations you'll see a set of rules that evolved from a very long and tragic accident history, which includes the requirements for a pilot's certificate. When someone short-changes a new pilot's training or the DPE ignores the oral and then administers a cursory half hour flight check it's the budding new pilot who has been cheated, because now he or she doesn't know what they can and can't do reliably. Then, instead of a license to enjoy uncommon freedom and a long flying career, they are set up for disaster. And unfortunately, as some of the accidents described show, quite often it's the pilot's closest friends or loved ones who are the unwitting victims.

It should be noted too that if someone *sells* you a pilot's license it's a felony and the newly licensed pilot becomes an accessory. Providing false information to your AME on your medical records is also a felony. Try getting insurance or a job with a felony conviction on your record.

Conclusion

As I hope you can see, becoming a competent pilot requires a structured regimen of academic instruction and a carefully planned flight training program. If you short-circuit the system because you're in a hurry, then it's you who can end up as an NTSB statistic. If you value your life and those of your potential passengers, you want all the training you can get. And beware the flight instructor whose teaching is directed towards "acing the oral and checkride" rather than understanding and comprehending the new information and learning how to fly the airplane competently and safely. The flight check with an FAA inspector or DPE is simply a validation of the adequacy of your training, knowledge and flying proficiency.

About three months after you finish training you'll find a lot of your new knowledge has become hazy, so a review of your ground school subjects is recommended. It's also very important that after receiving that new certificate you fly the airplane regularly. You can't go three or four months and then jump in an airplane and go somewhere. And after about 100 hours of flying with a new private certificate it's important to the new pilot's safety and longevity to begin training for an instrument rating. This is especially true for those who frequently fly at night. Because sooner or later, either low visibility or featureless terrain will introduce the new pilot to spatial disorientation, from which recovery is a matter of life or death.

As said previously, many accidents are preordained before departure. However, by reviewing these case histories, you'll be forewarned of your own potential *seed of destruction*—such as departing over the certified gross weight, flying VFR in marginal weather (scud running), low-level buzzing, departing with zero visibility, or "taking a look" below weather minimums to name just a few.

In the past, our system for licensing new pilots emphasized flying skills over judgment. But developing the ability to make sound decisions is the byproduct of extensive study of a variety of subjects. For example, we teach the student pilot how to accomplish a short-field takeoff then explain to him or her about slush-drag deceleration from rain or snow that can prevent getting airborne in the runway available. There's also the soft-field takeoff from a grass runway. The runway's softness is usually the byproduct of rain or melting snow. But how soft can a "soft field" be before it's too soft for a safe takeoff attempt?

Safe flying involves judgment and decisions founded on good flight training and in-depth academic study. It also takes continuous operational flying to maintain adequate flying proficiency. In aviation, the last thing you want is to learn something the hard way.

As emphasized in the beginning, you'll find that the Federal Aviation Regulations, like an airline's operations manual, provide a pilot with an excellent reference source for use in making decisions, because most of the rules are the result of someone's misfortune.

Meanwhile, *fly safe* and *fly smart!*

BIBLIOGRAPHY

These sources were consulted in the writing of this book. To read NTSB aviation accident and incident reports from 1962 and onwards, go to **http://www.ntsb.gov/_layouts/ntsb.aviation/index.aspx.**

Butler, Robert N. *Why Survive Being Old in America?* Baltimore: Johns Hopkins University Press, 2006

Carlisle, David. "Pilot Stress and What To Do About It," *Business & Commercial Aviation*, November 2001

Clark, Andrew, "Concorde: judges call in US airline," *The Guardian*, December 15, 2004.

Coffey, Richard A., *The Skylane Pilot's Companion.* Sandstone, MN: Sunset Hill Publications, 1996.

Covault, Craig, "Echoes of Concorde," *Aviation Week and Space Technology*, May 5, 2003.

Department of Transportation. Federal Aviation Administration. *Aviation Weather.* By C. Hugh Snyder and John W. Zimmerman, Jr. AC 00-6A. United States Government Printing Office, 1975.

Dornheim, Michael A. "Concorde report Uncovers Inflight Fire In 1979 Incident," *Aviation Week and Space Technology*, February 4, 2002.

Dornheim, Michael A., "Concorde had a Chance Until 2nd Engine Failed," *Aviation Week and Space Technology*, September 11, 2000.

Dornheim, Michael A., "Details Emerge of Earlier Fuel Tank penetrations," *Aviation Week and Space Technology*, August 28, 2000.

Federal Aviation Administration. *Pilot Age and Accident Rates Report 4: An Analysis of Professional ATP and Commercial Pilot Accident Rates by Age.* By Dana Broach, Kurt M. Joseph and David J. Schroeder. Oklahoma City, OK: 2003

Ferrera, Lee. "NTSB Recommends to FAA ATC Modifications to Reduce Possibility of Mid-Air Collisions Near Airports." *Airnation.net.* July 3, 2013. http://airnation.net/2013/07/03/ntsb-collision-recommendations/

Harriss, Joseph, "Concorde's Redemption," *Air & Space*, August/September 2001.

Hounsfield, Christopher. *Trailblazers: Test Pilots in Action* (Barnsley: Pen and Sword Books, 2009), 148.

Kannel, William. Interview with Larry King. *The Hidden Epidemic: Heart Disease in America.* PBS, 2006

Li, Guohua et al, "Age, Flight Experience and Risk of Crash Involvement in a Cohort of Professional Pilots," *American Journal of Epidemiology*, Vol. 157, No. 10, pages 874-880

Morrocco, John D., Sparaco, Pierre, "Concorde team Activates Return-to flight-plan," *Aviation Week and Space Technology*, January 22, 2001.

NASA Aviation Safety Reporting System. "Taxiing: The Task At Hand." *Callback*, 280 (January 2003)

National Transportation Safety Board. "Full Narrative: CHI02FA074"
http://www.ntsb.gov/_layouts/ntsb.aviation/brief2.aspx?ev_id=20020207X00196&ntsbno=CHI02FA074&akey=1

National Transportation Safety Board. "Full Narrative: CHI94FA050"
http://www.ntsb.gov/_layouts/ntsb.aviation/brief2.aspx?ev_id=20001211X13828&ntsbno=CHI94FA050&akey=1

National Transportation Safety Board. "Full Narrative: CHI99FA079"
http://www.ntsb.gov/_layouts/ntsb.aviation/brief2.aspx?ev_id=20001204X00018&ntsbno=CHI99FA079&akey=1

National Transportation Safety Board. "Full Narrative: DCA01M034"
http://www.ntsb.gov/_layouts/ntsb.aviation/brief2.aspx?ev_id=20010412X00738&ntsbno=DCA01MA034&akey=1

National Transportation Safety Board. "Full Narrative: DEN01FA070"
http://www.ntsb.gov/_layouts/ntsb.aviation/brief2.aspx?ev_id=20010321X00618&ntsbno=DEN01FA070&akey=1

National Transportation Safety Board. "Full Narrative: FTW01FA015"
http://www.ntsb.gov/_layouts/ntsb.aviation/brief2.aspx?ev_id=20001212X22152&ntsbno=FTW01FA015&akey=1

National Transportation Safety Board. "Full Narrative: FTW01LA091"
http://www.ntsb.gov/_layouts/ntsb.aviation/brief2.aspx?ev_id=20010404X00692&ntsbno=FTW01LA091&akey=1

National Transportation Safety Board. "Full Narrative: FTW04FA052"
http://www.ntsb.gov/_layouts/ntsb.aviation/brief2.aspx?ev_id=20040106X00018&ntsbno=FTW04FA052&akey=1

National Transportation Safety Board. "Full Narrative: FTW96LA366"
http://www.ntsb.gov/_layouts/ntsb.aviation/brief2.aspx?ev_id=20001208X06517&ntsbno=FTW96LA366&akey=1

National Transportation Safety Board. "Full Narrative: IAD96FA055"
http://www.ntsb.gov/_layouts/ntsb.aviation/brief2.aspx?ev_id=20001208X05411&ntsbno=IAD96FA055&akey=1

National Transportation Safety Board. "Full Narrative: IAD97FA060"
http://www.ntsb.gov/_layouts/ntsb.aviation/brief2.aspx?ev_id=20001208X07722&ntsbno=IAD97FA060&akey=1

National Transportation Safety Board. "Full Narrative: LAX00FA191"
http://www.ntsb.gov/_layouts/ntsb.aviation/brief2.aspx?ev_id=20001212X21025&ntsbno=LAX00FA191&akey=1

National Transportation Safety Board. "Full Narrative: MIA00FA265"
http://www.ntsb.gov/_layouts/ntsb.aviation/brief2.aspx?ev_id=20001212X22030&
ntsbno=MIA00FA265&akey=1

National Transportation Safety Board. "Full Narrative: MIA01LA080"
http://www.ntsb.gov/about/employment/_layouts/ntsb.aviation/brief2.aspx?ev_id
=20010222X00491&ntsbno=MIA01LA080&akey=1

National Transportation Safety Board. "Full Narrative: MIA02FA037"
http://www.ntsb.gov/_layouts/ntsb.aviation/brief2.aspx?ev_id=20011210X02372&
ntsbno=MIA02FA037&akey=1

National Transportation Safety Board. "Full Narrative: NYC94FA065"
http://www.ntsb.gov/_layouts/ntsb.aviation/brief2.aspx?ev_id=20001206X00973&
ntsbno=NYC94FA065&akey=1

National Transportation Safety Board. "Full Narrative: NYC99MA178"
http://www.ntsb.gov/_layouts/ntsb.aviation/brief2.aspx?ev_id=20001212X19354&
ntsbno=NYC99MA178&akey=1

National Transportation Safety Board. "Full Narrative: SEA02FA023"
http://www.ntsb.gov/_layouts/ntsb.aviation/brief2.aspx?ev_id=20020104X00037&
ntsbno=SEA02FA023&akey=1

National Transportation Safety Board. "Full Narrative: SEA03FA147"
http://www.ntsb.gov/about/employment/_layouts/ntsb.aviation/brief2.aspx?ev_id
=20030724X01192&ntsbno=SEA03FA147&akey=1

National Transportation Safety Board. "Preliminary Report: CEN14FA462."
http://www.ntsb.gov/_layouts/ntsb.aviation/brief.aspx?ev_id=20140827X25654

National Transportation Safety Board. "Preliminary Report: ERA14MA27"
http://www.ntsb.gov/_layouts/ntsb.aviation/brief.aspx?ev_id=20140531X32035

National Transportation Safety Board. "Probable Cause: ANC10MA068"
http://www.ntsb.gov/_layouts/ntsb.aviation/brief.aspx?ev_id=20100810X62027

National Transportation Safety Board. "Probable Cause: ATL95LA121"
http://www.ntsb.gov/_layouts/ntsb.aviation/brief.aspx?ev_id=20001207X03621

National Transportation Safety Board. "Probable Cause: ATL98FA060A"
http://www.ntsb.gov/_layouts/ntsb.aviation/brief.aspx?ev_id=20001211X09798

National Transportation Safety Board. "Probable Cause: CHI01MA011"
http://www.ntsb.gov/_layouts/ntsb.aviation/brief.aspx?ev_id=20001212X22136

National Transportation Safety Board. "Probable Cause: CHI81FA011"
http://www.ntsb.gov/_layouts/ntsb.aviation/brief.aspx?ev_id=28643

National Transportation Safety Board. "Probable Cause: DCA70AZ008"
http://www.ntsb.gov/_layouts/ntsb.aviation/brief.aspx?ev_id=2646&key=0

National Transportation Safety Board. "Probable Cause: DCA76AZ025"
http://www.ntsb.gov/_layouts/ntsb.aviation/brief.aspx?ev_id=51910&key=0

National Transportation Safety Board. "Probable Cause: DCA81AA007"
http://www.ntsb.gov/_layouts/ntsb.aviation/brief.aspx?ev_id=27730&key=0

National Transportation Safety Board. "Probable Cause: DCA88MA032"
    http://www.ntsb.gov/_layouts/ntsb.aviation/brief.aspx?ev_id=20001213X25040

National Transportation Safety Board. "Probable Cause: DCA92MA011"
    http://www.ntsb.gov/_layouts/ntsb.aviation/brief.aspx?ev_id=20001212X18578

National Transportation Safety Board. "Probable Cause: DCA93GA042"
    http://www.ntsb.gov/about/employment/_layouts/ntsb.aviation/brief.
    aspx?ev_id=20001211X12106

National Transportation Safety Board. "Probable Cause: DEN01FA041"
    http://www.ntsb.gov/_layouts/ntsb.aviation/brief.aspx?ev_id=20010126X00364

National Transportation Safety Board. "Probable Cause: DEN70AD046"
    http://www.ntsb.gov/_layouts/ntsb.aviation/brief.aspx?ev_id=4724&key=0

National Transportation Safety Board. "Probable Cause: DEN84FA089"
    http://www.ntsb.gov/_layouts/ntsb.aviation/brief.aspx?ev_id=20001214X38745

National Transportation Safety Board. "Probable Cause: ERA14FA288"
    http://www.ntsb.gov/_layouts/ntsb.aviation/brief2.aspx?ev_id=20010404X00692&
    ntsbno=FTW01LA091&akey=1

National Transportation Safety Board. "Probable Cause: FTW78FA011"
    http://www.ntsb.gov/_layouts/ntsb.aviation/brief.aspx?ev_id=44109

National Transportation Safety Board. "Probable Cause: FTW96FA027"
    http://www.ntsb.gov/_layouts/ntsb.aviation/brief.aspx?ev_id=20001207X04682

National Transportation Safety Board. "Probable Cause: LAX02FA041"
    http://www.ntsb.gov/_layouts/ntsb.aviation/brief.aspx?ev_id=20011226X02439

National Transportation Safety Board. "Probable Cause: LAX78FA029"
    http://www.ntsb.gov/_layouts/ntsb.aviation/brief.aspx?ev_id=43266

National Transportation Safety Board. "Probable Cause: LAX91FA132"
    http://www.ntsb.gov/_layouts/ntsb.aviation/brief.aspx?ev_id=20001212X16614&
    key=1

National Transportation Safety Board. "Probable Cause: LAX92GA128"
    http://www.ntsb.gov/_layouts/ntsb.aviation/brief.aspx?ev_id=20001211X14123

National Transportation Safety Board. "Probable Cause: LAX96LA302"
    http://www.ntsb.gov/_layouts/ntsb.aviation/brief.aspx?ev_id=20001208X06549

National Transportation Safety Board. "Probable Cause: MIA83FA046"
    http://www.ntsb.gov/_layouts/ntsb.aviation/brief.aspx?ev_id=20020917X04911

National Transportation Safety Board. "Probable Cause: MIA97LA088"
    http://www.ntsb.gov/_layouts/ntsb.aviation/brief.aspx?ev_id=20001208X07442

National Transportation Safety Board. "Probable Cause: NYC83FA087"
    http://www.ntsb.gov/_layouts/ntsb.aviation/brief.aspx?ev_id=20001214X42792

National Transportation Safety Board. "Probable Cause: NYC99FA213" http://www.
    ntsb.gov/_layouts/ntsb.aviation/brief2.aspx?ev_id=20001212X19616

National Transportation Safety Board. "Probable Cause: SEA95FA198" http://www.ntsb.gov/_layouts/ntsb.aviation/brief.aspx?ev_id=20001207X04586

National Transportation Safety Board. "Probably Cause: MIA00FA103A" http://www.ntsb.gov/_layouts/ntsb.aviation/brief.aspx?ev_id=20001212X20686

National Transportation Safety Board. "Safety Recommendation (A-92-81)." Vogt, Charles M. August 13, 1992

National Transportation Safety Board. *Aircraft Accident Report: Acceptors, Inc. Cessna Model 551, Citation II, N2CA, Mountain View, Missouri, November 18, 1982*. NTSB-AAR-83-04. Washington, D.C.: July 18, 1983

National Transportation Safety Board. *Aircraft Accident Report: COMAIR, Inc., Piper PA-31-310, Navajo, N6642L, Greater Cincinnati Airport*. NTSB-AAR-80-8. Washington, D.C.: 1980

National Transportation Safety Board. *Aircraft Accident Report: Delta Airlines, Inc., Boeing 727-200, N467DA and Flying Tiger, Inc. Boeing 747-F, N804FT, O'Hare International Airport*. NTSB-AAR-79-11. Washington, D.C.: 1979

National Transportation Safety Board. *Aircraft Accident Report: Jet Avia, Ltd. Learjet, LR24B, N12MK, Palm Springs, California, January, 6, 1977*. NTSB-AAR-77-08. Washington, D.C.: October 6, 1977

National Transportation Safety Board. *Aircraft Accident Report: Jaktoe Cessna 411A, N100KC, Wise, Virginia, January 12, 1975*. NTSB-AAR-76-05. Washington, D.C.: March 8, 1976

National Transportation Safety Board. *Aircraft Accident Report: Loss of Control on Approach Colgan Air, Inc. Operating as Continental Connection Flight 3407 Bombardier DHC-8-400, N200WQ Clarence Center, New York February 12, 2009*. NTSB-AAR-10-01. Washington, D.C.: February 2, 2010

National Transportation Safety Board. *Aircraft Accident Report: Loss of Control While Maneuvering Pilatus PC-12/45, N128CM Butte, Montana March 22, 2009*. NTSB-AAR-11-05. Washington, D.C.: July 12, 2011

National Transportation Safety Board. *Aircraft Accident Report: Midair Collision Mitsubishi MU-2B-60, N74FB, and Piper PA-32-301, N82419, Greenwood Municipal Airport*. NTSB-AAR-93-05. Washington, D.C.: 1993

National Transportation Safety Board. *Aircraft Accident Report: Runway Collision United Express Flight 5925 and Beechcraft King Air A90 Quincy Municipal Airport*. NTSB-AAR-97-04. Washington, D.C.: 1997

National Transportation Safety Board. *Introduction of Glass Cockpit Avionics into Light Aircraft*. Safety Study NTSB/SS-10/01. Washington, D.C.: 2010

National Transportation Safety Board. *Special Study: Light Twin-Engine Aircraft Accidents Following Engine Failures, 1972-1976*. NTSB-AAS-79-2. Washington, D.C.: 1979

Naval Air Systems Command, United States Navy. *Aerodynamics for Naval Aviators*. By Hugh Hurt. NAVWEPS 00-80T-80. Newcastle, WA: Aviation Supplies & Academics, Inc., 1996

Rose, David. "Doomed," *The Observer*, May 13, 2001.

Thalmann, E.D. "Decompression Illness: What Is It and What Is The Treatment?" *Alert Diver* March/April 2004. http://www.diversalertnetwork.org/medical/articles/Decompression_Illness_What_Is_It_and_What_Is_The_Treatment

Transportation Safety Board of Canada. "Aviation Investigation Report: A03A0022: Loss of Control and Collision With Terrain" http://www.tsb.gc.ca/eng/rapports-reports/aviation/2003/a03a0022/a03a0022.pdf (February 14, 2003)

U.S. Department of the Air Force. *Physiological Technician's Training Manual*. AFM-160-5. Washington, D.C.: U.S. Government Printing Office, February 1969

U.S. Department of Transportation. Federal Aviation Administration. *Instrument Flying Handbook*. FAA-H-8083-15B. Washington, D.C.: United States Government Printing Office, 2012.

Vann, Richard. "Altitude and Decompression Sickness," *Alert Diver* Summer 2011. http://www.alertdiver.com/Altitude_and_Decompression_Sickness

Werner, Bob. "Tragedy on a Mountain." *The Alaska Professional Hunter Magazine*, Winter 1996

INDEX

ABOUT THE AUTHOR

Author John Lowery first soloed at age 16 in a Piper J-3 Cub, at Auburn-Opelika Airport (AUO). After graduating from Auburn University, he spent the next 24 years in the United States Air Force flying a variety of high performance aircraft, including a brief break in service during which he flew for Western Airlines as a first officer. Upon returning to the Air Force he subsequently lived and flew all over the world. After Air Force retirement, Lowery spent the following 24 years as a practicing flight instructor and FAA designated pilot proficiency examiner in a Sabreliner corporate jet, ultimately accumulating 13,500 flying hours. In addition, he was for some years a designated pilot examiner in the Beechcraft King Air turbo-prop series and various light airplanes.

John holds an Airline Transport Pilot certificate with type ratings in the Sabreliner, Learjet, Citation, King Air 300, Beechcraft 1900, DC-4 and DC-3, in addition to single- and multi-engine seaplanes. As a flight instructor he is rated for single- and multi-engine, and instrument flying. Concurrently, he earned a master's degree in aeronautical science from Embry-Riddle Aeronautical University and taught both graduate and undergraduate courses in corporate aviation management and aircraft accident investigation for ERAU's night campuses at Mather AFB, McClellan AFB, and Travis AFB, California, as an adjunct assistant professor of aeronautical science.

Now retired in California, he remains active as an author of aviation books. Some of his previous publications include *Anatomy of a Spin, Professional Pilot* (Third Edition, 2008 ASA Inc.), and *Life in the Wild Blue Yonder: jet fighter pilot stories from the cold war.*